STARTING ON A SHOESTRING

Small Business Management Series
Rick Stephan Hayes, Editor

Simplified Accounting for Non-Accountants
by Rick Stephan Hayes and C. Richard Baker

Accounting for Small Manufacturers
by C. Richard Baker and Rick Stephan Hayes

Simplified Accounting for Engineering and Technical Consultants
by Rick Stephan Hayes and C. Richard Baker

Simplified Accounting for the Computer Industry
by Rick Stephan Hayes and C. Richard Baker

The Complete Legal Guide for Your Small Business
by Paul Adams

Running Your Own Show: Mastering Basics of Small Business
by Richard T. Curtin

Up Front Financing: The Entrepreneur's Guide
by A. David Silver

How to Finance Your Small Business with Government Money: SBA and Other Loans, Second Edition
by Rick Stephan Hayes and John Cotton Howell

The Entrepreneurial Life: How To Go For It and Get It
by A. David Silver

The Complete Guide to Buying and Selling a Business
by Arnold S. Goldstein

Getting Paid: Building Your Powerful Credit and Collection Strategy
by Arnold S. Goldstein

Choosing Your Sources of Venture Capital
by A. David Silver

Starting on a Shoestring: Building a Business Without a Bankroll
by Arnold S. Goldstein

STARTING ON A SHOESTRING

Building a Business Without a Bankroll

Arnold S. Goldstein

A Ronald Press Publication
John Wiley & Sons
New York • Chichester • Brisbane • Toronto • Singapore

Published by John Wiley & Sons, Inc.

This publication is designed to provide accurate and authoritative information in regard to the subject matter covered. It is sold with the understanding that the publisher is not engaged in rendering legal, accounting, or other professional service. If legal advice or other expert assistance is required, the services of a competent professional person should be sought. *From a Declaration of Principles jointly adopted by a Committee of the American Bar Association and a Committee of Publishers.*

Library of Congress Cataloging in Publication Data:

Goldstein, Arnold S.
Starting on a shoestring.

"A Ronald Press publication."
Includes index.
1. New Business enterprises—Management. I. Title.
HD62.5.G65 1984 658.1'141 83-23379
ISBN 0-471-88439-1

Printed in the United States of America

21 20 19 18 17 16 15 14 13 12 11

To my wife, Marlene, for the encouragement she gave me to write this book, and her tireless efforts in helping me to create it.

PREFACE

The signs of quiet desperation are everywhere. Corporate serfs and bored housewives, blocked executives and ambitious dropouts, real people, unhappy people from every walk of life are joined by the common goal to own their own business. They also share a common problem. Too little cash to make it happen.

The entrepreneurial mavericks will clear the hurdle. Whatever cash they need they find. And what they can't find they learn to do without. Lack of money is their handicap but never their obstacle. So armed with little more than hope, goals, and determination they buck the odds and defy the rules. In the process they build bootstrap ventures into profitable enterprises. These are the people who prove you can start on a shoestring—and succeed.

That's what this book is all about. I want to show you how you too can be a successful shoestring entrepreneur. As you turn the pages you'll share the experiences of those who safely travelled the road before you. It's through their experiences that you'll find the strategies and techniques to build your venture, and do it with far fewer dollars than you dreamed possible.

I've travelled the same bumpy road myself, starting several businesses with less cash than I care to admit. In recent years I've counselled many more with the same objectives and financial limitations. It provided the insight for this book. And it also convinced me a book such as this was long overdue. Countless others want and need the same practical guidance for starting on a shoestring.

What do these cash-shy but ambitious people want to know? They don't want inspirational pep talks about building castles in the air or how to magically go from rags to riches. Motivational books have their purpose; however, this book is designed to be instructional. You face the mundane problems of the real business world and need concrete advice to start, grow, and survive in the twilight world of creativity in place of cash.

Every start-up has its own blueprint for success. As we proceed through the book I'll ask you to set aside your opinions and misconceptions of what it takes to achieve a successful start. In Chapter 2, you'll see how to put your business idea to the test to see if it's right for you. Capital? Of course you'll need some, and you'll find the ten best sources and how to approach them. Finding equipment and inventory on 100% financing terms can be yours once you turn to Chapters 8 and 9.

As you claw your way to success you'll face numerous day-to-day problems. I'll guide you over these operational bumps with proven solutions. And I'll give it to you in easy-to-understand everyday language, avoiding textbook theory or technical jargon. When you put this book down, you'll have new insights and the information that any business person can effectively use and relate to.

Starting on a shoestring is a game plan—a strategy. But strategy is only one dimension. Your thought process, willingness, and desire to see the business through the inevitable challenges is the other. Success won't come with a wave of the wand. Every story in this book shows how another business was born, but the people involved didn't do it without plenty of hard work, sleepless nights, and a commitment to their own financial victory.

Professional confidentiality required me to change the names of many individuals and businesses in the cases. However, every one is true. As I have learned from their successes so will you.

ARNOLD S. GOLDSTEIN

Boston, Massachusetts
March 1984

ACKNOWLEDGMENTS

I express my sincere thanks to those who have made valuable contributions to this book. Special thanks to my associate, Barry R. Levine, for his critical reviews, to my editor, Michael Hamilton, for conceiving the idea for this book and his confidence that I was the individual who could best write it, and to my wife, Marlene, for her tireless efforts in producing the manuscript. No author could have a better team.

A book is seldom the work of one person. A special acknowledgment is extended to the countless individuals—accountants, attorneys, consultants, and shoestring entrepreneurs whose experience and insight provided the foundation for this book.

Perhaps I am most indebted to my many acquaintances and clients who have proven that you can start on a shoestring and succeed.

A. S. G.

Author's Note:

Every case and example in this book is true. To preserve confidentiality and privacy many of the names of individuals and organizations have been changed. Any resemblance of fictional names to actual persons or organizations is purely coincidental.

CONTENTS

1

YOU MAKE YOUR OWN MIRACLES

Monday, October 1, 1973.

Zero hour minus one minute.

It was my big day. With bright purple letters the proud banner flurried over the near-empty parking lot announcing the grand opening of Discount City. Beneath, cavorted two clowns anchoring dozens of colorful balloons for the crowds to come.

Thirty seconds to launch.

A shrill noise broke the air as three kids hired from the local high school band trumpeted "Dixie." Quite unusual I thought considering we were in Massachusetts, but then again, Discount City was an unusual store.

Zero minus ten seconds.

My eyes scanned the mountains of merchandise jam packed on a wide array of used fixtures painted a nauseating green to hide their disparate origins. "Who could resist?" I mused. To my left were the \$3.98 garbage cans and to my right, the crates of six-fingered back scratchers direct from Taiwan at the incredible 49-cent price. Wherever I looked there were bargains galore, hustled and conned on credit from every corner of the map.

Outside the cacophony of noise changed to the lively tempo of "Alexander's Ragtime Band." Everything was set. All was ready. It was the moment of truth.

Four . . . three . . . two . . . one . . . blast off!

The doors swung open to welcome swollen crowds. All that appeared was a little old lady in tennis shoes swinging an oversized pocketbook. Out she quickly marched with a deftly shoplifted $6.98 can opener safely tucked in her now heavier pocketbook. It was a start. Discount City was christened; the Discount City with $120,000 in unpaid-for merchandise heaped on $20,000 in fully mortgaged fixtures sitting on retail space with three months' deferred rent. It was the Discount City which came to life owing everybody for everything. But it was also the Discount City built on a financial deck of cards that somehow made the grade and mushroomed in three years to 12 more stores ringing up a profitable $6 million in sales. Best of all, it was the Discount City started on a shoestring with only $2600 of my own cash.

It's never easy. You wonder how it ever happened when so many people say it shouldn't and predict it can't. Sydney, my Valium-popping accountant, would label me the "lunatic with the big dream and the small bank balance." It hardly inspires confidence. And while you're in the trenches trying to turn a dream into reality, your family thinks you've lost your marbles and you find your friends scanning the auction pages anticipating your bankruptcy. They may send you flowers when you open, and with them their well wishes. Still, they never quite believe.

But that's the thrill of it all. You want a business of your own so you go for it. You connive, beg, borrow, hustle, and manipulate to get it together and keep it together. You work your butt to the bone to make it happen. In the process you thumb your nose at a world of non-believers, skeptics, pessimists, and conventionalists with their words of wisdom of why you can't or why you shouldn't. No, it's never easy, but when you're through and have the business off and running you stand tall and pat yourself on the back. You did it and did it on a shoestring. In short, you made your own miracles. It's quite an experience.

Flushed by my Discount City days, I journeyed into nine more shoestring start-ups. By then I had the money to invest, but I was spoiled. I didn't want to invest. My philosophy was simple and it never changed. Any idiot with a bushel basket of money can land himself in business, but also it doesn't take a genius to do it without cash. Chutzpah is a powerful substitute. Tight with cash but heavy on chutzpah, I wound up my entrepreneurial spirits, took a few working partners in tow, and opened two drugstores, a health food store, two greeting card and gift shops, a furniture manufacturing plant, and even a direct-mail firm for import items. Total personal investment? Less than $10,000. Were they all successful? Nope. Most came under the broad heading of "winner," but a couple were blunders and would have been the same blunders even if heavily bankrolled. The education was had and the lesson learned as these and so many other businesses capitalized with little more than heart, hope, and hard work have taught me. You can start on a shoestring and succeed.

ARE YOU THE ONE IN THE CROWD?

No longer is my office a dank corner of my first store, Spartanly equipped with a war surplus file cabinet and discarded door bolted to two orange crates. Today I'm in a high-rise office building. Directly across the road from my building—in easy view of my office—is a large tire plant employing thousands of people. At precisely 8:45 each morning they stream through the front door to punch a clock. The executives, salespeople, clerical staff, and factory workers—like bees abandoning a hive—all stumble out the same door at precisely 5:00 each afternoon.

How many are happy at their work? How many would rather be at the helm of their own business? You never know the answer. Some probably never even thought of their own business, quite content to punch a clock, pick up a paycheck, and head home to drink a few beers before the television. Others harbored the idea but are slaves to the illusive security of employment, afraid of the gamble, the inherent risks of running their own show. Still others, the timid and the tired, lack the self-confidence while they mistakenly believe management is magic. Whatever their reasons, these same people wouldn't venture out on their own under the best of circumstances. And they shouldn't even try.

No, we don't know who they are, but in that endless stream of people marching in to work every morning—there are the few who want their own business and have what it takes to run it successfully. There's only one thing holding them back—money. They have yet to develop the shoestring mentality.

Now let's turn the spotlight on you. With this book in your hand you're planning, or perhaps just thinking about, starting your own business. You too are wondering about where the money will come from. Now I know nothing about the type business you have in mind, but it doesn't matter. Shoestring start-ups are pretty much alike for all businesses. I have no conception of how large or successful it will become. That's for you to decide and achieve. My job is to show you how to put together your business and get it started without digging deeply into your own pockets. In the next several hours you'll see how. Your job is to take the ideas and turn them into action. But I know as well as anyone that it's easier said than done. Standing between you and success may be a lot of fuzzy thoughts and nonsense ideas of what it takes. That's what this chapter is all about. If you're the one in the crowd, it's time to develop your own shoestring mentality.

Let's get to work on it. And the only place to start is by knocking out a few dangerous myths.

MYTH #1: YOU NEED MONEY TO MAKE MONEY

People say it and people believe it. That explains why there are so many poor people. I agree that the rich may get richer, but that doesn't preclude a bit of success for the rest of us poor souls.

It's easier selling vacuum cleaners door-to-door than to sell people on the idea that they too can get started on a money-making venture without using their own money. Bob Allen, best-selling author of *Nothing Down* (Simon & Schuster, 1982), had just this problem when he tried to convince his readers that they could buy real estate with little or no money of their own. Now Allen was no fool. People could read, but would people believe? Not according to Allen. The skeptics were everywhere. So Allen threw out an interesting proposition, "Put me in any city," said Allen, "give me $100 for living expenses, and in 72 hours I'll return owning several properties without using a dime of my own money." The *Los Angeles Times* took the bait, handed Allen $100, and shipped him to San Francisco to turn his boast into proof. A few days later the triumphant Allen descended the plane, clutching a few deeds to some choice Frisco properties.

Oftentimes I'm tempted to match Allen's challenge by boasting that you can land me in any city or town and within one month I'll have a good, solid, healthy business started and running without spending a dime of my own. But who needs another business?

Now what's the message? It's not boasting, and it's not about either real estate or starting a business. It's about money. While you may need money to make money—it doesn't have to be *your* money. Better yet, it *won't* be your money.

Shoestring entrepreneurs understand it. So did Henry Ford. Henry was fond of saying that he might be flat broke but he'd never be poor. Armed with nothing more than a good idea, old optimist Henry would soon have all the money he'd need pouring into the venture from everyone else's pockets. You may not be Henry Ford, but his philosophy will work equally well for you. If you have that solid business idea, you'll find the money to make you money.

MYTH #2: A HEALTHY INVESTMENT MAKES A HEALTHY BUSINESS

Accountants always advise it, professors teach it, bankers love it, while the gullible swallow it. What nonsense!

Bob Kuzara knows how to punch holes in this fallacy. Bob started his successful North Pine Furniture with $80,000 in borrowed funds and today grosses $2 million annually, distributing his natural pinewood chairs, tables, and bookcases through local furniture stores and his own packed showroom. So as a shoestringer extraordinàire, Bob frequently joins me to address business start-up groups.

Not long ago a young lady attentively listening to Bob's pitch at a start-up seminar, jumped up and said, "If I don't invest a substantial amount of cash from my own funds, my business will collapse from excessive debt before it even has the chance to get off the ground. How can you dare suggest I do it on a shoestring?"

Bob had a ready answer. "First," he said, "whether your business makes it or not has little to do with your own investment. The secret is to structure the debt so it fits the payment capabilities of the business. You can safely start any type business with 100% leverage once you know how to program the debt. I agree. There's no such thing as the undercapitalized business, only the poorly planned business."

Bob overlooked the most important reason why a healthy investment does *not* necessarily make a healthy business. In fact, it usually creates a sick business. Owners throw more money into the business than it needs. It spoils them. They don't start out "lean and mean," and that leads to foolish expenditures. I'm reminded of a young MIT grad who started an electronics assembly firm with his wealthy father's generous $150,000 investment. A healthy business? Hardly. Six months later the Bankruptcy Trustee auctioned off its swanky furniture, a $38,000 Mercedes, and a $20,000 computer that was never needed. A healthy start would have been the father throwing his son $5000 to rent a garage and sit behind his own orange crate desk. If the business was destined to make it, it would make it building from the bottom rather than destroying it from the top. And the only way to build from the bottom is to lock up your checkbook so you do have to pinch pennies. And when you're borrowed to the hilt you'll have few pennies to pinch. It's therapeutic.

MYTH #3: DEBT IS BAD

Not by my book. I love debt. No, not when it comes to personal finances, but when you're talking in terms of business. And you can't really shake yourself clear of the first two myths unless you're willing to start in over your head and walk a financial tightrope until a business is eventually on its feet.

Most people are terrorized by the thought. They've been programmed to think of debt as a curse since they were old enough to understand the word. You may have the same problem. It's time to change your perspective.

About a year ago a young man retained me to help him start

a marina on Cape Cod. His grandfather left him some choice waterfront property so it was only a matter of construction. The demand was fabulous and boaters hearing of his plans were already lined up. Within a month we had the lowest construction bid—$250,000. "How much money do you have, Jack?" I asked. "About $10,000–15,000," he replied. No problem I figured. With the valuable land owned outright we'd have no problem finding a $240,000 construction loan from a local bank. And the numbers worked beautifully. Projected income would exceed expenses and mortgage payments by about $50,000. Jack would have a perpetual annuity and would hardly have to work for it. Do you think he did it? You know the answer. His mental block to signing a $240,000 note blocked his success. Eventually he leased the land to a "go-getter" who did build the marina and he's now the owner—mortgaged to the hilt—who's making the big money.

Sure debt can be scary. A cash-poor start-up puts you in the twilight world of constant bank overdrafts, overdue bills, sleepless nights, and robbing Peter to pay Paul. It comes with the territory. But you do it because it's the only way you *can* do it.

Look at it the way I do. On the tenth of each month I sit down and write out some pretty hefty mortgage payments and payments to suppliers. As I write each check I'm actually creating wealth. It's a simple philosophy. What I owe today I'll own tomorrow.

Think about it. How many wealthy people do you know who didn't start out up to their eyebrows in debt? It's the American way. For most of us it's the only way.

MYTH #4: STARTING ON A SHOESTRING IS STARTING SMALL

Not always. Remember my first Discount City? It opened its doors with over $200,000 in assets working for me. It was a shoestring deal because I had so little of my own money into it. That's the only definition of a shoestring start-up.

They say that Monsanto Chemical started with only a $5000 investors pool. It didn't start out as the industrial mammoth it is today, but it didn't begin in someone's basement either. It started at the logical size that could get it off and running as a viable company.

Plenty of shoestring start-ups are nothing more than cottage industries with industrious entrepreneurs moonlighting at a kitchen table or tinkering in the basement. For some it's the best place to start. Small can be beautiful as the saying goes. In a year or two many of these same businesses will have graduated to full-time, full-scale ventures. Others will begin operations with considerable assets behind their launch. As I write this book I'm consulting to a husband-wife team who developed and patented a "zip-lock" rainhat. It's an interesting device to provide a rainhat that folds to the size of your thumb. You'll find them hard at work in a spare bedroom, slaving away behind two used sewing machines. All it needed was $1200 to start, and when it comes time to grow they'll find plenty of backing.

Ever hear of Boston-Bio/Tech? You will. At least I think you will as soon as we can find the final $200,000 to complete a $1,300,000 capitalization package. Behind it are two bright Harvard Ph.D.s holding some interesting genetic engineering patents.

Right now they're busy cloning frogs but they evidently assured plenty of investors they'll soon be cloning money once their capital intensive laboratory is complete. And it'll take every penny of the $1,300,000 to put it together—scrimp and save as they may. What are our bright Harvard boys investing? Only an assignment to the company of their patent rights. Here's a case where large is logical, while showing shoestring start-ups come in all sizes and shapes.

Later in this book you'll see how to shape your start-up to just the right size. And it may be healthier looking than you think.

MYTH #5: MY BUSINESS CAN'T BE STARTED ON A SHOESTRING

Sure it can. It'll work for any type business. Now that's a bold statement considering I have no idea of the type business you have in mind. But I make the statement because I have seen it work in just about any type business, and the few that haven't crossed my path are no different. Service businesses are a snap. They usually require so little start-up capital that it hardly pays to read a book about it. Retail shops? They account for about 70% of the shoestring start-ups. And they're the most fun because you can bootstrap them in so many interesting ways. Whether it be a bookstore or a bagel bakery, if you can't shoestring it your creativity is on the blink.

Whenever you talk to people you hear some fascinating tales. Some people can be so darn creative they belong in jail. I was once giving the "if you can name it—you can do it" pitch at a women's club. A middle-aged lady sprang to her feet and said, "Mr. Goldstein's absolutely right. A few years ago I wanted to open a pet shop in a nearby mall, but I could only raise $1800 cash. It was only enough to build the cages and buy the sign—but I managed." Everyone in the room was curious. "How did you manage?" I asked. "What did you do for inventory?" "Oh, that was the easiest part. I went to the animal shelter and picked up 16 mongrel dogs for free. I then gave them exotic names. One bitch, for example, who was half German Shepherd and half Dalmatian became a Mongolian Laphound selling for $350." "What's a Mongolian Laphound?" I asked. "I just told you," she testily answered. "It's half Shepherd and half Dalmatian. But next week it may be half Irish Setter, part Poodle, and part Spaniel. I just picked up a few more dogs. Do you want to know what a Peruvian Llama dog is this week?" I didn't.

How about starting your own manufacturing plant? From aircraft components to zipper factories, thousands have started on a shoestring, although it's always a bit more of a challenge when you consider how capital intensive and risky they can be. Scan the list of Fortune-500 companies. Trace their histories. Check their pedigree. Whether it be Atari or Zenith—most started with less capital than you can probably raise right now.

MYTH #6: ONLY WHEELER-DEALERS NEED APPLY

This is the biggest myth of all. Experience and watching hundreds of ordinary people bootstrap their way into business have taught me otherwise. Wage earners who don't know the difference between a profit and loss statement and balance sheet have done it. Housewives who have never signed a check have done it. I've witnessed a group of high school kids do it. My own eleven-year-old daughter is doing it. Just last week she hit me for a $20 "loan" to launch a lemonade stand at her school picnic. Starting her out "lean and mean" I demanded 50% of the profits and a guarantee of repayment from future allowances. Business is business.

Northeastern University did a bit of research to find out just who shoestring entrepreneurs are likely to be. They discovered the best bets were people who were never in business before, had no business education, and were cash shy. In plain language, they didn't know any better and couldn't do any better. It once again shows that what you don't know can't hurt you. To solidify the case, the least likely people to start a thinly capitalized business were MBAs, or people with extensive business experience. You'll find them hiding behind a desk at General Motors, believing businesses are really started "by the book." They've been reading the wrong books.

Speaking of books, A. David Silver recently wrote an excellent one titled *The Entrepreneurial Life—How to Go for It and Get It* (John Wiley & Sons, 1983). It shows what makes an entrepreneur tick. Now most people starting out in business don't consider themselves entrepreneurs any more than they perceive themselves as "wheeler-dealers." I point that out because I sometimes use the word in this book. It may throw you off track as it does conjure the image of a dashing promoter overseeing a vast conglomerate that he started three weeks earlier and will probably bankrupt three weeks later. But that's not you either. All you want is your own little shop to open with short money. Wheeler-dealers need not apply.

WHAT IT TAKES

Starting a business with little or no cash of your own is more than a technique, a mathematical formula, a way of business, or even an objective. It's a state of mind.

After you finish this book you'll know the techniques and the strategies, but to turn it from theory to practice requires a unique individual. It's not everyone's cup of tea.

Precisely what does it take to go for it and succeed? I offer no long shopping list of personal attributes or managerial skills. It doesn't work. Too many times we have seen the village moron end up owning the largest and most successful business in town while the smartest kid on the block ends up his bookkeeper. So put away all the books giving you self-tests and prodding your managerial IQ. It's only filler and doesn't mean a thing. You never know if you have what it takes until you actually do it.

Neither does it matter why you want to do it. Most people don't really know why they want their own business. Their mind plays nasty tricks on them. Ask them why and they'll say money, when it's really the challenge. Or they'll say the challenge when they can't bring themselves to admit it's only to break away from an overbearing boss. It may be an ego trip or a combination of a hundred reasons. What difference does it make? If you want it—or only think you want it—then do it. Either you'll swim like a fish in water or decide it's not for you. But at least you'll have it out of your system and stop wondering about it the rest of your life.

I will tell you this. Whatever any reasonably capitalized business takes to succeed, it will take more to succeed in a shoestring start-up. There's no such thing as a free lunch. In one way or another you pay the price for going it on a hope and a prayer. And the two absolutely essential ingredients you must provide are:

1. Double determination.
2. Ten times the work.

"Bull," you say. "You can't scare me." Well that's good. It shows guts. And you'll need plenty of that also to succeed. Earlier in this chapter I called it chutzpah, a precise word with an imprecise Anglo-Saxon equivalent made up of equal parts of aggressiveness, courage, daring, and plain moxie. I've yet to see a shoestring business succeed without it.

DOUBLE YOUR DETERMINATION

You never quite know what the word *determination* means until you try to build something from nothing. You can't do it with half-hearted attempts. That's one reason why so many bootstrap deals do succeed—once the doors open. An enormous determination brought it that far and that same determination usually carries it over the survival stage. It's a far cry from the owner who mortgages his home to the hilt and plows $40,000 into the business on a whim. That's not determination. It's only a mortgaged house. When you knock on a hundred doors, tell a hundred stories, and with sweat on your brow try still another door—then you know what determination is. It turns the soft metal of ambition into the tempered steel of resolve.

I opened this chapter telling you about the first day in the life of Discount City. Words are easy to write, but it wasn't quite so simple. The mountains of inventory didn't just appear at the loading platform. Without cash and without credit it was a mighty tough sell. We had to bang on the doors of 980 prospective suppliers before we could find 38 who would gamble on us and ship on lenient credit terms the business could handle. We had to listen to 300 suppliers laugh us out of their offices before the first order was accepted.

It's enough to send you back to the time clock. It was the same for everything the business needed. Fixtures? We scoured 27 auctions before we landed an assortment of gondolas, showcases, and counters we could buy dirt cheap and on credit. Location? It was the hardest part. We needed both a high-traffic location and a landlord who'd wait two to three months for his first check. Mission impossible. Finally, after two months, we found a strip shopping center whose landlord would take a chance on us in return for a higher rent in the later months. Heck, we couldn't even afford the $900 for an electric deposit. Using a borrowed portable generator we had the lights to operate for several weeks until we could cover the $900. It may sound like war stories, but that's how it happens in the real world when you don't have money behind you.

Others have their own stories. Don Pendergast is an interesting example. Don designed a new style boat anchor offering the twin advantages of lighter weight and greater holding power than conventional anchors. Boating firms and enthusiasts endorsed the anchor, but it wasn't enough to help Don raise the $200,000 he'd need to start production. Since 1979 he has been banging on doors. He contacted over 200 venture capital firms and 60 banks. Still no money. But Don never threw in the sponge. Early in 1983 his determination paid dividends. An investor from Spokane heard about the anchor, investigated, and decided to capitalize the start-up for a 50% interest. Think about it. Over four years between dream and reality.

I came across plenty of people with business ideas and limited or no capital. It's interesting to test their determination. Many will make a few feeble attempts to raise a few dollars from a bank or relatives, and when they come up empty they walk away from the idea. It's a blessing in disguise. If they can't walk the extra mile to get it going they don't have the determination to work it through the trouble spots and make it succeed.

THE ONE-TENTH PRINCIPLE

Jerome Goldstein (no relative), publisher of *In Business* magazine, wrote a terrific editorial in a past issue of his journal. He captioned it the "One-Tenth Financing Principle." I borrowed the term because he did aptly sum up what I'm now about to say. You can start a business with one-tenth the capital normally required (or even no cash at all), but in return you must work ten times as hard to make it succeed.

Any business—even the heavily capitalized firm—takes plenty of commitment and elbow grease to make it. That's common knowledge. The shoestring start-up needs more. Lots more. It all comes down to doing things for yourself instead of using precious capital to have other people do it for you. You find yourself working around the clock, and typically, your family by your side. Every penny saved is a penny less you need to start. Before you know it you're a genuine workaholic.

Peggy Lebow is. She admits to working 16–18-hour days to

make her artificial flower distributorship hum. "It's all economics," says Peggy. "I spend evenings making the flowers instead of buying them ready-made at double the price. During the day, I'm out selling rather than paying commissions or salary to someone else." She's not alone.

Hard as you may work it's all to your advantage. Control is one. Nothing escapes your eye because you are involved in every phase of the operation. You measure costs, control waste, and don't hesitate to knock three hours from a stockboy's schedule if you can. Costly mistakes are far and few between because you realize you can't afford mistakes. As you grow you do it with extreme caution because you remember where you came from.

While studying for my MBA I burned the midnight oil with two brothers. One went on and is now a regional manager for Coca Cola. The other scraped together a few dollars and started a wholesale bakery firm. "You know," he said, "I work morning, noon, and night and my brother, the Coca Cola executive, never understands why. And he'll never understand it until he's in his own business—a business he enjoys. Then and only then will he realize that it only looks like work."

THE TIME IS ALWAYS RIGHT

Behind my desk is a framed self-portrait of an elderly gentleman named Harold, poised with a palette in one hand and a paint brush in the other. Neither the artistry or a deep personal relationship with the artist compelled me to buy the painting. It was his smile. It carried an important message, and I wanted that smile to be my continued warning that hopes can grow old.

I met Harold while visiting my grandfather in a nursing home. As a patient he'd spend his day painting and smiling. Striking up a conversation with him, he confided the reason for his ever-present smile. "You know," he said, "when I was a young art student just out of high school, I wanted to open an art gallery. My father wanted me to be a dentist instead. Well, I spent six years getting through NYU Dental School, hating every minute of it and wishing I owned my own art gallery instead. I wanted a career in art, not pulling teeth. But life plays nasty tricks. First came the Depression, so I drilled teeth to make a living. Then came the war, and the Navy needed dentists. When I got back I had a wife and two kids to support, so I pushed aside my dreams of an art gallery and resumed my dental practice. When I hit 50 I figured it was time. My kids were on their own and I had money in the bank. My wife called it mid-life crisis and my kids thought I was insane to give up a lucrative dental practice to open an art gallery. So for the next 20 years I continued to push aside the idea of my own gallery and drilled more damned teeth. Well now I'm 73 years old and too ill to start an art gallery so I paint instead. You wonder what happens to all the years and all your dreams." I never wanted to forget those words.

People always have reasons for pushing their ambitions into the future. Excuses come easy. If you really want your own business you'll face only one real enemy—procrastination. You can read this or any other book 56 times and memorize every word, but what good does it do if you don't put it into practice?

The procrastinator always has a reason. How many times have you heard someone say "the time isn't right," "the economy is bad," "money is too tight," or " I want to make certain there'll be no war in the Mideast." The list is endless. Year in and out the procrastinator reasons while someone else makes the money.

One thing is certain, my friend. Nobody is going to knock on your door, lead you by the hand, and do it for you. Nobody is going to give you the push to get started today. Why should they?

So let's face facts. Some of you will never start your own business. Your dreams are nothing more than fantasies. You'll hope for it, think about it, and fabricate ten more reasons why you can't do it. And you shouldn't. Whatever you want from your business your business will need more from you.

Then again, you may be one of the few who are ready. Perhaps you've been in business before and know what it's all about. Maybe it's your first time and you have kicked aside all your fears and doubts and are anxious to tackle it. Welcome to the club. Someday you'll look back at your own grand opening—your first day at the helm of your own business. And when you do, you'll also stand tall and give yourself a hefty pat on the back. You'll deserve it. You made your own miracles.

2

CHECKING OUT YOUR WINNING IDEA

You can imagine the pained expression on the faces of Gary Dahl's astounded bowling buddies when he announced his plans to package ordinary sandstones in cage-like cartons and market it as everyone's favorite pet—"The Pet Rock." Who in their right mind wants a rock for a pet? It can't curl up on your lap, beg for a treat, or fetch a newspaper. In fact, it can do none of the heartwarming things we've come to expect from the more animated variety of household additions. About all it can do is slumber in its clever striped box with the $4.98 price tag and hope people would learn to love it. And they did. "Rocky" ranks third as a household pet, after Fido and Tabby. As one proud master asks, "Why can't you love a pet rock? Did you ever see a rock bite?"

Marketing experts scratched their heads in predictable disbelief, while psychologists threw up their hands in mock surrender. Saner people laughed, while the rest of the world bought. It was the story of one more idea—and one more instant millionaire.

So who wants to be a millionaire? Not Beverly Zintgraff, who at 32 is still scraping together a few dollars to open a lingerie shop in Cleveland's swank Shaker Heights suburb. "I'll be happy if I can someday take out enough money from the business to have a home without a leaky roof, a mortgage that doesn't pinch, a Buick in the driveway, and a few bucks for my kids' college." You'll also find Ken Engour on the slow track to success. "I'm not looking for a quantum leap to a fast fortune. What I do want is a sideline business to augment my salary as a flight engineer. And that sideline business is a newsletter to corporate pilots." Listen to the stories. It's the stuff the American dream is made of. Ordinary people in ordinary businesses, however, do make very unusual stories. But it makes you wonder. How many are selecting their right business? Are you?

THE ONE MOST IMPORTANT DECISION

This year 500,000 people will start their own business. Burt Nicholas, a career consultant estimates that 60–70% will select the wrong business for them. That's why so many people do fail. There may be nothing wrong with the business idea itself, or their own management capabilities, but still the owner and the business may not fit together. And when that happens the venture never works out. The first ingredient for success is the perfect match between the entrepreneur and the enterprise.

I enjoy talking to entrepreneurs planning their first venture. It's interesting to probe their thoughts and discover how they came to choose their intended business. One young man recently told me he looked at various opportunities over a two-year span. He considered everything from a restaurant to a franchised real estate office, finally settling on opening an automobile tire and accessory shop. "So why did you pick that business?" I asked. "Easy," he replied. "*Entrepreneur Magazine* predicted auto-related businesses will be the best money-makers in the years ahead." Maybe so. But will it be *his* best money-maker?

It's an easy trap to fall into. Some are blinded by what they see as the best way to make money. Others mistakenly look for prestige or glamour. Many others simply go into the easiest entry business. And with less thought behind it than in selecting a new car, they somehow think it will work for them. Too often it doesn't. Take some advice:

Doesn't everyone want to run a restaurant? Kirk Begogian thinks so. Kirk manages a Boston brokerage firm specializing in restaurant sales, and will tell you that the money motive can be a killer—and everyone thinks the biggest, fastest, and easiest money can be made in the food business. "Not so," Kirk adds. "The restaurant business is the world's toughest business, and for every millionaire it produces there are 100 bankruptcies. Still they line up knowing nothing about the business except the delusion it's their pot of gold."

"Whenever we sell a business brokerage franchise," reports one unnamed executive of a franchise brokerage system, "we do sell opportunity, but we're also selling prestige and glamour. Seventy percent of our franchisees have no business trying to sell a business. Mechanics, assembly line workers, route delivery people, and other blue-collar types are always dreaming of the day they can trade dirty work jeans or a soiled apron for a three-piece suit and a chance to sit behind a desk. Most of them don't belong behind a desk. They belong in dirty work clothes or a soiled apron doing what they do best. But they will shell out $30,000 for a chance to grab what they see as prestige."

"We can put people into a franchised food store for as little as $4000 down," claims a supermarket executive who started a successful program for licensing convenience stores. "So as you'd expect we have a waiting list of hundreds of willing food store operators. If you cull the list you'd find out that 90% are interested only because we do give them the opportunity to get into business with so little cash. How many are on the list because they really want to operate a convenience store? Damn few. That's why we have such a high turnover of franchisees."

You can't fault many of these people who opened in haste and repented in leisure with little to show for it but boarded up store fronts, going-out-of-business sales, and broken dreams. Choosing the right business is one of the most important decisions of your life, and before I show you how to start on a shoestring I want to help you check out what you intend to start. Let's make it a winner.

NARROW THE RANGE

Start-up entrepreneurs can be divided into two categories. First are those with a reasonably precise idea of what their business will be. They know the type business, size marketing approach, and general location. They have a fixed mind-set. They can close their eyes and visualize it—make it come alive. Some do even better and have it all reduced to a comprehensive business plan nailed down to its smallest detail. Well, that's good. It's a starting point and the essential starting point for this chapter and the chapters to come. If you're such an entrepreneur you have your own mind made up. That doesn't mean that what you have in mind is a right or logical choice, but it *is* the starting point. We have something to test. We can kick its tires and see if it'll stand up. When we're through you may decide to go ahead with it, re-shape it, or abandon it altogether. Keep an open mind.

The "shoppers" are the second category. Their mind is far from made up. In a maze of indecision they wander through a wide selection, hoping to narrow the range to the one best choice. If you're a shopper make a list of businesses you're most interested in. Rank them so you too have your starting point. Let's see how your list looks when we complete the chapter.

CREATING THE PERFECT MATCH

When is there a perfect match between entrepreneur and enterprise? I recommend a four-part test:

1. Can you *enjoy* the business?
2. Can you *manage* the business?
3. Can you *earn* from the business?
4. Can you *afford* the business?

Doesn't it make sense? These four points answer the question of what you can bring to the business, and in return, what the business can do for you. As with any relationship you and the business must mesh together to create a workable bond, and it only happens when you score on all key points. Consider them one by one.

THE PSYCHIC REWARDS

For Gary Gygax, forming his own company TRS Hobbies, Lake Geneva, Wisconsin, was like a return to his childhood. "The real motivation is I like games," he reports. "I've been playing chess and Parcheesi for longer than I can remember, so I made a business out of my hobby." You probably know Gary through his now popular "Dungeons & Dragons" games. Although I never met Gary I bet he's a man who whistles while he works, and that always means a man in the right business.

Most people think money is the number one priority in selecting a business. Put it on the bottom of your list. The psychic rewards—enjoyment—head the list. When you enjoy your business the success and money are bound to follow, but it never quite works in reverse. And if you happen to make serious money in a business you don't enjoy, I'll guarantee you'd make twice the money in a business—any business—that does get your adrenalin flowing.

So what business would you enjoy? No quick answer is needed. It may be the line of work you have experience in, but in a real sense you're never sure what will provide the greatest pleasure because you are limited by your own experiences. The unknown may be even better.

Starting your own business may be breaking away from your working past. For many, it signals not only the transition from employee to entrepreneur but from "what they have been" to "what they really should be." And for many, it's like being reborn. But for many others, breaking from the past for the challenge of a totally new career path is too much to tackle and there's always the few with their blinders on who never really think about it.

One of my brightest associates in our law firm had this problem. Peter would sit behind his desk pouring over legal briefs but always thinking about marketing an adult game he was developing. He'd walk into my office and talk games while I wanted to talk law. Finally I asked him why he didn't quit the practice of law and go into the full-time business of promoting his game? It wasn't money or security. Peter, lucky enough to be born to the right parents, had more money than any senior partner in our firm. It was his own self-image. "My folks would have a heart attack if they found out their son the lawyer was selling toys." So Peter's not selling games. And as an unhappy lawyer he's not living much of a life either.

Peter's story isn't unique. People everywhere are so busy making a living they think they can't switch gears to have a more enjoyable career. Not long ago we were asked to handle the legal work for a 42-year-old gas station attendant about to open his own service station. So you talk and you learn. What I learned was this chap was a photography buff. Pumping gas was his life. It wasn't easy to convince him to give up his idea for a gas station and go for a photo shop instead. With 25–30 productive years ahead of him, why waste it on a business he didn't enjoy? Today you'll find him operating not one but three camera shops and loving every minute of it. You only live once.

I've been in many businesses. Some I thought I'd enjoy and learned to dislike, while others I enjoy more than I thought I could. That brings us to the other side of the coin. Sometimes the grass only looks greener.

One misadventure of mine was a movie theater. I was a movie fanatic since I can remember and can tell you who won the Academy Awards in 1956. So when I had a few chips to spare and another adventure to conquer, it was only logical a movie theater would catch my eye. That's when I learned you don't know a business until you're in it, work it, and live it. While I thought I'd be partying with movie stars, I discovered it was a headache business, hassling film distributors, chasing rowdy kids, and working weekends. It cost me $30,000 to find out that you have to look before you leap.

Look *before* you leap. Important advice. Since my bygone days as a movie mogul I fight like a madman with clients going into a business he or she doesn't know, just as I'll push to get a client involved to test an untried business. Then, and only then, do you know whether the business will give you a psychic reward or a royal headache.

This may be your best opportunity to experiment and try your hand in several situations of interest to you. Why jump into unchartered waters? When Taylor Lynch decided to leave his job as a dispatcher for a freight-forwarding firm his target was to open a travel agency. As Taylor admits, he knew nothing about the travel business. While keeping his daytime job he learned fast, working in a local office evenings and Saturdays. It still interested him but he had his doubts. Taylor never realized how difficult it was to satisfy the vacationing public. "I didn't think I had the patience to handle it," says Taylor. "Not after a lady phoned me from the Bahamas screaming that her plane was late for take-off. When you're in the travel business everything's your fault." But that's what it's all about. When you're on the outside looking in any business can look good. You have to crawl inside to feel the pulse, see the problems, detect the difficulties, and see if it's for you. Try it on the installment plan.

Every aspect of a business can add or detract from its enjoyability. The type of business—and nature of the work—is only one factor to be considered. "But even a slight modification from what the entrepreneur is comfortable with can throw him off balance and make him a fish out of water," says Burt Nicholas. "Some people are totally inflexible. For example, a manager of a high-class steak house reasons he can enjoy operating any type restaurant. But throw him into a different type restaurant with a different clientele and you may as well put him into another business. On the other extreme are entrepreneurs who can happily adapt to a wide range of opportunities within or beyond a given field. The entrepreneur has to discover this about himself."

The structure of the firm is one more dimension to consider. Frequently people will hunt for a franchise for management support because it offers a financially attractive opportunity, and never consider the control they have to surrender. A franchise can make a free-wheeling entrepreneur's life miserable or it can be a bonus to a less secure type happy to exchange decision making for firm guidance. The same can be said for partners.

Don't overlook business hours or travel demands. Frequently the opportunity for travel is an attraction because it is a novelty. The novelty wears off as so many people discovered, and spending half your life away from family can quickly destroy enthusiasm.

When you're in the right business there is a thrill to it all. You see the business born. You nurse it through the survival stage. You navigate it to its apex. And when you're through you'll probably sell out if only so you can start again and enjoy it again. It sure beats going to work.

Will you enjoy your business?

MEASURE YOUR MANAGEMENT MENTALITY

What management mentality will your start-up need? Plenty. And it will need considerably more than the venture started with a healthy investment, because when you start on a shoestring you don't have any margin for error. And as the Bankruptcy Courts can tell you, entrepreneurs don't always use the right yardstick when they do measure their management mentality.

Elliot Galahow, a small business consultant, says, "It's not so much a matter of *what* the entrepreneur can manage as much as *when* he or she is ready to manage the start-up they have in mind." So it's timing and prior experience rather than capability that's usually the decisive factor. "And while you're learning you can be nickeled and dimed to death with 100 small but nevertheless fatal mistakes," adds Bill Portnoy, who confesses to making enough slip-ups in his embryonic Philadelphia restaurant to teach a course in "mis-management" at the Harvard Business School.

Just as a business can look like *fun* to operate, it can also look *easy* to operate. Illusion on the first point means only less fun. Illusion on the second means failure. And few businesses are as easy to operate as it may appear. But still the naive optimists beat their drums, "What do you have to know about running a pinball arcade, shoe store, or coffee shop?" I don't know. I never operated one. But why don't you ask someone who has? Take your notebook along and be prepared for a long and hard education. Every business has its tricks.

It amazes me how many people have never worked in a business, know nothing about it, and with a refreshing mixture of chutzpah, enthusiasm, and sheer optimism throw their life's savings into the venture. What's more amazing is that some people actually make it. They're the fast learners. The slow learners are wise to make their mistakes with an employer's money, so they'll make a few less with their own.

Experience alone does not magically transform itself into management ability. Years of experience coupled with narrow responsibility still deprive the enterprise of the broad skills necessary to master the operation.

One characteristic of a shoestring start-up is the ability of the entrepreneur to parlay his managerial strength into financing. Creditors have their own perception of your management ability and when you're collateral shy it becomes the major selling point. One wholesaler comments, "We helped a young fellow get started in his own liquor store with a lenient credit line. We had confidence in him because he managed a large liquor store for one of our accounts and did a hell of a job building the business. In fact, we knew him better than we did his boss. It's a different story with someone off the street who wants to try his hand in the liquor business."

So the message is clear. If you don't have the experience in the type business you have in mind, then don't try to open it just yet. Defer it until you can obtain valuable "hands-on" experience as an employee. You may have to moonlight to pick up the experience or sacrifice some income for a few months but it will be a much smaller loss than what you will sustain by operating a business you know nothing about. There are some other steps to consider:

1. A franchise is one. A major selling point of most franchises is that they will train you and then provide the close supervision to keep the business on track. It works well in the fast food fields, but I question whether it's enough background in more complex fields such as business brokerage. Watch the economics. If you're essentially buying the "training" you're over-spending. The reason to pick up a franchise is because you want the name and system a good franchise can offer.

2. Partners are another possibility. I have seen many cases where a partner provided the experience and management "know-how." A partnership can also be ideal for a larger business requiring either a broader span of management or a division of responsibility. It also has its downside as you'll see in Chapter 7.

Don't be what I call a "minimum-wage manager." What's a "minimum-wage manager"? Anyone who knows so little about a business that all he or she is worth is the minimum wage. Few can take an idea and make it a winning idea.

LIVING WITHOUT A LIVING

"Tighten your belt and don't expect to eat for a few years," comments Pat Mone who is still waiting for enough money from her struggling bookstore to finance her first legitimate meal in as long as she can remember.

Nobody can, with a straight face, predict how wealthy your business will make you 10 or 15 years from now. That's up to you and the business. It's the first year, or two or three, that counts. That's when the mismatch between what you need from the business to live—and what the business can afford to give you—takes its toll. And the answer can only be found with a realistic look at the business itself.

The mismatching process continues. Entrepreneurs, for example, will leave a $25,000-a-year position and start a bootstrap business that can only generate $6000 a year for the first year or two. For some people it's not a problem. For the guy who *needs* $25,000 to support a wife and three kids it's a $19,000 problem. Common sense? Maybe. Usually, however, it's a wildly optimistic type who either overestimates his earnings potential from the business or somehow thinks he can live on less.

It's endemic with all shoestring start-ups. You pay a price for starting poor, and the price is staying poor for some time to come. But what entrepreneurs don't realize is that some businesses will keep you poorer longer than others. An example: When Phyllis and Barry McLean decided to leave their respective jobs as teacher and commercial artist to start their art gallery, they knew they would immediately sacrifice $53,000 in combined income. "We had several options," explains Phyllis. "One of us could have remained with our job until the business was large enough to need us both, but we wanted to start with myself handling retail sales while Barry went after corporate sales. But even with the two of us pitching sales we knew our art gallery was a business with a very slow take-off. So to create a larger cash flow—and base to draw a salary—we altered our plans and made it a combination art gallery and greeting card and gift shop. It required very little additional capital to triple our sales but now the numbers begin to make sense."

Take off your rose-colored glasses when assessing the short-term income potential of your business. What you need is a cash flow statement that shows how much you can safely draw from the business. And with your rose-colored glasses beside you look at it with a jaundiced eye. Whenever I project income I deliberately underestimate projected income by 20% while over-estimating expenses by 10%. It usually takes you closer to reality.

Here's another mistake to avoid. Don't think you can defy the odds. Even shrewd management isn't magic. Three years ago I was taking two young partners through the exercise of projecting their cash flow and take-home income from a planned tool rental shop. Admittedly, a cash flow statement is at best a guesstimate of what a business actually will do, but even under the best of circumstances the business couldn't afford more than $10,000 a year for each of its two partners. That's not how they saw it. Working backwards they conveniently pumped up the projected sales to give them the bottom line they were looking for. It's an idiot's game.

Frequently a partnership produces a greater strain on the question of earnings. While a single-owner business can juggle personal finances to subsidize what a business can pay, it's rare that two partners can perform the same juggling act. So with one partner willing to bite the bullet and take home less, the other needs more. It's not only poor partnership planning but poor business planning. The solution is usually a larger business.

Don't concern yourself with the income potential a few years into the future. The business at maturity may be too small or unprofitable to provide the income you want. In itself it's not the criteria for defining your business. You can always expand, sell-out, or trade-up. What you want now is a threshold business. Something to get you started.

Ron Chisholm, who started many bootstrap companies and most notably a four-store phono record and stereo chain, says it's all a matter of "staying power." "When you recognize how little a business can afford you can plan for it—deal with it. I went for broke in my first record shop and instead of opening a small 1000-sq.-ft. store, I gambled all the way on a 3000-ft. operation. With a larger store I'd have a larger cash flow and that always translates into more cash to take home. Why die on the install-ment plan?"

There are a hundred ways to shape a business—or shape a situation—to make ends meet so you have staying power. Thou-sands of successful start-ups had their owners moonlighting to keep their income flowing so the cash could remain in their business. Others live on cash reserves. Still others, the retired or bored housewives, may not need present income. The same is true if you have an income independent of the business. But when you can't shape the situation, you do have to shape the business to give you the income you do need.

CAN YOU AFFORD IT?

I'll have considerably more to say about this in the next chapter, but capital is the *least* important factor in selecting a business or in defining start-up size. Perhaps that one point is the central theme of this entire book. You can start just about any type business, regardless of how much capital you personally have, once you know how to put together what you do want with everyone else's money.

A case in point: Overlooking Cape Cod's Buzzards Bay you'll find several very successful restaurants. But the largest and most successful was started with absolutely no owner's cash. Several years after it opened I came to be friendly with the owner and he confided, "I came to the Cape from New York not only penniless but $300,000 in debt from an aborted business deal. I was ready to go bankrupt, but decided to wheel and deal just once more. Either I'd bail myself out or go bankrupt with a few more creditors. So I decided a restaurant would be my logical choice. Now, of course, I couldn't afford to open even the smallest restaurant so why not go for the largest? It's my way of making the illogical logical. Within six months I put together a syndicated partnership. The 20 investors each contributed $40,000 for a total of $800,000,while I retained 50% ownership as the mastermind. But I looked ahead and gave myself the option to buy out my partners for $1,200,000 payable over five years. Within a year of the opening I exercised the option and just finished paying down my ex-partners. Now it's worth $2.5 million and it's all mine. You don't start a business on what *you* can afford—you start the business with what others *let* you afford."

It was an interesting story and I never forgot it. Neither should you.

What do these four points really come down to? Self-assessment. Admittedly it's never easy to be objective when you're asking the tough questions about yourself. But when you do know your own goals and needs, strengths and limitations, you have one part of the matching process. And only then can you define your perfect match.

THOUSANDS OF SUCCESSFUL NEW VENTURES

The small business movement is on the march. The 500,000 start-ups this year (the highest number since the Second World War) will grow to an estimated 750,000 new ventures for 1990.

Why the groundswell of entrepreneurial activity? New consumer trends and recent technology, coupled with the fact that more people than ever before want to be their own boss, create the momentum. And while large corporations can't or won't respond to the needs, it leaves vast pockets of opportunity for the small venture.

I simply don't understand people who want to start their own business but complain the opportunities don't exist. They're wrong—dead wrong. Not only do more opportunities exist today than ever before, but even newer opportunities are on the horizon for tomorrow.

Consider all the new businesses surrounding you. A nearby shopping mall tells part of the story. Almost half the tenants are operating businesses unheard of only five years ago. Specialized shops—a designer jean store, a video shop, a store devoted only to jogging shoes, to name a few—are peppered throughout the mall. Turn to the yellow pages, 40% of the listings are businesses in embryonic industries bypassing the imagination of yesterday's entrepreneur. Did you know that more than 50% of all service businesses offer services that only recently came into demand? The computer revolution alone created its own tidal wave of opportunities. I can point out 30 publishing firms, for example, riding on the coattails of a public clamoring for computer information. Not one of these firms was around in 1975.

If the future presents its opportunities, the past makes its own contributions. Traditional businesses are being re-shaped into brand-new opportunities as people discover new ways—better ways—to do business and grab their healthy share of a market from traditionalists who won't change.

You can't find one industry that won't go through a radical re-styling in the next several years. Society is on too fast a track for anyone to stand still. And as always the change will be pioneered by enterprising individuals who can see opportunities while others see none.

So your winning idea is more than an inward look at your own talents, interests, and motivations. You want to find a market niche for a viable, successful venture. And thousands of opportunities await you.

HOW OTHERS FOUND SUCCESS

How do people find success? What formula do entrepreneurs use to discover opportunity and their perfect business? There is no one answer, but a wide range of approaches. For some it came after months of active, deliberate searching and sifting, while for others the transition from personal interest to business took place so gradually that they were surprised to discover themselves actually in business. And not a small number will tell you that "something snapped—an idea was born."

Let's meet some of these people as they tell their stories.

A visit to the dentist to cure a cantankerous molar was the launching point for Gary Klein, a shipper for a New York firm. "While waiting for the novocaine to put me out of my misery, I studied the deplorable condition of my dentist's aquarium. It was a natural observation for me," says Gary "because I'm an aquarium buff and have a few fish tanks of my own. My dentist clearly didn't have the time or inclination to keep his fish happy so I offered to—for $25 a month. Within three months he referred me to several other professionals with their own problem aquariums. By moonlighting I could handle about 50 calls a month, and at $25 an office visit (still less than what my dentist charges), I was soon making more money by moonlighting than from my regular job. Before jumping into the business full time, I advertised for new accounts in local professional magazines, and surprisingly, obtained a slew of new customers. Now I have two panel trucks on the road, and a full-time assistant helping me handle 300 accounts a month in the New York boroughs. It's still a small business—grossing about $100,000 a year but the net profit is fantastic because I'm only selling a service. Within the next year or two I plan to triple the number of "office calls" and perhaps open a retail aquarium shop. For me it all started with a toothache."

Ask Bob Crisafi if he expected to open his own business. "No way," voices Bob. So how was it that one month later Bob was the stereo king of Cambridge's Harvard Square? "I owned a small block of stores near Harvard and one of my tenants was a highly successful stereo shop pushing hi-fis to the college crowd. And I knew just how successful they were because their rent was based on sales and that gave me a look at their books. One blustery winter evening the store had a fire, destroying most of the inventory. Although the partners in the business collected insurance, they decided not to re-open and instead part company. Well, that gave me an empty store. I lined up another tenant in a hurry, but when it came time to sign the lease my hand froze. I kept getting flashbacks to the income statement from the stereo shop and simply said, what the hell—I'm going into the stereo business. I didn't agonize over the decision, I just knew what I had there and the idea wouldn't let go. Since I knew nothing about the business I hired a top-notch manager away from Tech Hi-Fi and never regretted the decision."

A warehouse loaded with imported neck pendants was the starting point for Dave Scribner's Royal-Wear Jewelry, a mail-order firm nicely chugging along at the clip of $500,000 annually. Dave explains how the company came to be: "My father was a commercial auctioneer. Very often he'd bid in himself for the merchandise and re-sell it later at a profit. Evidently a large jewelry firm in Providence folded and my dad purchased $60,000 worth of jade and gold neck pendants for about $10,000. He planned to sell the merchandise to a few department stores when he unexpectedly died. At the time I was just graduating from Brown University and had the task of liquidating my dad's estate—including the warehouse loaded with jewelry. So I toyed around with several methods to unload the merchandise and finally settled on a mail-order campaign. I gave the neck wear the 'Royal-Wear' name and had a Boston free-lance ad man work me up several ads for *Cosmopolitan* magazine and the *Ladies' Home Journal*. We tested the ad in one or two journals and found they pulled orders. It's a great feeling to look in your mailbox and see it stuffed with 200–300 envelopes—each with a $15.95 check. Within two months the inventory was gone and we had a $20,000 profit. It was then I decided I thoroughly enjoyed mail-order promoting and wanted it as my career. Borrowing my share of the inheritance I scouted out new direct-mail items—from digital watches to a unique collapsible hunting knife. Of course, I had to change the name of the firm to 'Royal Sales' because I was no longer just in the jewelry line. Growth has been deliberately slow. Mail order is a tough business, and you need the instinctive touch for gauging the market. Now that I've been in the business several years, I'm developing the touch and expect the company to reach the $1 million mark within two years. It's interesting. I was forced into the business by circumstance, and I always wondered what I'd be doing today if I wasn't left a warehouse full of jewelry."

For Martha and Joe Beaumont everything about their decision was slow, painstaking, and deliberate. "We knew we wanted our business to be a family affair," says Joseph, a burly ex-marine with a service pension. "We had no particular skills but we knew that the business would in some way be connected to food, because both Martha and I enjoy cooking. Opening a small restaurant or even a coffee shop looked like our logical choice until we took a trip to New York and spotted a crowded gourmet shop selling delicacies from around the world. We immediately liked the idea because it was not only the food business—but one with an exciting twist. Best of all, our neck of the woods in southeastern Massachusetts didn't have a comparable business. Rather than rush into it we spent a full year talking to suppliers, reading specialty food journals, and checking out similar businesses on the east coast. And the more we learned the more we were convinced it was our *right* business." Today, the Continental Gourmet has 12 employees and sales of $800,000—but you'll still find Martha and Joe behind the counter explaining to yet another amateur gourmet the secret pleasures of their 27 blends of imported coffee.

You won't read about these people in the *Wall Street Journal*. But each in their own way found their path to success. Gary Klein perhaps says it best when he philosophizes, "Somewhere in the zigzag of life, you snare your enthusiasm on an idea. That's when you've found your opportunity."

GIVE YOUR IDEA THE ACID-TEST

Do you have the *right* business idea? Don't look for the answer in this book. If I had the foolproof crystal ball I'd be too busy sipping piña coladas in the Bahamas to tell you. And nobody else (except for the few quacks who pretend to have all the right answers) can tell you either. That too is part of the fascination of business. It bears its similarities to the Las Vegas slot machines.

Ask Gary Dahl, "Mr. Pet Rock," how many people believed

that not all his rocks were to be found in cardboard cages. Ask Henry Ford about the 400 MBAs with 198,000 pages of "market research" who *proved* every American wanted an Edsel in the driveway.

So, my friend, being an entrepreneur is being a gambler. But there are ways to stack the odds in your favor. Put your idea to the test.

Test One. The Test of Time. Stay with the idea at least several months before you take the plunge and commit to the venture. If the idea fades before then, it doesn't necessarily mean it was a bad idea, only an idea that you didn't believe in strongly enough to make work.

Test Two. Measure the Market. Identify, isolate, and rate the potential users. Plenty of ideas collapse, not because the market isn't there, but because it's too small or poorly defined to turn into a money-maker. This advice extends to even traditional retail stores who may enter under-populated or overly competitive areas. Are the customers there to support your business?

Test Three. Test the Pulling Power. You may see a huge demand out there for your winning idea, but the way to turn demand into dollars is to convert your demand to *demand pull*. In other words, come up with the selling point. Nobody sells a product or service. We all sell a "benefit." How will customers benefit from what you have to sell?

Test Four. Test Your Reach. Even with a well-defined market and an approach with pulling power, you need the means to reach your market. Many start-up firms stumble on this one, underestimating what it takes in advertising or promotion costs to capture the interest of a sufficiently large percentage of users to make the venture worthwhile.

Test Five. Pre-Test the Idea. This is a particularly important point in product marketing. Always pre-test the idea. Try it out on a small scale with select advertising, or try to line up your customers before you commit yourself to the business. Gary Klein pretested the demand for his aquarium service business before he ventured into it on a full-time basis, and so do the largest corporations. Always test the gamble first with a few disposable dollars.

Test Six. Game-Plan the Entire Venture. Acid-test the basic assumptions on which your business will be built. Market potential is only one of many assumptions. Check the others: Can you obtain the product? Can you buy—and sell—at the right price? Do you know your costs? Will the numbers work? Every business is a long chain of integrated factors, never stronger than the one weak link.

Test Seven. Test Your Knowledge. This is the key to it all. Businesses fail because the entrepreneur at the helm didn't know enough about the business to psyche out and correct the weaknesses or exploit the potential strengths. It's all in the homework. And while you never come up with foolproof conclusions there's no excuse for overlooking the obvious. So become a sponge, soaking up as much information as you can about the business, because eventually you'll need it all.

KEY POINTS TO REMEMBER

1. Your success—or failure—will depend more on selecting the *right* business than on any other decision. It's your most important decision.
2. Don't chase illusive reasons in deciding upon a venture. Money, prestige, and easy entry are never strong reasons.
3. Develop the mind-set of what your business will be. Visualize it in as much detail as possible so you can evaluate it.
4. Match the business to yourself before you match it to the market. Remember you want a business you can enjoy, manage, and earn from.
5. Don't limit your sights by what you *think* you can afford.

6. There are more opportunities today than ever before. Bootstrap pioneers are invading traditional fields and pathfinding new industries.
7. There's no one right way to come across your perfect opportunity. In the zigzag of life, you too will snare your enthusiasm on a winning idea.
8. Put your idea to the seven-point test. It can improve your odds, but never expect foolproof results.

3

SHOESTRING ECONOMICS

Shoestring economics? Don't look for it in the catalogs of the Harvard or Stanford Business Schools. Yet this year over 150,000 bootstrap entrepreneurs will enroll and sweat through the course on the self-study plan. Their laboratories are the countless shoestring enterprises started with high hopes and low cash. The exams come fast and furious, testing skills on how to make a cash-shy business come together and stay together. Tuition? The willingness to dig in and do whatever's needed to survive. Four out of five drop out. The graduates never receive a sheepskin but do win a successful business. The class motto: "Who needs cash?"

Building a shoestring enterprise demands mastery over numerous problems ignored by the well-capitalized entrepreneur. Essentially they can all be boiled to one—an acute shortage of capital to follow conventional economic rules. You plan differently and operate with different priorities. Survival is the ability to always compensate for lack of cash.

The economic theme is the same during each of the four stages of the venture's development: the planning stage, the start-up stage, the survival stage, and the growth stage.

During the planning stage, the entrepreneur conceives and roughly shapes the idea for the venture. He may do preliminary research on a fixed idea or seek out opportunities. It's at this stage that most shoestring ventures become "still births," as the entrepreneur concludes either that the idea is in itself unworkable, or the capital needs too excessive. For every business that is started many more are put on hold or dropped because the entrepreneur didn't analyze how the business could come together using the right economic perspective.

At the start-up stage, the organization begins to take form. During this period the entrepreneur begins to assemble financing, assets, locations, and personnel. It may be a methodical approach or the venture may simply stumble together as a pre-destined event. In either case, the later success of the enterprise is chiefly dependent on whether the organization is formed on a financial foundation to get it through the early years.

The survival stage can be roughly measured as that period between commencing operations until the business is both profitable and operating with a surplus cash flow. For most firms this represents at least the first two or three years. During the survival stage the focus is on the operational decisions to build sales, and cash flow to stay ahead of the cash demands. It's during this period that most failures occur because either the entrepreneur couldn't achieve this objective or the financial commitments made during the start-up stage were too burdensome to begin with.

The growth stage may, in reality, be more an expression of stabilized operations rather than actual growth. The majority of small ventures do not expand much beyond their original size and scope and for them "growth" is only the "light at the end of the tunnel" when they can declare themselves free of a constant cash crisis. It's at this point that the shoestring start-up begins to converge with the economics of the well capitalized firm. Still, 20% of the small start-ups will considerably expand. Here then the economic decisions are on both the timing and the growth strategy.

Each stage presents its own economic pitfalls. That's what this chapter is about. Although you can't anticipate all the booby traps, most are predictable and face every type venture. So let's put you through a primer course on what I see as the fourteen essential economic lessons to be learned by every shoestring entrepreneur.

FOURTEEN ESSENTIAL LESSONS FOR EVERY SHOESTRING ENTREPRENEUR

Lesson #1: Set Realistic Goals

Pinpointing the right size and scope for the start-up is the essence of a successful blueprint. While every business can begin within a broad range, you eventually reach the extremes when the planned venture is too large or too small.

Those who go beyond the reality zone are entrepreneurs who either try to match their venture to their dreams or try to match the venture to their pocketbook.

The ambitiously large and grandiose blueprint brings about self-defeat during the planning stage, since the entrepreneur can seldom reconcile the financing needed with the financing available. Rather than lower his or her sights from the desirable to the attainable, the idea is on perpetual hold. These are the dreamers.

The danger is not necessarily in thinking big, but in refusing to think smaller by carving a fall-back position that is attainable. I have seen many shoestring entrepreneurs put together six- and seven-figure start-ups, but for every one who can there are ten other entrepreneurs who plan on the same scale only to run into stonewalls. Reality for them is the ability to re-design the venture on a smaller scale. There's an old adage that advises: "You never know what you can afford until you try." It was tailor-made for the shoestring entrepreneur.

Thinking too small is an appreciably greater danger than thinking too big. While the stubborn dreamer simply doesn't start, the overly cautious entrepreneur finds it easy to start—only to fail. From my viewpoint, the majority of shoestring ventures do fail because they began on too small and unrealistic a scale. The venture simply didn't have enough momentum to get off the ground. It's not necessarily true with service and sideline businesses that can flourish from microscopic beginnings, but it certainly is so with retail ventures dependent upon internally generated profits for survival and growth.

The anemic start-up is almost always the creation of the entrepreneur whose plans are based on his pocketbook rather than the profit potential of the venture. What he thinks he can afford overrides the question of what makes sense. So with a few dollars he whips together a few assets and expects it to turn miracles. That's not planning a business but planning a disaster.

When is your venture the right size?

1. When it's *small* enough to be financed.
2. When it's *large* enough to give you a healthy start.

Stay within this range and you have the correct yardstick.

Lesson #2: Nail Down Start-Up Costs

The actual start-up is always the end point of converging costs with financing. While you may have an approximation of what the business will be, you can't seek financing until you have nailed down the cost components of the start-up.

Don't proceed with vague ideas of what the costs will be. Even a small venture can demand $100,000 or more to be properly capitalized. Conversely, many entrepreneurs overestimate start-up costs because they didn't make the effort to seek lower-cost alternatives.

The first step is the preparation of a detailed and itemized schedule of all the beginning assets required. For example, when I plan a retail operation, I divide inventory down into product lines, and can estimate within 5% what the actual beginning inventory will be. It's the same with fixtures and equipment, listing even items as small as office supplies.

The Small Business Administration (SBA) has prepared this excellent start-up costs worksheet. It lists several start-up costs frequently overlooked.

The shoestring objective at this point is two-fold. First you want to go through the detailed list of what you *think* you need and reduce it to what you *actually* need. There can be a substantial difference. The characteristic of the shoestring venture is that it

WORKSHEET NO.1

ESTIMATED MONTHLY EXPENSES Item	Your estimate of monthly expenses based on sales of $ ______ per year	Your estimate of how much cash you need to start your business (See column 3.)	What to put in column 2 (These figures are typical for one kind of business. you will have to decide how many months to allow for in your business.)
	Column 1	Column 2	Column 3
Salary of owner-manager	$	$	2 times column 1
All other salaries and wages			3 times column 1
Rent			3 times column 1
Advertising			3 times column 1
Delivery expense			3 times column 1
Supplies			3 times column 1
Telephone and telegraph			3 times column 1
Other utilities			3 times column 1
Insurance			Payment required by insurance company
Taxes, including Social Security			4 times column 1
Interest			3 times column 1
Maintenance			3 times column 1
Legal and other professional fees			3 times column 1
Miscellaneous			3 times column 1
STARTING COSTS YOU ONLY HAVE TO PAY ONCE			Leave column 2 blank
Fixtures and equipment			Fill in worksheet 2 and put the total here
Decorating and remodeling			Talk it over with a contractor
Installation of fixtures and equipment			Talk to suppliers from whom you buy these
Starting inventory			Suppliers will probably help you estimate this
Deposits with public utilities			Find out from utilities companies
Legal and other professional fees			Lawyer, accountant, and so on
Licenses and permits			Find out from city offices what you have to have
Advertising and promotion for opening			Estimate what you'll use
Accounts receivable			What you need to buy more stock until credit customers pay
Cash			For unexpected expenses or losses, special purchases, etc.
Other			Make a separate list and enter total
TOTAL ESTIMATED CASH YOU NEED TO START WITH		$	Add up all the numbers in column 2

Figure 1. SBA Start-Up Costs Worksheet.

always begins on a Spartan note, confining assets to the bare essentials.

The second objective is to find ways to reduce each item cost to the absolute minimum. This is particularly so with fixtures, equipment, and leasehold improvements where there can be enormous price spreads. In Chapters 8 and 9, I show you specific ways to slash start-up costs on these items, but for the moment the strategy is to shop alternatives and price until you know what each item will stand you.

"Knowing your costs is the key to financial planning," advises Steve Carmoy, whose first business was an ice cream shop in a resort town. "My original estimates were that it would take $30,000 to equip the shop and another $12,000 to install plumbing, electrical, and leasehold improvements. Another $8000 was budgeted for signs and furniture. The $50,000 price tag came from talking to one fixture supplier, but it's only when I began to shop around that I found ways to cut costs to about $12,000. Used equipment was located for $7000 and the particular store I had in mind offered the plumbing and electrical service with very little additional cost. It's a different ball game when you're trying to put together a $12,000 deal compared to a $50,000 proposition."

Legwork is also the science of uncovering unanticipated costs. One dismal story involved a small manufacturer who scraped together the assets to produce an organic fertilizer only to shut down when town officials required installation of a $150,000 waste converter to avoid pollution. Hidden start-up costs are an ever-present problem with manufacturing and technically oriented start-ups who face a host of regulatory requirements. For this reason I always suggest bringing in someone who knows the technical problems that may escape the entrepreneur unexperienced in the industry.

The same can be said of marketing costs. All too often an entrepreneur will accurately predict product demand while overlooking the capital really needed to push the product through the channels of distribution.

Lenders and investors may detect a business plan hurriedly rushed together without adequate homework and research. Typically it is a case of not uncovering all the costs or not putting a realistic price tag on them.

The well-capitalized firm can cope with a few unanticipated expenditures. Not so with the shoestring enterprise with a taut financial tightrope. Guesswork doesn't count. Know your costs.

Lesson #3: Put the Money Where it Counts

When you do have limited cash and borrowing power, the objective is to deploy them where it will do the most good. An overexpenditure in one area is likely to result in a forced underexpenditure in another.

Balancing investment between "fixed assets" (furniture, fixtures, and equipment) and "working assets" (inventory and working capital) requires special consideration with the shoestring enterprise. The successful start-ups throw as much money as possible into the working assets and as little as possible into fixed assets.

There are two reasons for this strategy: First, it's the working assets that create the lifeblood for the shoestring venture—sales and cash flow. The second reason is that the carrying costs on expensive fixtures is a fixed cost the struggling shoestring venture can well do without.

I have seen many start-ups, particularly in the retail trades, with the fanciest fixtures in town and reciprocally the least amount of inventory in town. The lesson is that customers buy inventory not fixtures. My philosophy has always been that I'd rather see twice the inventory on used fixtures instead of half the inventory on spanking-new fixtures.

Upgrading the physical plant can always come later when the business is on a more solid plane, but during the start-up stage your money should be in the assets that will work the hardest for you.

Lesson #4: Financing is the Sum of its Parts

Financing a business is a misnomer. You never finance a business. What you do finance are the individual assets needed for the business. The sum of the parts always produces more financing dollars than could be achieved by financing the whole.

Consider financing much as you would a giant jigsaw puzzle—one small manageable piece at a time. The strategy allows you to exploit each asset for its maximum borrowing power. And you'll be amazed to see how much of the venture is financed once the pieces come together.

The conventional financing path on a $100,000 venture is to borrow perhaps $50,000–60,000 from an institutional lender and add the difference from investment capital.

The shoestring strategy can't follow the conventional niceties. Leverage is putting together every financing block possible to build a total pyramid with few of your own dollars.

This has been the key to my own shoestring ventures. Using the schedule of assets needed for the start-up, I'll go down the list item by item asking, "What's the best way to finance this asset with the fewest upfront dollars?" Merchandise is a matter of wrangling trade credit from suppliers, as I discuss in Chapter 9. Fixtures and equipment go through the same exercise. For example, on a cash register I'll not only negotiate price, but negotiate to buy it on terms, lease, or financed through a finance company. However I do it, it typically means that I'm spending few or no upfront dollars.

As you go through this book, you'll see the various ways to exploit the credit potential of the assets needed in your business. Once you're fully familiar with all the sources of money that can take the place of your own cash, you may find that the available financing blocks come remarkably close to 100% of total start-up costs. Experience will not only let you design a 100% financed pyramid, but in many cases you'll have sources of financing actually competing for a place in the financial pyramid.

Only *after* you have exploited sources of credit offered by the respective assets should you consider institutional financing. For example, you may line up credit for 90% of the start-up costs through a potpourri of trade credit, leasing, or equipment financing, and be shy the 10% to complete the package and for working capital. Now you can reasonably borrow for these purposes and probably can borrow enough to create a healthy cash reserve.

That's one advantage of using bank financing as the capstone of your financial pyramid. Once you've amassed the assets with supplier credit, you can use bank financing for working capital. And that's when the sum of its parts can exceed the whole.

Lesson #5: Building the Best Financial Pyramid

Achieving 100% financing—or as close to it as you can reasonably come—is only one part of the strategy. You need a strong financial pyramid, and every building block has its own characteristics—its own advantages and disadvantages.

The trade-offs must be considered both from the point of view of the business and yourself. The ideal financing block will:

1. Provide the longest payback period.
2. Carry the lowest interest rates.
3. Require little or no collateral.
4. Demand no personal liability.

No one source of financing will display all these characteristics. Bank loans may give you an adequate payback period, but the downside is your personal liability and tying up the business assets as collateral. Supplier financing ordinarily won't involve personal liability but may require a speedy payback. Partnership funds will satisfy all these points but require you to give up a piece of the action.

Considering these conflicting characteristics, the objective is to shape each so that it both makes sense to the business and yourself. For example, I'm risk-conscious so I won't take on more bank financing than I think the collateral can safely cover. My next objective is to select financing with the longest payback. For the shoestring venture, reducing cash flow demands is considerably more important than a slightly higher interest rate or whether the debt is secured. Supplier financing is conventionally short-term, but properly negotiated it may be an excellent source of long-term financing. But at what point is short-term debt still so excessive that you're forced to retrench either to more long-term bank financing or partnership funds with their own inherent disadvantages?

It's always a matter of profiling your interests with the business. Understand your priorities before you seek financing.

Lesson #6: Navigate by the Numbers

Cash flow controls every decision in the shoestring process. Cash flow is the name of the game and the only way to navigate during every stage of the start-up.

Don't be your own navigator. Preparing a legitimate cash flow projection takes both objectivity and competence. It's the role for your accountant. Your role is to make planning and operational decisions based on what fits within the cash flow framework.

A start-up without a carefully planned cash flow statement is a ship without a rudder and a compass. You neither know nor can control where you're heading. It explains why so many small ventures do fail. It's not a matter of being undercapitalized, but in failing to properly plan the undercapitalized operation.

While in broad terms the cash flow statement measures projected income against the outgo of cash (operating expenses and the paydown of debt), its initial function is to test the viability of the financial pyramid. Only the cash flow statement can tell you whether you're top-heavy on short-term debt, necessitating a switch to more long-term financing. You live by the numbers.

"Mastering the shoestring start-up is really a matter of mastering cash flow under the worst of circumstances," says David Dube, a management and financial consultant to small firms. "It's a twilight world of constantly trying to get money in so you stay ahead of what you're forced to pay out. When you achieve that constant objective—you survive. When you fail—you sink. It's all in knowing how to go about it."

I agree. A cash flow orientation takes the place of even a bottom line orientation during the start-up and survival stages. It's only when you're in the growth and stable periods that decisions can be made to enhance profits instead of cash flow. Entrepreneurs sometimes stumble over this one. They'll start a venture and every decision is directed to profits. Yet the decision that's right for the bottom line may be counter-productive from a cash flow viewpoint. The two don't always coincide. Only when the business becomes strangled does the entrepreneur become forced to focus on cash flow. By then, however, it may be too late.

That's the overview. Shoestring economics is the ability to master your own cash flow game. The next several lessons can show you how.

Lesson #7: Test the Timing

There's a right time and a wrong time to open a business. This is particularly true when the venture is cyclical in nature or in a seasonal location. And not surprisingly, many shoestring start-ups are small ventures in tourist areas or selling goods of a seasonal demand.

The ideal opening date is about one month before the peak selling season begins. The month's lag gives you time to work out operational problems before the bustle of the season, yet the launch coincides with the positive cash flow of high sales. And you need that positive cash flow to get you through the dry seasons.

While it may be common sense, many entrepreneurs overlook its importance and begin the business based on their own convenience or when a location becomes available. Bob Braunstein, a bankruptcy attorney practicing on Cape Cod, reports, "Any business can make it through a Cape Cod summer. But come October half the businesses are gone. It's amazing to see how many new bootstrap ventures quickly take their place and fold before they even reach the summer season."

I share the same observation. Many of the ventures that withered on the vine with an ill-timed start might have had the staying power if they started strong with a strong beginning cash flow. Momentum is the best word for it, and when you don't have the cash to play the waiting game you wait until you can bring in the cash.

Opening at the right time is only one part of the "timing" strategy. The second objective is to smooth out cash flow by structuring payments to coincide with income. For example, a business may open on Cape Cod and have plenty of money to cover expenses and financing payments. When you ride the crest of the wave there's always plenty of money to go around. Then the tide ebbs, cash slows to a trickle, but the heavy note payments continue. When the cash reserves are frittered away, the business heads for trouble.

Handling a cyclical business requires both planning and discipline to reap the harvest and save it for the off-season. Even squirrels know that much. It's a point overlooked by too many entrepreneurs. For this reason I suggest structuring note payments and other fixed obligations to parallel income. Few lenders will refuse and it can keep your cash flow on a steady course.

Lesson #8: Prime the Pump

Since your venture faces a cash drain from the moment you open your doors, make it a goal to build sales as rapidly as possible *before* you open as well as after you open.

Many ventures have an exceptionally slow sales curve. How long it will take to reach respectable (if not profitable) sales depends on the nature of your business, location, competition, and your own ability to prime the pump through promotion.

Of course, every sensible business person wants the fastest increase in sales. The difference with the shoestring entrepreneur is in what he or she will do to achieve it. More than an objective, it becomes a business-saving necessity.

When I opened a retail pharmacy I estimated the business needed $6000 a week to break even and cover note payments. We couldn't wait the eight months or a year to gradually build sales. Up to our neck in debt, we had to quickly turn dollars. Every week was another promotion. Flyers advertised "specials" at our net cash price and coupons for a $5 savings on prescriptions. We probably lost 5% on sales, but we quickly grossed $10,000–12,000 a week. We could afford a paper loss of $500 a week, but what we couldn't afford was an income of $4000 a week while we were obligated to pay out $6000 a week. So our objective was to turn dollars.

Priming the pump before you open can pay dividends. It was handled the right way by a friend of mine who planned an awning installation business. Before he set up shop he had over 100 orders guaranteeing him a fast income of over $40,000. His cash flow began to roll the moment he opened his doors. Sure it was smarter than opening his doors and chasing his first dollars while the bills began to mount.

Creating fast sales is so important that we allocate twice as many dollars to a launch promotion as is standard in the discount industry. Make your own commitment "to go after those fast nickels—particularly when you can't afford to wait for the slow dimes."

Lesson #9: Plan on a Lean Year

Since cash flow projections are only a "guesstimate" of what you *think* will come in, measured against what you *know* will be going out, it's wise to hedge by planning on a lean year.

Any cash flow statement can look rosy on paper if you want to be the confirmed optimist expecting to start with a boom. That's typically the anatomy of a failure. The entrepreneur says to himself, "The business will gross $500,000 the first year and $700,000 the second." With these self-deluding numbers in mind he takes on financing to match. One year later the venture sputters to a stop, grossing $200,000. Nine out of ten entrepreneurs are optimists, which explains why there are so many entrepreneurial ventures and so many entrepreneurial failures.

The right way to project sales is to ask yourself, "What's the *least* the venture can gross?" Make it a worst-case situation. Check industry averages and comparable businesses. You may be a better butcher, baker, or candlestick maker, but few of us are the geniuses to defy the odds.

Underestimating sales has a pleasant cure. You can always take surplus cash and reinvest for faster growth. The process is not reversible. Locked in with excess financing and expenses predicated on higher sales requires either very understanding creditors or a journey to the Bankruptcy Court. Since the first is improbable and the latter unthinkable, plan on a *very* lean year.

Lesson #10: Don't Choke on Receivables

Few shoestring firms are sufficiently capitalized to sell on terms and wait for their money while watching accounts receivable build. It's the fastest way to strangle cash flow.

If your business is in an industry that typically sells on credit, this puts you at a decided competitive disadvantage. It may even be the controlling factor in not selecting a particular type business—with plenty of justification.

Fortunately, most shoestring ventures are retail or service firms that can limit sales to cash. Manufacturing and distributing start-ups are another story. Their ability to finance the launch depends on their ability to either operate without extending credit—or make arrangements to finance the receivables.

The common method to finance receivables is by factoring the receivables to a factor who will pay you up front, while holding back a reserve for bad debts. Despite the liquidity the arrangement does offer, it still places an added strain on the thinly capitalized firm. Factoring receivables can be expensive both in terms of interest charges and bad debts that you eventually have to absorb. Cash receipts can still be delayed for 30–60 days while you wait for the factor to take over the receivables and pay you. And even a "hold-back" on 20% of the receivables as the factor's cushion for bad debts puts a sizable crimp in cash flow.

Credit and collections is beyond the scope of this book, but if you do plan on a business with receivables, I suggest you read my *Getting Paid* (John Wiley & Sons, 1983). It can show you many ways to accelerate payments and reduce losses, always key considerations for the shoestring entrepreneur.

Lesson #11: Keep Fixed Costs Down

For the small start-up, fixed costs are dead weight. You can't afford it. To the extent possible, every dollar in expense should be directly tied to income. It's only when income and expenses follow parallel paths that the business escapes a cash drain.

Commission sales people are safer than salaried. Direct ads with a measurable dollar pull are better than institutional ads that only add to good will. A rent based on a percentage of sales can preserve more capital during the survival stage than will a fixed rent. Every expense item has its own possibilities.

David Dube of Silverman & Co., a Boston CPA firm specializing in small business finance counsels says, "The strategy is always to open with the smallest committed overhead. From that point expenses can grow only when you have a favorable cost-volume relationship."

Whenever I'm called in to rescue a start-up venture my first step is to evaluate whether there's enough gross profit for the business to be viable. Assuming it has the right margin, the next step is to see how it's dissipating the difference. What I normally find is a venture pregnant with needless overhead expenses eating more dollars than the business can produce.

Above all, the one common characteristic of successful shoestring entrepreneurs is their "lean and mean" attitude. They seldom spend a nickel unless they're sure it will quickly produce a dime.

Lesson #12: Protect Gross Profits

Strategizing gross profits for the bootstrap firm must of necessity follow a different route than with the well-financed counterpart who can afford to buy on better terms and price lower.

"What it comes down to," says Elliot Galahow, "is being smart enough to know you can't stand head-to-toe with the big boys and slug it out. You need a counterstrategy to corner a niche of your market that allows for higher prices and leaner inventories."

Many entrepreneurs go after increased sales—always a worthwhile objective—but give away too many profit points in the process. The business that should operate on a 35% profit structure finds itself crippled with a 20% profit on sales. Usually it's an entrepreneur who thinks he'll set the world on fire with the lowest prices in town. While one eye is on sales the other isn't focused on gross profit. The profit given away seldom matches the sales increases.

There's always the temptation to recapture margins on discount prices by buying deals to save an extra 5–10%. The shoestring operation can't afford it, because it only builds inventory and further strangles cash flow already strained by a leveraged beginning inventory.

The priority must be on turnover and buying lean quantities so the goods move fast enough to pay for themselves. Set a minimum price spread that not only insures reasonable sales, but also reasonable profits to cover overhead and note payments. Industry averages can show you what your right numbers should be. Try to maintain gross profits at least equal to the industry averages and improve turnover by 20–30% to give the business the best balance between profitability and turnover needed for cash flow.

Lesson #13: Cultivate Creditors

The shoestring enterprise rarely fails because it starts out with too much debt. It fails because the entrepreneur couldn't cultivate the creditors and put them on hold until the venture gained a financial foothold.

The undercapitalized firm has remarkable staying power. And it can stay alive with beginning debt that would have the financial experts shaking in their boots if it follows common sense strategies.

1. Intelligently structure debt from the beginning. The secret of the leveraged start-up is not the amount of debt you take on, but how long you have to pay it down. Financing an opening inventory on 100% trade credit terms becomes a problem only if the payback period isn't logically tied to a cash flow projection.
2. Don't let debt panic you. No matter how carefully you plan, you'll journey through the survival stage with desktops heaped with unpaid bills. It's the price you pay for using creditor money instead of your own to finance the start-up. The cure for your sleepless nights is the reality that the stack of bills is dwindling as cash flow and profits take hold.
3. Communicate with your creditors. Creditors will remain patient, provided you keep them abreast of the venture's

progress. If you can't stay on schedule let them know about it before you default. You may begin the venture with one idea on how the debts can be liquidated and be forced to re-negotiate several times before the reality of the situation dictates how you *can* pay.

4. Future business and even a dribble of cash toward older bills can keep a creditor satisfied. Creditor problems become serious when you buy on credit only to shut them off and ignore what's owed.
5. When you lay your problems on the line with creditors, you'll have to accept the risk that one or more nervous creditors will go for the jugular and try to push you over the brink. Try to get your major creditors behind you. They can be very persuasive in controlling the smaller creditors who are likely to be more troublesome.
6. Set up a pecking order to give certain creditors priority. Essential overhead—rent, payroll, and utilities—always comes first. Next come payroll taxes. The IRS plays rough. Suppliers selling the essential lifeline merchandise for your business also stand at the head of the line. Banks and other lenders holding security also require priority because they do have the immediate remedy of foreclosure. Cash flow problems are invariably handled by delaying payments to secondary suppliers.

The goal of the shoestring entrepreneur is to make it through the survival stage, albeit under considerable pressure of trying to make ends meet. Many don't succeed because they can't find the path to a profitable business. Others manage to create a company heading in the right direction, but give up too easily under mounting creditor pressure. Staying power is the realization that drastic problems demand drastic solutions. Thousands of small struggling start-ups have made the grade only through a major restructuring of their debt. It may be an out-of-court composition settlement or a Chapter 11 reorganization through the Bankruptcy Court, but saving the business may be a logical sequel to starting the business.

Are you the type who can comfortably exist in the twilight world of too little cash and too many creditors? Before you answer you may want to read *How to Save Your Business* (Enterprise Publishing, Wilmington, Delaware, 1983). It tells you the inside story of how to put any financially troubled business together again.

Lesson #14: Take Total Control

Most entrepreneurs, being creative types, dislike accounting and finances, preferring to make "seat of the pants" decisions, or as I sometimes say, "decisions from the gut," instead of from the cerebral cortex. Nobody who has been in business will suggest you can run a business entirely by slide rule or computer, but when your margin of error is somewhere between slim and non-existent—as it is with the shoestring enterprise—you hedge your decisions with numbers, numbers, and more numbers.

It's all part of taking control—knowing where you've been—where you're going, and how fast you're getting there. What controls will you need?

1. Cash flow statements head the list. Break it down by month, and project ahead at least a year in advance. These pro forma predictions are even more important than past performance records because they help you plan, spot problems, and devise solutions in advance.
2. Work up a tight budget for purchases and your controllable expenses. Without budgeting you're likely to overspend in these areas, destroying the validity of your cash flow projections and profit planning. Don't hesitate to adjust budget as the conditions change. A new start-up may go through many "ups" and "downs" within a brief period, and you need a budget to control outgo, not restrict growth.
3. Calculate your break-even point. That's the magic number that tells you when the venture crossed the line and is making money. Your accountant can approximate your break-even point with very little work, and it then becomes your target. Plot your growth toward break-even. Monitor

the sales curve. It's the easiest way to see if your business is heading in the right direction—and moving fast enough.

4. Profit and loss statements should be published monthly. You can't afford to wait for semi-annual or end-of-the-year reports. The start-up needs immediate corrective action to cure excess expenditures, sluggish margins, or weak sales. Only up-to-date and timely statements can tell you where you've been and the steps necessary to keep you on track.
5. You should get a readable warning flag report. Program it into the sensitive areas of operations. At a minimum you want constant readouts on working capital, inventory levels, accounts receivable, accounts payable, orders on hand, slow collections, out-of-stock situations, and customer complaints. Keep your finger on the daily pulse of the venture to detect dangerous changes from the norm.

Having the right information is only one part of the equation. It has value only when turned into action. You'll make your mistakes, and the best reporting system won't change that. What it will do is keep your errors down to a manageable minimum.

Check out any small start-up that grows and thrives and pays its bills, and somewhere within you'll find someone who's something more than a creative entrepreneur with an idea. He or she may be one part Scrooge and one part Simon Legree, but it's someone who can keep a cold, calculated eye on the numbers and squeeze every nickel for all it's worth. It's intrinsic to all money management. When you're a shoestring entrepreneur and understand the economics of the situation you squeeze harder.

Your Shoestring Economics Final Exam

You've been through a cram course. And there's plenty more to learn, but those lessons will be in the laboratory of your own small venture as you try to turn theory into practice. Are you ready for it? Try a quick pre-test.

1. Review the business you have in mind. Is it within a range that's both attainable and desirable?

2. Do you know your true start-up costs or are you just guesstimating?
3. Do you know how to deploy your capital amongst assets to create the healthiest start?
4. Are you ready to exploit each asset for its own borrowing power to achieve a shoestring start-up?
5. Do you know your priorities—and the priorities of the business—so you can build the best financial pyramid?
6. Have you tested your financing against cash flow projections?
7. Are you planning to open the business at the right time to quickly tap maximum cash flow?
8. Do you know the steps you'll take *before* you open and *after* you open to maximize sales and help the business to fast sales increases?
9. Have you based your financial projections on sheer optimism or the reality that you may have a lean year?
10. If you plan on selling on credit, have you tested whether you can support the receivables?
11. Are your fixed costs slashed to the rock bottom so you can operate "lean and mean"?
12. Do you have a solid policy of capturing sales without sacrificing needed profit margins?
13. Are you ready to do combat with creditors to keep the business afloat until it is healthy?
14. Are you ready to take total control so you can make "thinking cap" decisions?

Find some interesting answers?

4

STARTING SMART

Entrepreneurship is risk. Starting smart is the awareness that your venture has only a 20% chance of making it through the first five years, and taking shrewd steps to protect yourself from the contingency of failure before you start.

HOPE FOR THE BEST—PREPARE FOR THE WORST

Who ever heard of planning for failure? Open any business book and you'll see rosy pictures of fat cats in plush penthouse suites sipping cognac and "wheeling and dealing" their way to a fortune. They're not the people I see in my office a year or two after they entered the business arena. What I see are discouraged, frightened people who have lost everything they owned and face the prospects of personal bankruptcy.

These people are invariably the full-time dreamers who only see the "benefit" side of the equation and never the "downside" risk. They ignore the possibility of failure until it's too late. Most dreamers don't start smart by taking at the outset the precautionary steps to protect themselves against a less than prosperous business future.

Realists on the other hand don't fall victim to the "rose-colored' glasses syndrome." Instead they do everything possible to reduce their risks. Realists understand and prepare for possible defeat. They define and prune their potential losses. They objectively weigh the "benefit/risk" ratio of their deal and only move ahead when the possible gains outweigh what they stand to lose.

Whenever I journey into another venture I pull out a pad of paper and draw a line down the center. In the left column I try to assess the possible financial gain from the deal. In the right column I list my investment and what I stand to lose if the deal goes sour. It's a form of playing "what if," as I try to assess the best and worst case. But I don't stop there. While you can never measure the equation with complete predictability you can take positive steps to control loss.

Be objective. You have to look at yourself as one entity and the business as another. The relationship between the two must make economic sense. How many times have you seen eternal optimists mortgage their home to the hilt and cash in their savings to move into a start-up? How many ask themselves the two important questions: Can this business possibly provide sufficient return to risk what I am gambling? Are there steps I can take now to reduce what I can lose?

That's what this chapter is all about. It will show you how you can minimize risk because it will:

1. Keep your personal investment to a minimum, protecting what you do invest.
2. Protect valuable personal assets from hungry business creditors.
3. Free you from personal liability on business debts.
4. Put you in the best defensive posture so you, and not your creditors, have the upper hand if the business goes sour.
5. Keep your personal resources intact so you can bounce back and try again.

WHY A CORPORATION IS A MUST

Starting smart means choosing the correct form of business organization and no chapter on risk-reducing strategies would be complete without mentioning that greatest of risk-reducers—the corporation.

About 50% of all small businesses are operational as sole proprietorships or partnership forms of organization. Without the benefit of a corporate umbrella, these individuals are literally saying to their business creditors, "If my business doesn't pay your bill you can come after my personal assets to satisfy the obligation." If you assemble all the non-incorporated entrepreneurs you'll be looking at a long line of dreamers. They never fail, so why do they need the protection of a corporation? Dream on.

If you were to review many of the personal bankruptcies you'll find they were needlessly caused by the failure of the business person to incorporate. One of my first cases, fresh out of law school, involved a liquor store owner who operated his business for seven years as a proprietorship. His former attorney had said, "Why incorporate and go through the hassles of extra paperwork and tax returns?" It was costly advice several years later when his business finally failed with $200,000 in unpaid bills. With a few quick attachments the creditors had my client's home and my client moved to a third floor walk-up apartment to ponder the most expensive advice he ever had—"Why incorporate?" It was the first of a long list of similar experiences.

Look at incorporation as just another form of insurance. You may pay $300–600 to initially incorporate (although later in this book I'll show you how to incorporate for far less), and you may have to pay your accountant another $200 a year to file corporate tax returns. But those modest premiums isolate and protect all the personal assets you have worked so hard over the years to accumulate. You can't find better insurance.

Every business book seems to dwell on the relative advantages and disadvantages of a corporation over other forms of organization. From my viewpoint it's no contest. The limited liability benefits of the corporation overshadows other considerations. Any attorney who disagrees is an attorney without broad experience in handling business failures.

Aside from the personal protection of a corporation, there are the other advantages. A corporation can provide valuable, tax deductible "fringes," including sick pay, medical and dental insurance, life insurance, and even travel and educational expenses. Workmen's compensation is another big benefit. The only way to obtain personal protection is by incorporating.

The advantages continue to mount. Unlike a partnership or proprietorship, a corporation continues after the death of its owner. No liquidation of the business is necessary. Do you want to bring in partners? Selling corporate stock is the cleanest way to divide ownership. Expansion? Only the corporation offers the flexibility to attract diverse types of financing.

Taxes are the war cry of the uninformed. It's safe to say the majority of small business people aren't incorporated because they think they'll face double taxation—a tax on corporate profits and a personal tax on withdrawn income. Years ago they were right. Today the tax code is slanted in favor of the corporation. Not only can you take advantage of the numerous tax savings only a corporation can offer, but you can even be taxed as a proprietorship (or partnership) by electing to be taxed as a "Subchapter S Corporation." This point is best discussed and decided by your accountant, but as an attorney who has seen over 2000 entrepreneurial defeats let me tell you that if you want to start smart, you'll start with a corporation.

SMALL INVESTMENTS MEAN SMALL LOSSES

While optimists always ask how much they can make from a venture, realists ask how much they can lose. And the answer, of course, is in how they formulate and control the investment decision.

That too is what starting smart is all about. Shoestring ventures are not only the creation of entrepreneurs with few dollars to invest, but are equally the creation of people who can invest more but intentionally choose to start with less because they want to risk less.

But even shoestring entrepreneurs can lose a bundle when they lose sight of their objective and begin to make irrational investment decisions. Typically their investment policy is ill-defined to begin with and totally abandoned once the business is underway. It's easier to throw money rather than objectivity into the cash-hungry start-up.

"Unbridled enthusiasm can wreck you financially," admits Pat Dwyer who parlayed an expected $10,000 investment into a $125,000 loss. Pat's story? "I had my sights on starting a small Syrian-style restaurant in a Detroit suburb. My initial $10,000 investment estimate was workable because I had a fixture company who would lease me the equipment on near 100% terms. But then you become like a kid in the candy store. I decided to upgrade the decor and throw more money into advertising. So my initial investment of $10,000 very quickly became a $28,000 investment. Sluggish sales caused me to mortgage my home for $25,000 to cover operating losses. A start-up can absorb money like a sponge if you let it, and to keep the business afloat I threw in another $60,000 or more over two years before running out of money or ideas on how to get the business off the ground."

It's too common a story. And it's not hindsight or playing "Monday morning quarterback." Uncontrolled losses are always the result of uncontrollable optimism.

The intelligent approach to the investment decision is to focus on four questions *before* you start the venture.

1. How much *can* you invest?
2. How much *should* you invest?
3. How much *will* you invest?
4. *When* will you invest more?

Let's see if we can help you find your right answers with the four-step process.

1. *How Much* Can *You Invest?*

This helps define what you're prepared to lose on a venture. Contrary to what many entrepreneurial books suggest, starting smart is not exposing all your personal assets to risk but gambling only with what you can realistically afford to lose. I handle it by dividing my assets into the classical "touch" and "don't touch" piles. For example, I'll confine my entrepreneurial investments to only 25% of my liquid assets. That's the formula I'm comfortable with, but you need your own formula. Once you set aside precisely what you are prepared to risk, you know your maximum investment capability while preserving your fall-back position. Setting limits is the only way to control losses.

2. *How Much* Should *You Invest?*

Within the limits of what you can afford to risk is the decision of what the business can justify as an investment. Consider the return on investment the business can offer and make certain it bears a rational relationship to the capital at risk. Many entrepreneurs make sizable investments only to discover the low earning power of the venture. Others understand the financial return won't quite measure up, but go ahead because the business offers psychic enjoyment or a better lifestyle. It's a fair trade-off if that's all you expect from the business. When financial return is important, your goal should be a minimum of 25% annual return on investment. The inherent risk of a small business doesn't justify less. What price tag would you put on your venture?

3. *How Much* Will *You Invest?*

What the business can logically justify as an investment and what you *will* invest are two different numbers. The goal is to prune investment to the smallest possible amount. Cutting investment not only cuts losses but provides a better return on what you do invest. In many of my own ventures I'll target the optimum investment at perhaps $10,000–15,000 and then see how I can accomplish the start-up goal with absolutely no money of my own. Why not? Every dollar you invest is a dollar you might lose. Starting smart means investing as little of your own money as possible.

4. When *Will You Invest More?*

Over-investment is most likely to occur after the business is in operation. Many shoestring entrepreneurs start the venture with a reasonably small and prudent investment only to throw caution to the wind as they continuously feed the cash-hungry enterprise. Starting smart is to define the criteria for a later capital infusion.

It takes tremendous discipline to deprive a thinly capitalized business of more owner-provided capital. As Pat Dwyer discovered, you can't succumb to the pressures of what the business needs, but must keep your eye on what is justified investment.

One reason to invest small initial capital is to hold further funds in reserve, feeding them slowly and judiciously to the enterprise once it shows promise. Admittedly, the decision on whether to feed or starve the business is the most difficult of all management decisions. You wonder whether it's "good money after bad," or whether the few extra dollars will propel the business over the start-up hurdles on its way to success.

The only approach to the problem is to set performance standards that can justify adding more working capital. Before I start a venture I project sales. If the business is at or close to its targeted goal, I may loosen my pocketbook to release a few more dollars, but my eyes are always on the financial indicators. If the venture looks like a loser the investments stop. That's the one cardinal error of so many shoestring entrepreneurs. Rather than admit defeat, they think that adding money is the cure. It's expensive medicine.

PROTECT YOUR INVESTMENT

No matter how little you do invest, once you have put together your creative financing package, the next step is to protect even that modest investment so you can recoup it should the business fail.

And there is a right and wrong way to invest money in your own business. The wrong approach is to use your entire investment to buy shares in the corporation. Assume your investment is $20,000. Your investment would be characterized as "equity" or "capital contribution." Should your business fail, you can only recoup investment after all creditors have been fully paid. Considering its improbability your plight becomes obvious.

Starting smart is splitting your investment so you use a small fraction of the investment to buy the shares, while loaning the balance to the corporation. Not only does this give you creditor status against your own business, but you can repay yourself the loan without taxable consequence, except for the interest charges.

The very best way to protect your investment is to loan the

money to the corporation on a secured basis. By holding a mortgage on the business you are the first to be repaid should the business turn sour. With 70–90% of your investment secured you have very little to lose.

This strategy requires careful planning. Don't lend the money directly to the corporation. Bankruptcy decisions have disallowed stockholder loans, granting priority to "arm's-length" creditors. The right way to handle it is to lend the money to a close friend or relative who in turn would loan the money to the business, taking back a mortgage. Should the business fail, your mortgage-holding relative would be repaid and could then repay his loan to you. A loan from a friendly intermediary is safe, provided he can prove he actually loaned the money.

This strategy is perfectly legal. Should the idea of putting your own economic interest ahead of your creditors shock your conscience, that's morality not business. You follow your own conscience; however, starting smart will at least give you a choice. Review this point with your attorney and accountant.

A second objective is to pass losses on to the IRS. Why not? The IRS is never shy about sharing your profits so why not make them a partner when you lose money? You can do just that if you take advantage of the little-known Section 1244 of the Internal Revenue Code. Section 1244 provides that once you purchase your shares, you can deduct any loss on your investment as an ordinary loss. If you're in the 30% tax bracket, and invest $20,000 for your stock ownership in the business, you can deduct the entire $20,000 loss from income, saving yourself $6000 in taxes.

Without this valuable provision in your corporate books you can treat the loss only as a capital loss, which means you can only "write off" $3000 a year.

All it takes to benefit as a Section 1244 stockholder is a clause in your bylaws stating the shares are sold to you under this IRS Code provision. Even experienced attorneys may overlook this, so make it a point to review it when you do incorporate.

How important are these capital-saving techniques? One case can show you. A client decided to invest $20,000 to capitalize a small convenience store in a local resort town. Splitting the investment, he used $4000 to acquire the shares as Section 1244 stock and through an intermediary loaned the corporation $16,000 secured by a mortgage. Two years later the business folded and liquidated for $18,000. Since $16,000 was still owed on the note, the intermediary recouped the entire $16,000 balance, and in turn, repaid my client, leaving the $2000 balance to satisfy other creditors' claims. The $4000 investment for the shares was lost, but by deducting the loss from present income my client saved $1000 in taxes. So with a few pieces of paper my client only lost $3000 on the venture. As he'll tell you, "It beats losing your entire investment." That too is what starting smart is all about.

ASSETS YOU NEVER HAVE TO LOSE

Turn to the bankruptcy auction pages and scan some of the ads. Look closely at the assets going under the hammer. Many valuable assets could have been saved had the owners used common sense by placing title to the assets in their own name rather than under the business.

Frequently you'll find entrepreneurs prematurely transferring valuable personal assets to their start-up corporation, needlessly exposing the assets to risk of loss should the business fail. It happened recently to a young engineer who developed a patented circuit breaker component and decided to go into business manufacturing the item. Several years later the business folded, and since the patent was now the asset of the corporation, it was sold by the Bankruptcy Trustee for $140,000 to satisfy creditor claims. The shrewd buyer immediately licensed the rights to the product and is now collecting over $30,000 a year in royalties. Had the engineer started smart he would have personally retained ownership of the patent and licensed it to his own corporation. Had he done so he would now be the one collecting the fat royalty checks.

Business people seldom consider the point, but a transfer of a personally owned asset to the business is the same as a cash investment. It's still an asset at risk. The more common error is made when new assets are acquired. That's when the decision must be made as to whether it's best to buy the asset through the corporation or instead buy it personally and lease it to the corporation.

One entrepreneur who started smart was Cal Sullivan. Cal's venture was a small printing plant in an industry noted for its high failure rate. The key to his operation was a sophisticated piece of high-speed printing equipment that cost $60,000.Cal purchased the equipment in his own name for $15,000 down, financing the balance. He then leased the equipment to his printing corporation for a fair monthly rental fee. Five years later the printing plant collapsed under $100,000 in debt, but all Cal had to do was to go in and repossess the machine that now had a $30,000 equity.

In many start-up situations, the tax considerations are the deciding factor in whether an asset will be personally or corporately owned. Frequently an accountant will suggest personal ownership of depreciable assets because it does provide the best tax breaks to the entrepreneur. From my experiences the deciding factor should not be the tax angles but the risk of loss should the business fail. Only in later years when the business is stabilized should the decision be based on taxes.

Look over your own situation. If your corporation plans on acquiring real estate, high-cost equipment, motor vehicles, or even a valuable intangible asset such as a patent, trademark, or copyright, starting smart may mean personal, not corporate ownership of these assets.

SIDE-STEPPING DANGEROUS GUARANTEES

Starting smart means reducing the risk of personal liability and loss by side-stepping personal guarantees. When you are on the personal hook to creditors it's very much part of the risk side of the equation.

As a shoestring entrepreneur you may achieve your number one goal of risking little investment capital and still face a mountain of personal obligations should the business fail. Your second objective then is to confine the debts to the corporation.

Creditors, for their part, have the annoying habit of always pushing personal guarantees under your nose. Who can blame them? They know that if they extend credit to your corporation, they severely limit their options in the event it goes bust. They're always happier when they have a shot at your personal assets. That's why they want your personal signature on the dotted line.

When I was in law school I had a cantankerous but wise professor who defined a guarantor as an "optimisitc moron with a fountain pen." Twenty years and 2000 cases later, I must confess that more times than not his definition fit.

Personal guarantees are an integral part of entrepreneurial life. Banks and other institutional lenders won't lend to a small start-up corporation without the owner's guarantee. Suppliers are equally wary of the new venture without a credit history to rely on. This leaves you in the position of deciding beforehand just how far out you're willing to stick your neck to back up business obligations.

Poverty can be a friend of the shoestring entrepreneur with few assets to lose. The well-heeled entrepreneur is the one with hard decisions to make as he measures the maximum personal exposure he'll submit to.

I look at investment and risk on guarantees collectively in weighing the total risk factor for the venture. For example, I may invest $10,000 in cash and be personally bound on $15,000 in guaranteed debt. The downside on the deal is realistically $25,000. It comes back to the question of whether it's an amount you can afford to lose.

There are several steps you can take to reduce your own personal exposure.

1. Structure your financing the right way. In Chapter 6, you'll see the correct procedures in greater detail, but the approach to take is to make certain the bank (or other lenders) loan the money to the business and secure the debt with a mortgage on business assets. In the event the business fails, the bank is first to get paid, decreasing your exposure on the note. Second, make certain the liquidation value of the collateral is comparable to the balance owed the bank on

the note. You don't want business assets yielding the bank only $30,000 if the note shows a balance of $50,000. They'll chase you for the $20,000 and that's when guarantees become dangerous.

2. If you take on partners, make certain they also sign the guarantees. This is particularly important to remember if your partners come on board after you guaranteed the note. Your partners enjoy the benefits of the business so why not the risk? Another point to consider is the ability of your partners to equally pay on a guarantee. You don't want to be the one with the deepest pockets left to pay the creditors. I can tell you one sad story of a 25% owner of a restaurant who guaranteed an $86,000 loan without "bothering" the other three partners. You guessed it. When the restaurant failed, his partners walked away, leaving him to satisfy the debt. Overlooking the common sense points can spell financial disaster.
3. Risk is a decided factor in shopping suppliers. Some suppliers will insist on a guarantee while others won't. From my viewpoint I'll always go with a supplier willing to gamble on the business alone, even if price is slightly higher or other terms less attractive. If you want to substantially reduce your risk you'll shop around, negotiate, and even bluff suppliers—but you won't put your signature on their guarantees.
4. Learn the negotiating points to avoid guarantees. A supplier may be willing to accept a mortgage on business assets in place of a guarantee. It's a wise trade-off. If you must, provide a guarantee then insist on the supplier accepting a mortgage to shield you from excess exposure. Conversely, you may be able to bypass a guarantee by negotiating a smaller credit limit. You may also agree to a postal guarantee confining your liability to a fixed amount.
5. Make it you policy never to guarantee an *existing* corporate debt. Why should you? You have nothing to gain. When your shoestring venture falls behind in supplier payments, credit managers will chase you for a guarantee

to solidify their position, and that's when the unwitting entrepreneur is most likely to place his or her personal assets on the line.

6. Always monitor your risk. If you have personal guarantees outstanding and the business shows signs of a false start, then begin to think of reducing risk by reducing the personally guaranteed debts. Your objective is to pay them before the business collapses so they (and ultimately you) will incur no loss.

Entrepreneurship may be risky, but it doesn't have to be a game of excess risk. And the distinctions between the two are your guarantees.

HOW DEEP ARE YOUR POCKETS?

Smart players realize that no amount of care or caution can prevent personal liability and lawsuits from following them home once they've closed down a defunct business.

You never know what creditors will come knocking on your door. It may be creditors holding your personal guarantees or the IRS chasing you for unpaid withholding taxes. It may even be your partners with an invented claim against you. In fact, it's a rarity when an entrepreneur can shutter a business without a few skeletons lurking from its closet.

So starting smart is starting poor and staying poor so "would be" creditors can't find any personal assets to take once the lawsuits begin. The strategy is to "judgment proof" yourself by deploying your assets so they always lie beyond the grasp of creditors. You may be a multimillionaire but if none of your assets is in your name, you enjoy the financial vulnerability of a pauper.

Whenever I represent an entrepreneur about to embark on a business venture, my very first move is to "judgment proof" him or her so personal assets are fully protected no matter what happens in their business pursuits.

People are surprised to find there are numerous—and perfectly legal—ways to insulate what they own from business disaster.

Looking ahead and planning for the contingency of failure is the key. As I write this book I'm wrestling with the problems of a businessman who stands to lose over $300,000 in personal assets because he never did quite plan for defeat. As a partner in a mid-sized manufacturing plant going through liquidation he now knows what trouble really is. As typically happens, the business fell behind in federal and state taxes, and he now has over $200,000 in tax liens against his property. A creditor holding a $50,000 guarantee has an attachment on his bank account and on his vacation cottage. Several other creditors are suing him personally on $20,000–30,000 for bad checks and are also moving in to attach his property. In the final tally my beleaguered client will lose virtually everything he worked so hard to accumulate over the years.

Could it have been avoided? Certainly. Had he started smart he could have:

1. Deeded his home or cottage into a real estate trust that he could control as trustee. As trust property it would be free from creditor attack.
2. Taken advantage of the homestead laws provided by many states. These laws protect all or a share of the equity from creditor claims if you follow the requisite steps.
3. Transferred stocks, bonds, and even cash to either a trust or perhaps a specific corporation set up for that purpose.

These are only a few of the common techniques available to achieve the goal of staying rich while you appear poor. On paper you should look so poor that creditors are more likely to send sympathy cards than subpoenas. The quickest way to defuse a rambunctious creditor is to convince him he's spinning his wheels, chasing a worthless judgment.

Timing is critical. Don't expect to incur substantial debts and try to protect your assets two days before the sheriff comes calling. Creditors can successfully claim it is a fraudulent transfer and set aside the conveyance. That's why you "judgment proof" yourself *before* you go into business and incur debts.

Discuss this with your counsel. Request that he or she take all necessary steps to protect and insulate what you own. Nothing obligates you to be a debtor with "deep pockets." You can legally, safely, and morally shield your assets. Starting smart means having nothing to lose.

YOUR STARTING SMART SELF-EXAM

It's time to test yourself. Take a few moments and review your situation, then ask yourself these questions:

1. Did you look at both sides of the coin, preparing for success *or* failure?
2. Do the potential benefits of the deal outweigh the risks?
3. Have you taken every known step to keep your investment as low as possible?
4. Will you operate your business as a corporation?
5. Is your investment to be protected by a loan against business assets?
6. Will you purchase your shares by taking advantage of Section 1244 of the IRS Code?
7. Have you defined the maximum liability you will accept as a guarantor of business debts?
8. Have you taken all the steps to reduce liability on personal guarantees?
9. Have you defined the assets you will own in your own name rather than under the business?
10. Have you protected your personal assets by "judgment proofing" yourself?
11. Have you carefully reviewed these points with your attorney and accountant?

If you answered "no" to any of these questions, you have work to do. It won't take long to prepare for the worst. Then you can spend all your waking moments planning and working for success.

5

BUYING ADVICE AT A BARGAIN PRICE

Today's small independent, to be successful, must know a little about a lot of things—including when to seek outside help rather than tackle a job himself.

Even the smallest business is complex. Whether you run a small restaurant or a mom-and-pop retail shop, you face such diverse tasks as inventory control, merchandising, credit and collections, hiring and firing, bookkeeping, budgeting, and marketing. On top of it all are the varied problems of keeping up with the rapid changes in your field and staying out of trouble with laws piled atop laws in a towering layer cake of confusion.

So say goodbye to being a rugged individualist and say hello to an army of people who can give you the right answers at bargain-priced costs.

Few entrepreneurs reach out for help with a welcoming hand. The average business person thinks of outside advice only when the business needs an instant solution to give it a quick fix. Others ignore outside advice even then, while they wrestle with their ego. It's an expensive mistake. Hyperthyroid take-charge loners may build companies, but when they think they have all the answers they can just as easily wreck their company. Shrewd entrepreneurs know they need answers and know where to look for them.

Expert talent is a double must for the shoestring entrepreneur. You not only need the everyday advice of an established business person, but you need more—and need it earlier—because you can't afford a few costly start-up mistakes. The margin for error just isn't there when you're leveraged up to your eyebrows.

What's amazing is how much valuable help—free or for small pay—you can get from the vast world of outside experts. They're everywhere and can guide you with just about any problem. You'll meet many of these people in this chapter. But don't stop there. There are as many sources of low-cost assistance as there are people who know something about your business. And these people mean business.

TAKING ON TOP-GRADE TALENT

In the market for a savvy consultant to check out your business plans or solve a few specific problems? Forget Booz-Hamilton or Arthur D. Little, the masters of managerial wisdom who peddle their services to the Fortune-500 companies. You want *free* help from people who someday soon may work or perhaps have worked for these or other high-powered consulting firms.

With a phone call you can have a bevy of top-notch MBA students anxious to burn the midnight oil guiding your business. More than 300 universities are members of the Small Business Institute, partially funded by the SBA. The SBA contracts with the university to provide free consulting services for small enterprises that want it, under the supervision of a faculty coordinator. And it's not necessary to be an SBA borrower to qualify.

While students get valuable experience by applying classroom knowledge to actual business problems, your business will benefit from the fresh perspectives these ambitious students can provide.

MBA students are high on my list of free advisors. Bogged down by two years of steady theory they may not know the practical intricacies of your business but they earn top marks in finance, money management, production, and marketing.

As a young MBA student, I enjoyed working on many "hands-on" projects, especially for small start-up firms. From that viewpoint it was an eye-opener to see how few people understood the economics of their business or had a financial grasp on where the business was heading. Fewer still knew even the rudiments of reaching their market. Invariably it was a turkey shoot of problems so we had plenty of work.

Now that I'm on the other side of the fence, I still have two or three MBA students at my side. One student is researching manufacturers' advertising allowances available to my discount stores. I anticipate he'll find $10,000–15,000 in annual promotional bonuses I didn't have time to ferret out. Another student is analyzing our organizational structure to pinpoint responsibility to profits. A third, a young lady from the Northeastern University School of Business, is hard at work on some new merchandising lines.

Think what these young but talented students can do for your start-up, when in a year or two they may be swinging a briefcase at $100 per hour. Today their price is right. Very right.

The SBA is another excellent source of free consultants. It now offers several hundred management assistance officers who counsel both start-ups and established businesses. In addition, the SBA's SCORE—Service Corps of Retired Executives—has a roster of close to 10,000 retired executives and entrepreneurs on standby to help you with every imaginable start-up question from location analysis to pricing. As with MBA students, they are strong on managerial theory, but you want the candidate who has experience in your type business.

The best way to find your right sharpshooter is to shop around. Define the areas you think you need help in, but don't be too restrictive. You may think you have a solid marketing plan and need bolstering in the finance area only to find out the reverse is true. So give these people a reasonably free hand to roam around into all areas of operation while targeting them for specific projects. Interview several candidates. Look for talent that has experience in your type business.

"No business is too small for a helping hand," says Marcia Kavick, now operating a successful interior design firm by the same name. "You think you have all the answers until someone walks through your front door with a few more questions."

Marcia lived the experience. Two MBA students walked

through Marcia's front door—a third floor walk-up loft—and helped her build it to a $600,000-a-year money-maker. As Marcia adds, "It doesn't have to cost for it to pay."

BORROW SOME SUCCESS

Who are the success stories in your field? Your objective should be to borrow some of their success by hiring them on as paid consultants to put you on the right track.

Why not? Most people journeying into their own business check out successful competitors by trying to learn whatever they can about their operation. Go a step further. Don't merely try to steal a few of their ideas when you can steal them all. And if you play it right you can buy plenty of profitable strategies at a very low price.

A good example was a friend of mine who planned to open a gourmet restaurant in Vermont's booming ski area. Although my friend had years of experience as an assistant manager of a family-style restaurant, he was the first to admit a gourmet restaurant was more than another kettle of fish. So my young friend borrowed success from an owner of a fashionable New York culinary paradise, trading $1000 for a three-day intensive course in starting and running a profitable gourmet restaurant.

My friend called it the perfect solution to the "everything-you-always-wanted-to-know-but-didn't-know-who-to-ask" problem. And my friend wanted to know plenty—everything from how many shrimp in a shrimp cocktail justify a $4.95 price to the best sources of veal.

But it's those small details that spell the difference between success and failure. Books can only give you basic theory. No book, seminar, or general consultant can give you the 1001 tricks of your trade. To pick up the fine points, you need the people who proved through their own success that they do have the answers.

Whenever I venture into a new business for the first time, I chase down two or three people to teach me a few lessons. Usually I bring on board a seasoned manager but he's not enough.

Three heads are better than one. When I started my first greeting card and gift shop I imported the owner of an unusually successful Chicago store to help me out in everything from layout to seasonal promotion. He showed up with a computer printout listing his best-sellers by product line. For $800 and travel expenses, my consultant from afar infused 20 years experience into my two-week-old business.

Can you borrow success? Of course. Look for operators in your line with a proven track record. Go well beyond your trading area in your search. You can't expect competitors to show you the ropes. Put your relationship on a firm business footing right from the start. Don't try to ferret free information.

Most of the people you approach will be happy to consult with you—and at surprisingly low costs. They don't really consider themselves as consultants, and the idea you want to borrow their brains for two or three days can be flattering. And for you it can be the key to a profitable start-up.

SUPPLIERS WHO SUPPLY INFORMATION

"I don't know what the independent pharmacy would do without top-notch assistance from his supplier," comments George Maloof, President of New England Wholesale Drug Company. "We provide more than drugs at wholesale—we provide one-stop information on how to start and operate a successful drug store." Whether it be advice on layout, inventory control, promotion, or an automatic order entry system, Maloof's customers consider him to be the umbilical cord to a healthy start.

Vendors in every industry are gold mines of information and start-up assistance. And it's no longer just a sprinkling of information as more and more firms beef up consulting or customer support services to hold a competitive edge.

When considering suppliers, ask about their management assistance programs. There may be a difference amongst suppliers. Of course, business is business and you want the best deal you can strike, and valuable start-up assistance is very much a part of the deal.

What can your suppliers do for you? Shop around. Sometimes you have to prod a supplier to throw in some start-up help. And sometimes it pays to push a bit harder to get even more. In fact, suppliers will do anything in their power to help you if you look like a profitable customer, and do push for extra assistance.

I have talked wholesalers into sending crews in to stock shelves with the initial order. Another supplier with computer capabilities may give you velocity reports on what's selling in your business. Another may send in a design firm to work with you on layout. If you think they can do it then ask for it. They seldom refuse.

Make a supplier a co-conspirator in your success. It may be a friendly afternoon discussing your merchandising plans, pricing, promotion, or whatever he can contribute to. Maybe you'll buy his suggestions or perhaps you won't. But whatever comes of your conversation, you have an ally. He's likely to be more lenient on credit or give you the extra inch when times are tough.

Salespeople are talkers, and when they talk you listen. You'll learn plenty. The advice and favors they throw your way can be more important than help from the top. I don't care how busy I am, I always have time for salespeople. In the time it takes to share a cup of coffee they'll give you the pulse of your industry. If they hear about new lines, promotional ideas, problems, or what your competitor down the street is doing you'll know about it before you empty your cup. And don't sell them short. An experienced salesperson can know as much about your business as anyone. Some of my best merchandising strategies were offered by salespeople. And when they're on your side, they can work wonders as troubleshooters between you and their company.

Discuss your proposed plans with potential suppliers. Don't wait until you open your doors. By then it's too late for suppliers to give you the start-up guidance you need.

TEN THOUSAND HEADS ARE BETTER THAN ONE

Every industry has its local, regional, and national associations. While some are glorified political clubs, many others are a warehouse of information and can be extremely useful to a start-up.

The larger associations gather specialized technical or marketing data to save you research time. One of the associations I belong to publishes average operating data for comparable businesses in my field.Another offers low-cost training programs to employees and management seminars to owners. One of the most useful pieces of information I pick up from the association are monthly profiles on the fastest moving lines in the discount industry and retail prices charged by minor chains.

You can also save money on the associations' group buying. Health and accident insurance may be at a fraction of the individual subscriber rate and aggressive associations will offer group member discounts on everything from equipment to supplies and credit reporting. One local association in my area offers discounts on rent-a-cars and even a security service to check internal pilferage.

The biggest benefit of membership is the ability to chat with other people in your field. You make contracts, swap problems and solutions, and learn what's going on. You can't operate in a vacuum and expect to make the grade. Ten thousand heads are better than one.

Too many business people ignore the trade journals. They should be high on your reading list. Once a week I set aside two hours to pore through every journal in my field to pick out a few tips I can put into practice. Many associations publish their own magazines, and you may be able to subscribe without membership.

Don't stop with your own trade associations. Join, if you can, your customers' associations. Learn about the problems they're having and the opportunities it offers you. It's not a bad way to meet some good customers either.

Nathan Goldberg, executive director of the Boston Association of Retail Druggists, is one association exec who agrees that new entries into the field miss the boat by ignoring associations. "Only 20–30% of the new entrepreneurs in our field take the time to join. It's surprising, considering the wide range of services we can provide a start-up and most of the services are absolutely free."

FREE PRODUCT IDEAS

The federal bureaucracy is itching to help you turn new products into success. They'll even help you find and develop new products, then bolster it with tons of marketing information.

Interested in new inventions ripe for development? There are two places to shop. The U.S. Patent Office will send you descriptive lists of new inventions, many available for licensing or outright sale. The SBA also publishes a monthly "Products List Circular," while a similar list of fertile new product ideas, grouped by industry, are available from the office of technical assistance.

Many of the products and inventions on these lists can be exploited by your business at a nominal royalty charge. You'll also find some developed by the government available to you absolutely free on a nonexclusive basis.

A small army of government researchers are ready to hit the books to come up with answers to just about any question involving a product, process, or invention. How do you put these federal employees to work as your market research department? Write the Science and Technology Division of the Congressional Library, Washington, D.C. State your problem or what you want researched, and in a week or two you'll have a fully researched written report either for free (if it's a small research job), or for a few dollars if it takes some legwork.

Other agencies compete for the privilege of doing your market research for a pittance. Do you have a new energy-saving device? Nobody is more excited about the prospects of saving energy than Uncle Sam. Why do you think he gives those big tax bonuses to taxpayers who conserve fuel? But he also loves the people whose business it is to create and sell the energy savers. The U.S. Department of Energy are the people to call. They'll not only test and evaluate your product, but help you develop and improve it. And when your product is ready to go they may even guarantee a bank loan to help you start.

Consider all the sources of free or low-cost government assistance to move your product along. Washington is loaded with bright technically oriented engineers and scientists on the public dole and they have one job—to be your product development specialist.

EXPORT EXPERTS FOR HIRE

Do you have a product that can be sold abroad? Uncle Sam hopes so. He's hoping to balance the growing onslaught of imports by showing the rest of the world the good old U.S.A. can still turn out a few good products. And he's working harder than ever to prove it. If you think you can top a foreign market you'll have plenty of friends in Washington.

First stop is the Export-Import Bank at 8111 Vermont Avenue, N.W., Washington, D.C. Eximbank, as it's known, offers every conceivable export service and can be your bloodhound leading you to all the right markets abroad. It can even arrange credit insurance to protect you from credit losses in dealing with foreign customers. Write the bank for details.

Another agency hard at work assisting exporters is the Commerce Department Bureau of International Commerce. It offers a long list of foreign buyers, agents, and distributors to work with you. If you are looking to market someone else's product, then ask the Commerce Department for the American International Traders' Index. The index lists over 25,000 manufacturers who want to sell abroad, and your name can be added upon request.

An added feature in working with the Commerce Department is its new product information service. The agency will promote your product free of charge and test foreign interest. They'll even arrange to have your product displayed at U.S. Trade Centers abroad.

The states have their own export services to offer, particularly the larger industrialized states of California, New York, Ohio, Pennsylvania, and Massachusetts. Check your state and you'll probably find a helpful hand within a specific agency set up to help its resident firms go after foreign sales. Most states limit themselves to answering specific questions on exporting, but they can put you in touch with all the right people to produce a successful export program. Massachusetts helped one of my clients become a millionaire. As a manufacturer of artificial bricks made by a patented process, he wanted to expand into Europe and Japan. Freight costs prevented shipping the brick, so a representative from the state's Commerce Department coordinated a meeting with several foreign firms who were interested in licensing the process. Today the artificial bricks are also manufactured in Florence, Italy and Kyoto, Japan, and negotiations are underway to license the process in England. Income from foreign sales has tripled the company's profits. And all it took to get the ball rolling was a ten-cent phone call.

Travel to Los Angeles and visit its World Trade Center. It doesn't cost much to participate, but when you do you'll have access to an "export hot line" and ready answers to your every export question.

When you talk about "exporting," people jump at the chance to help you. They have to. Their job is to make sure your product finds a new home abroad and more money in your pocket.

TO MARKET, TO MARKET

"Build a better mousetrap and the world will beat a path to your door." That's the saying, but it's wrong. The only people about to beat down your door are the people who want a mousetrap and know you have a better one to sell. So the name of the game is marketing. To win the game you'll need plenty of marketing information to identify and reach your potential customers. And marketing information can cost you an arm and a leg unless you know a few cost-cutting maneuvers.

Now let's suppose you do develop a better mousetrap. How can you develop first-class market intelligence at third-class rates?

1. Government agencies are likely to have plenty of answers. The Pesticide Division of the Department of Agriculture, for example, has a rundown on the rodent population by city and state. "Big Brother" knows everything. That's why

the government needs so many buildings to store its files. And the right agency will have the right answer to your questions—if you know the right questions.

2. The Commerce Department and Treasury Department have established a data base profiling every imaginable industry. They have all the statistics to show sales, market concentrations, and number of firms in the field. For a few dollars you'll have a full report on the mousetrap industry.
3. Your trade association has plenty of full information. Did you know there are five associations catering to mousetrap manufacturers?
4. Call the U.S. Census Department. Every industry has its demographics—the breakdown of its market by consumer classification. Once you know who your customers are likely to be, the Census Bureau will tell you where they are—and for free.
5. Public libraries are another good source. But you don't have to do the work yourself. Metropolitan libraries have researchers on their staff who pluck answers to specific questions as part of community service. In a few days they can provide information and more sources than would take you a month to find.
6. If your competitors are publicly owned corporations, ask for their 10-K reports filed with the SEC. They will tell you everything you want to know about your competitors for the price of a postage stamp.
7. Professional information-gathering services will do your market research at a per diem rate of about $200. The typical firm can land all the data it needs to make "thinking cap" decisions for less than $800.
8. Dun & Bradstreet can give you business data on your competitors if you are or know a subscriber. It's one way of finding out how your smaller (non-publicly traded) competitors are making out.
9. The National Science Foundation will do all your market research for free—if you have a big project that can benefit

the community, such as ecology, education, new drugs, or help for the handicapped. In other cases they'll give you a grant to hire the professional marketing staff.

"Any start-up company can have a complete data base of information to make intelligent marketing decisions," says Dr. Barry Bleidt of Northeastern University. "And it's not expensive to do once you know the information you're looking for and where to find it. Most entrepreneurs, however, are weak on marketing. Their wisest investment is \$200–300 to hire an MBA student or a few more dollars to retain a professional firm."

PROMOTING FOR A PITTANCE

Your firm's advertising budget may not be big enough to interest a top-dollar advertising agency or public relations firm, but there are other ways to get equally good results for small dollars.

Manufacturers routinely help retailers design ads featuring their products, and in many cases they'll even pay for part of the ad costs. Many retailers overlook the advertising dollars available to them by not knowing which manufacturers offer cooperative advertising money. A direct inquiry is one way to find out. Trade journals listing deals should also list the promotional allowances in buying the deal. And, of course, salespeople should let you know about it.

A health and beauty aid store in our area, grossing \$600,000 annually, reports that it spends \$20,000 a year on advertising—but more than 75% of the ad costs is reimbursed by the manufacturers whose products are featured. Think about it. You may have the most aggressive ad campaign in town, courtesy of a supplier anxious to push his products from your business.

Wholesalers, voluntary chains, or cooperatives organized by retailers undertake collective advertising for participating retailers. Twenty retailers operating under a common banner can create more punch for each advertising dollar spent.

Point-of-purchase promotional material is another area where suppliers can spare you a few of your own dollars. Many will provide free display racks while firms such as Coppertone, Kodak, Coca-Cola, or Pepsi may even pay for a store sign.

No need to look like an amateur with homemade advertising. There's an art and science to an ad that pulls. Newspapers, radio stations, and other media have specialists on their staff who'll help you create dynamic ads. Don't go it alone. They'll work even harder for you if you plan a long ad campaign and offer a one-year contract, which will save you money.

Free-lance ad and public relations specialists are naturals for shoestring entrepreneurs. Cost is one factor. You can hire an imaginative free-lancer for a very small fee of $75–100 a day, and if you have a sufficiently large advertising budget their 15% commission may entice them to work free. What I enjoy about free-lancers is their imagination. Some can be considerably more creative than larger ad firms. In a sense they have to be to get mileage for their clients working with too few ad dollars.

Where do you find free-lancers to whip together a powerful campaign? Every city has free-lancer's clubs and associations. Interview a few. Look over some of their work. Try to find a pattern of success with a business like yours.

Do you have a unique product or story to tell? If it can spark public interest then you need a public relations free-lancer to spread the word around.

Crazy fads such as the Pet Rock have generated millions overnight with exposure on network TV and write-ups in the national press. You may not have another Pet Rock but still have a newsworthy story for your local paper. But here you should pay only for results. Work up a fee schedule with the P.R. free-lancer, agreeing to pay specific sums only when your story breaks.

Turn to other imaginative entrepreneurs, and you'll see other ways to make your business come alive. And when you have the right people by your side it can come to life for very little cost.

FOUR WAYS TO FREE EMPLOYEE TRAINING

Another area where Uncle Sam is spending huge dollars is in employee training. Uncle Sam wants people off the welfare and unemployment rosters and on your payroll. And he'll train them for you—or pay you to train them—as your part of the bargain.

Many women, minorities, and handicapped need a chance at "entry level jobs." And many will become excellent workers once they've been properly trained. Here are four programs to investigate:

1. The Comprehensive Employment and Training Act (CETA) provides federal funds for training unemployed or underemployed workers. If you hire a CETA worker the government reimburses you a share of the wages and for the cost of training and training materials. CETA instructors are also on hand to help you train. You can find out more about the CETA program by stopping in at any local CETA office.
2. Project transition is a brainstorm of the armed forces. The Defense Department will help you train servicemen about to be released from the armed services. If you are interested in hiring veterans, and want some assistance from Uncle Sam, then contact the Defense Department.
3. Physically or emotionally handicapped workers can be trained through a wide range of government-sponsored vocational rehabilitation programs. Some offer wage subsidies while all provide training grants or payments. Check it out. The handicapped have high scores for reliability and loyalty.
4. Write to the Labor Department's Bureau of Apprenticeship and Training if you want to set up an apprenticeship program. They'll provide plenty of free assistance.

These programs are excellent, especially for start-ups in the manufacturing and service industries. A small electronics firm in our area started with 60 assembly workers provided by CETA and two state-sponsored vocational programs. The government paid $180,000 for its share of the training and had four instructors in the plant for one month to turn these willing workers into top-notch producers. Management estimates it would have cost the firm over $300,000 to hire and train on its own. Do you need help finding and training employees?

LAWYERS: A NECESSARY EVIL

Lawyers are a necessary evil. You can't do business—or start a business—without one. While the lawyer is necessary his legal fee is evil. And legal fees are becoming more outrageous every day. It's not anti-lawyer talk because I'm a practicing attorney myself, but I will tell you that unless you know how to find and feed your lawyer you can go for a bundle. How big a bundle? Partners in large law firms typically bill at $150–200 an hour. Novice legal pups with wet ink on their diplomas put a price tag of $60–100 for their wisdom. So while your lawyer is hard at work incorporating your business, negotiating your lease, posturing with your partners, and reviewing the financing agreement his time clock is happily ticking away. A month later you have your corner store and a $3500 legal bill. Wouldn't you be happier with a $500 bill? Let me show you how to slash your legal fees without sacrificing quality representation. And you can do it if you follow these fee-saving tips:

1. Shop for the right attorney. And what you want is someone with broad-based business experience to handle you while you grow, yet hungry enough to be flexible on fees because he wants your future business. You can't stereotype, but the largest firms are usually a mismatch for the small start-up. You never mean quite as much to them as to the smaller firm. Besides, large firms typically have fixed fee schedules and rigid payment policies. The sole practitioner has his own limitations of inability to handle a wide range of problems or churn out work quickly if you need it. Chances are you should look for the mid-sized, 3–10 lawyer firm.
2. Look for the business specialist within the firm. Today's lawyer is a specialist. You may have been referred to someone who primarily practices divorce, criminal, or

negligence law. And they may agree to represent you. It's a bad choice. You want the lawyer who spends the day representing businesses—and preferably the smaller firm whose problems may be somewhat different from the large corporation. The right attorney can help you mastermind a start-up. Don't forget, yours is not the first business he helped create.

3. Involve your lawyer early in the game. Don't run to him after you signed an agreement, lease, or bank note. You want advice and not a report card on your own legal brilliance. I see it all the time. Two partners will strike a cockeyed deal so the lawyers spend triple the time reworking it, or financing was improperly structured so it's back to the bank.
4. Discuss fees *before* you retain counsel. This is the most important point. Be candid. If you have very limited capital let your counsel know about it. Work out a budget for legal costs so your counsel knows what he has to work with and you know what your bill will be. Be fee-conscious. If your lawyer has to quote fees before you retain him he may quote on the low side to land you as a client.
5. Don't shop fees on the basis of an hourly charge. It doesn't mean a thing. A $100 per hour attorney may be twice as fast as a $75 lawyer. Negotiate an estimated total fee based on stated services he *must* provide for you. But remember it can only be a "ball park" estimate. Extra work may be required, as unanticipated problems can crop up. If extra work is needed ask your attorney to clear it with you but don't tie his hands. When you hold your counsel to a firm $2000-fee quote he has little incentive to spend the added few dollars to do the best job.
6. Lawyers will defer their billing. Ask them in advance so you both know the ground rules. Many of our clients ask us if they can pay their bill over several months and we always agree. In fact, we consider it a sign of a creditworthy client. Deadbeats never ask if they can pay it out since they never expect to pay.

7. All a lawyer has to sell is his time and advice. Keep your phone calls to a minimum and keep office visits to the point. Every lawyer has horror stories of clients who eat up costly hours on trivia. One way or another you pay for it.

The very best way to cut legal fees is to use alternative services. Incorporating your business is one place you save a small fortune. The average legal fee for a corporation is $500 (plus filing fees). Commercial firms set up corporations for a fraction of the price. The Company Corporation, 725 Market Street, Wilmington, Delaware, is one of the best. For $150 (and filing costs) they will set up a corporation in any state and in a matter of a few days. If your attorney will match the price then it may be more convenient for him to do it. Otherwise give The Company Corporation a call and pocket the difference.

Close to one million entrepreneurs have set up their own corporation using Ted Nicholas' *How to Form Your Own Corporation for Less than $50* (1978). It's easier than you think. You can buy this best-seller at any bookstore or order it from Enterprise Publishing, 725 Market Street, Wilmington, Delaware, 19801.

Federal and state agencies live in a world of forms. You'll need forms for everything from obtaining a tax number to registering your business name. You don't need your lawyer to obtain and fill out these simple forms. Your accountant can handle it at less cost. A better idea is to contact Simon & Schuster Rockefeller Center, New York, New York. It publishes a unique product—a portfolio of start-up forms on a state-by-state basis. For $15 you are sent all the forms you need with instructions to complete them. It can save you several hundred dollars.

Speaking of forms, you won't need your attorney to prepare the everyday legal and business documents for your business. Order *The Basic Book of Business Agreements* (1983), from Enterprise Publishing (see address above). For $49.95 you'll have hundreds of ready-to-use agreements and documents for every business need. It's a terrific money-saver. I know, I wrote it.

Common sense is the key to the effective use of an attorney. Don't be your own lawyer on complicated or potentially costly transactions. It's false economy. Just save where you safely can. The dollars can add up.

FINDING AN ACCOUNTANT TO NAVIGATE

A good accountant is the most important single outside advisor a small business has. Navigating by the numbers is even more important for the highly leveraged start-up.

The first rule is never to scrimp a few dollars on accounting services. Many small business people limit their accountants to the preparation of quarterly and year-end tax returns. They don't have financial navigators, they only have tax preparers. It's not the way to navigate your business.

What you do need is tight financial control. That means budgets, cash flow statements, expense analysis, product costing, and numbers, numbers, and more numbers to tell you where you've been, where you're going, and how you're getting there. And if you can't put these numbers together for yourself, you'll need some financial types who can. And they're not hard to find.

Most start-ups look for CPAs. As with any other professional group some do excellent work and others are a waste of money. A small business generally doesn't need a CPA because certified statements aren't necessary. Only the larger firms with heavy bank loans or publicly traded corporations require certified statements, so you may end up paying for a title you won't use.

The best way to get the most service for the least money is to divide the accounting function. Long-range financial planning and tax counselling should be left to the CPAs. They're still the best qualified for the important decisions. The operational accounting should be delegated to someone else.

I've had excellent results with General Business Services, a franchised accounting system. For $60 a month, my GBS accountant works with me on budgeting, forecasting, and cash flows, and sets my business up with a precise but easy-to-use daily bookkeeping system. Once a month he shows up with a computerized profit and loss statement and balance sheet for the prior month. He then spends an hour or two reviewing the problems and working with me to plan for the month ahead. He offers just the right information I need to navigate and it's a terrific bargain. I have found few CPA firms to offer the same intensity of service for so low a price. There are probably other equally good accounting services. Comprehensive Business Services is another comparable franchised system with offices throughout the country, and many others have started in recent years to answer the needs of the small business. Compare several franchised systems in your area.

A larger firm in the $300,000–800,000 sales range may need a part-time comptroller. Some comptrollers do free-lance on a part-time basis, serving several clients. Local universities with accounting programs have many students and recent graduates who qualify. Your own CPA firm may have a junior associate available. But don't have his services billed through the firm. You want him or her on a moonlighting basis without the firm's override. Your local newspaper will also list bookkeepers and accountants looking for per diem work.

Unquestionably the most important factor in selecting an accountant is his willingness to stand up to you and fight for financial decisions he believes are right. You can't afford a "yes" man. One of my earlier accountants would listen to whatever plans I had, shake his head in agreement while thinking he was scoring points. He wasn't. I fired him. My present accountant is the type pro you need. He'll listen to my plans and fight me tooth and nail if he thinks I'm steering in the wrong direction. It doesn't matter who's right. I may be the captain of the ship, but he's still the navigator. And as long as he is, it's his job to keep the business off the shoals. Don't look for titles. Look for the accountant who'll grab the wheel from you.

BUY THE AGENT NOT THE INSURANCE

Lawyers and accountants aren't the only professionals you need on your side. Your insurance agent is the third leg in your professional tripod. Unfortunately few people realize it, thinking all agents, like all insurances, are the same.

It's not so. Insurance is too complex today. You'll need your insurance agent for more than casualty and liability coverage, to guide you in the rapidly expanding areas of pension plans, Keough and IRA accounts, and a host of other tax-inspired insurance-related investments. And even the simpler forms of insurance are no longer quite so simple. How many different types of insurance do you need? You have about 50 different choices when buying liability insurance alone. You can buy wisely or buy foolishly. Only your insurance agent can tell the difference.

So you don't buy insurance. You do buy the insurance agent. And what you need is the agent who'll work to get you just the right coverage at the right price. But he has to work for you and not the insurance company. That's the key.

I don't recommend the agent representing only one insurance underwriter. He can't shop around for the best buy and his allegiances are too strong. Look for the agent handling multiple lines. He can play one company against the other until he puts together the best possible package.

Call in several multiple-line agents and compare their proposals. But look beyond their proposals. Look to see if they're trying to sell you insurance or trying to sell you savings.

Insurance, even for the small start-up, can be $8000–10,000 a year.It's a major expenditure and you can save 35–40% with the right agent. Like most laypeople, I don't know a good plan from a bad one and I never quite trust the agent no matter how trustworthy he may be. So I use a retired insurance broker as my personal consultant. For $100 a year he reviews my insurance and tells me whether my agent is doing his job. It's a great investment. Several years ago he pointed out areas of duplicate coverage, saving me $4000. When you have a pro working only for you, you know what you're buying.

Some business people prefer to buy insurance from one of the several underwriters who sell on a direct basis. It's true that you can save 15–25% but I don't recommend it for two reasons. First, you don't have the expert advice of an agent. You're likely to end up with a poorly designed program. An even more important reason is that you don't have an agent to fight for you when a claim arises. That's when you'll know whose side the agent is on.

MORE PEOPLE FROM MORE PEOPLE

How many sources are there for free or low-cost assistance to make your business a success? Entire books have been written on it. One of the best is the *Small Business Survival Guide* by Joseph Mancuso (Prentice-Hall 1980). It lists hundreds of valuable resources. It's recommended reading.

But you can take a page from the stories of other entrepreneurs who know how to put people to work without putting them on the payroll.

John Richards had an entire class of MBA students game-plan his idea for starting a foundry to manufacture wood burning stoves. The students used it as a case study and within a week Richards had 42 feasibility studies complete with marketing and financial projections. Thirty-eight students decided it wouldn't work. But it did work. Today the Hyde Park Home Energy Center grosses $2 million annually. "I still learned plenty about the business," says Richards, "even if I had to prove these budding executives wrong." Wouldn't your business idea be a welcome change for "B" school students using stuffy old textbook cases? Sure it would. Talk to a professor about it.

Do you realize that your electric bill can be sliced dramatically with a few simple techniques? Hub Foods did. It found an electrical engineer whose specialty was rewiring businesses, charging 50% of the first year's savings. But saving money is what a start-up needs. You can find firms who will show you how to also save on heat, air conditioning, and telephone costs—all on a percentage of actual savings. Your utility companies will tell you who they are.

Interested in profitable reading? The Government Printing Office has a library of over 35,000 fact-filled books on every type business. If you'd like an overview of the pamphlets and books available to you, write the Superintendent of Documents, Government Printing Office, Washington D.C. 20402. It has been called the best business library around.

This chapter only scratches the surface of all the people who can help you. Its real mission is to let you know the help is there if you look for it. You're not the only one who wants your business to succeed.

KEY POINTS TO REMEMBER

1. You can't do it all yourself. You'll need help—and the right help.
2. Your best consultants are free or low-pay consultants. They mean business.
3. Suppliers are ready to provide you with a wide range of assistance—if you ask for it.
4. Don't overlook associations. Their only purpose is to help you succeed. Tap their information-rich resources.
5. Uncle Sam can help you develop and market new products at home and abroad. He shares in your profits, so make him work to produce your profits.
6. Small firms can pack a powerful promotional punch, once you have the right people showing you how.
7. Expensive talent—your professional team—is never quite so expensive with a few cost-cutting steps.
8. The difference between failure and success may be one more answer to one more question.

6

FINDING THE MONEY

Wearing well-worn jeans, running shoes, and a T-shirt, he sports a full blond beard nestled beneath over-sized sunglasses. An ever-present frayed but dated Brooklyn Dodgers' cap sits tilted on his bushy blond hair. Scrambling from thought to thought he reminds you of Woody Allen while constantly pushing his glasses on his nose. Cradles in his left arm is a large, gray, contented cat, in sharp contrast to his animated master.

Would you lend $100,000 to this man?

Thirty-seven bankers said "no." So did the SBA, nine finance companies, and a slew of prospective private backers. They just didn't know Bernie Simon, the youthful chairman of the board of Simon Industries, grossing several million dollars annually in the laser light entertainment field.

Chairman Simon now occupies a spacious suite overlooking Boston's waterfront and you'll still find the Dodgers' cap perched on his head as the link to his Brooklyn past. But to the kids who storm the halls to have their eyes strained by psychedelic laser lights dancing on a screen and their ears punctured by local rock bands, he's still "Big Bernie." Indeed, Boston's teenyboppers have made "Big Bernie" a very wealthy man.

Boston's financial community was less enthusiastic. "You can't take some guy in a pinstripe suit hiding behind a mahogany desk and expect him to understand what your deal is all about. Not when it's an untried idea, and they can't back the loan up with hard collateral," explains Bernie. "Bankers aren't gamblers. So they warily shake your hand like you're a Martian and wish you well. Two minutes after you leave they're spraying Lysol around their office."

So who was it that gambled on "Big Bernie" and his "Magnificent Laser Light Show"? Quite a few people. Ten investors each shelled out $5000 for 4% of the business. Bernie was halfway there with $50,000 and still owned 60% of the company. With some fancy footwork, Bernie talked the equipment supplier into loaning him $10,000 and another $10,000 loan came from the concession operators promised the opportunity to hawk hot dogs and Coke to the adolescent appetites. The final $30,000 loan came from another entrepreneur who recently struck gold in a high-tech business. With the $100,000 in hand, Bernie's "Magnificent Laser Light Show" opened in three suburban theaters and can now be seen in cities dotting the East Coast. Bernie remarks, "You need your own style to find money. Willie Sutton the famous bank robber did it with a gun. I do it with enthusiasm. Sometimes it's contagious."

Can you infect a financial backer with the "contagious enthusiasm" to fork over your start-up capital? Successful entrepreneurs agree that the answer depends on three essential ingredients:

1. How long you look.
2. Where you look.
3. What you look for.

Here's a close-up view of each:

1. *How long you look: Check your staying power*

Finding start-up capital is never easy. Forget the nonsense rags-to-riches books that tell you the streets are lined with deep-pocket capitalists ready to throw money at you. It doesn't happen that way. Not if you're armed with only an idea and lack collateral to back up the loan. "And when you have little or no money of our own to throw into the deal it makes it that much tougher," says "Big Bernie" of laser light fame. "It's not impossible, but your fingers do get tired walking through the yellow pages," recounts Bernie, who struck out 52 times before landing his first few dollars.

Perseverance and sufficient commitment to your idea to knock on still another door is the key. Too many people with perfectly valid business plans underestimate what it takes to locate leveraged financing, and with a few turndowns, sigh a discouraged note aborting their plans.

Look at it realistically. Financing is a competitive process and the start-up comes in at the bottom of the heap in the bid for available cash. First in line are successful ventures seeking expansion capital, followed by buyers of going businesses. When start-ups are considered, priority goes to the venture that is both well capitalized and readily collateralized. Funding an idea alone is always a challenge because lenders are skeptics and every start-up must pierce through a stone wall of skepticism to pierce a lender's vault. And lenders should be skeptics. They know that between idea and successful operation too many things can go wrong.

To turn to a positive note, you only have to consider the two million new businesses opening their doors this year. It's proof positive start-up capital is available and in many of these cases the business idea had little more to offer lenders than entrepreneurial enthusiasm. Bernie Simon was one story. Amy Shapiro is another. Today Amy operates a large restaurant near Groton, Connecticut, but not without the helping hand of a potpourri of lenders ranging from the SBA to a $3000 loan from the cigarette vending firm anxious for Amy's promising location. "It took me almost two years to build my financial pyramid," says Amy, "and that represents 700 days of bending the ear of anyone who could possibly be interested in making a small loan. Most people weren't interested. A few were. But the 'few,' and the perseverance to find them, is what it takes."

2. *Where you look: Capitalists in the crowd*

Matching your money-making idea to the right financial backer is half the battle. And there are plenty of capitalists in the crowd who don't sport pinstripe suits.

You can't stop with banks, the SBA, and other conventional

lenders. Sometimes it's a waste of time to even start with them—particularly if you don't have strong collateral or a heavy personal investment to wave before them. As Bernie Simon says, "Banks don't gamble. And what can be a bigger gamble than someone short on cash and collateral dreaming of his or her own business?"

So where does the seed money come from to start your bootstrapped money tree? Non-institutional lenders. Friends and relatives are obvious candidates. Others are high tax bracket individuals looking for a high return buttressed with the consoling thought the IRS will share their losses. Still others are suppliers, customers, and even landlords with a vested interest in having you open your doors. The list is endless.

Andy VanBuskirk, with a string of successful businesses behind him, endorses the point. "I didn't have a dime to open my first donut shop, but I had the tenacity to nibble away at plenty of people who did. A bank loaned $10,000 against the value of used equipment, three suppliers each chipped in $3000 and a finance company backed me with $4000 credit. Sharpening my bite I landed $5000 from the boys at my poker club and another $2000 from a college chum who would never have made it through Chem 101 without me. But that's how it is when you need money. You don't leave stones unturned."

3. *What you look for: Dealmaking*

Just as you have to abandon your idea of conventional sources you'll also have to abandon your idea of conventional terms. In reality there's no such thing as "conventional" loan terms when you talk about shoestring start-ups. Your deal is what you can bargain for.

"To tap the money sources you have to be a bit of a wheeler-dealer," says Mark Winn who specializes in financing leveraged start-ups. "Every lender has his own motivations and expectations, and you have to talk and think in their terms to cement a deal. Too many people can't roll with the punches."

Private backers, for example, won't settle for 18% interest if a profitable loan is their objective. They want the high 24–26% interest proportionate to the high risk. Some want a piece of the business as a bonus. Suppliers are sold on the basis of a profitable account. Interest is secondary. Friends and relatives are yet a different breed. You never know what will make them happy.

It all points to one word: salesmanship. As Mark Winn adds, "The successful borrower targets a prospect and knows how to put together a proposition and sell it like you would any product. And when you know the right words it invariably leads to a 'yes.' "

Keep these ground rules in mind as you go through the next several pages and learn to play the game to win your needed financing.

YOU CAN'T BEAT BORROWED MONEY

Walt Disney once said, "I must be successful; I owe seven million dollars." So you're not Disney, but that doesn't suggest you shouldn't go after as much capital as you need. In fact, the cornerstone of shrewd financing is to borrow 100%—or as close to it as you can—while using little or none of your own money. And contrary to what theorists preach, it's both workable and advisable. Here's why:

1. You need your money as a reserve. Typically a start-up will be financed by an owner depleting his or her cash reserves and borrowing the balance to complete the capital needs. But you can never estimate with total accuracy what your business needs for a successful start. During the first year or two you'll have cost overruns and a host of unexpected expenses. It's too soon to go back to your lenders for more cash, and with your own money tied up, the cash bind begins. A higher debt level to begin with would allow you to hold your cash as a "cushion" to clear the unanticipated hurdles.
2. Taxes are another factor. With funds borrowed by your business, the interest payments are deductible. If you plow money into the business you can only take it out as taxable income or interest.

3. Debt is a safety net. It's difficult for laypeople to understand but the more debt your business has the more patient creditors will be with you. The reason is simple. If your business fails, creditors stand to see little or nothing. A business with a high liquidation value in relation to secured debt will yield a healthy dividend to creditors and make you a more vulnerable bankruptcy target.
4. Emotion is part of it. When your own money is at risk you may make warped business decisions worrying more about what's "safe" for your money than what's "right" for your business. Of course, when your home or savings account passbook backs up a loan, it's still money "at risk," but with further shopping and bargaining you may find ways to finance while keeping your cash and assets intact. It's the best of all worlds when you're finally in business with everything to gain and have nothing to lose in the process.

If you follow the 100% of leveraged philosophy you'll be in the strongest of all positions. You can sit back and objectively assess the performance of the business. If it's going well but needs periodic cash infusions, you have your cash reserves to handle it. But now you're making the investment decision based on performance and not projections. It's far safer.

How will financial backers take to the notion of 100% financing as you jockey to avoid putting any of your own money into the business? It depends on the backer and your reasons. When lenders are convinced the reason is because you don't have the cash to invest you retain credibility, but your backers will take an even more skeptical look at the validity of your business plan. Obviously suspicion reigns when you do have capital and let it be known that you'd simply prefer to play with everyone else's.

There are several ways to handle either situation. Honest disclosure of your limited finances is a start. Don't allow lenders to think you're holding back and afraid to risk your own capital. If you do have available capital then explain that your cash is committed for working capital and can't be used for fixed start-up costs. It won't be of primary concern to private lenders whose loan decision is usually independent of owner's capitalization;

however, institutional lenders are another matter. In fact, most institutional lenders require that an entrepreneur put up at least half the start-up capital from his or her own funds. Many banks don't really care how much you actually invest, provided their loan does not exceed 50% of the needed financing. That leaves the door open for secondary financing and subordinate lenders and your own "no cash" investment. Others are satisfied if you pledge personal assets as collateral for the loan.

Many entrepreneurs overcome the "owner's capital" question by contributing personally owned equipment, vehicles, or patents to the business. It satisfies most lenders, testing your commitment to gamble on your own business. "But commitment doesn't necessarily have to be in the form of owner's cash," admits one New York banker. "We look for other clues. How much effort went into the planning? Is the applicant leaving a high-paying job? How serious about the business does the applicant appear to be? It all comes under the heading of 'sweat equity,' and it may mean more than some clown toying with a half-baked idea and a pocketful of cash."

NEGOTIATE YOUR WINNING TERMS

Buying money is no different than buying any other commodity. You want the best terms available, and to win the best terms, take a short course on the bargaining points to watch for and negotiate in your favor.

Many a lender will tell you that "eager beavers" entering into their first business are so intimidated by the lending process—or so thrilled about obtaining a loan—they never think to haggle. It's a mistake. Even a few fine points bargained in your favor can add up to big savings. And it's all part of one-upmanship. Beggars don't land financing.

So whether you're negotiating with a bank, finance company, supplier, or your next-door neighbor, keep this negotiating check list before you.

1. *Do* structure the loan properly. And this means the loan is

made directly from the lender to your corporation. Don't have the loan go to you while you in turn invest it or loan it to your business. You may have to personally guarantee the loan or perhaps back it up with personal collateral, but the business should be the borrower. Consider the advantages: with the loan directly between the lender and your corporation, the lender will have recourse against your business which may shield you from needless or excess personal liability. Taxes are a second reason. With the business paying the loan directly, you have no adverse personal tax liability as you would if you had to take money out of the business to pay your loan. Review this advice with your attorney and accountant.

2. *Do* ask for more money than you need. Many lenders arbitarily cut you to a smaller amount so by starting high you may end up at just the right amount. A good rule of thumb is to ask for 25–30% more than what you hope for. The danger in going beyond that is that you lose credibility if the loan request is obviously in excess of what the business demands.
3. *Do* negotiate interest. With institutional lenders you should start by checking prevailing interest rates to comparable start-ups. Available collateral will greatly influence interest rates, so take this into consideration. Here are a few specific tips to follow. Always try to bargain a lender down 2–3% from the offered interest. Most banks, for example, start with flexibility, expecting your counteroffer. Another strategy is to reduce the interest as the loan balance is reduced. Why not? The lender's risk is now reduced. Watch interest based on an inflationary high prime rate. For example, when the prime rate was 15% many start-ups were charged 5 or 6 points over prime or 20–21%. As I write this book the prime is down to 11%, but these loans are still locked in to a high 20% interest. Bargain for a "floating prime" rate that cuts your interest when the prime rate comes down. A point or two on interest can appear insignificant, but doesn't one percentage point on a

$100,000 loan put $1000 in your pocket each year the loan is outstanding?

4. *Do* demand the longest loan possible. This is a critical point with all business borrowing and it's particularly important with a shoestring start-up. A bank, for example, may offer a three-year note. Can your business pay it down in three years? Forget rosy projections. You need loan payments that coincide with a conservatively drafted cash flow statement prepared by your accountant. Some lenders have a maximum three- or five-year loan as a matter of policy. One alternative is to schedule payments on the basis of a longer loan and be obligated to pay the balance upon maturity of the loan. By then your loan should be low enough and your business stable to re-finance. But in the meantime you may cut your monthly payments by 30–40%. Extending this same strategy a step further, see if the lender will accept interest only for the first year or two. Retaining the payments on principal can do wonders for an anemic cash flow.
5. *Do* pledge business assets as collateral if you personally guarantee the loan. Auction proceeds may satisfy the lender so he won't go after you personally. Conversely, don't use personal assets as collateral without a fight. Lenders are collateral hungry and will demand whatever you own to reduce their risk, but it's always a negotiable point and you may be surprised how much you can borrow without fear of losing your home.
6. *Don't* settle for the first loan offer. There are plenty of lenders once you know where to look, and they're all in competition to "sell" you money. Having spent the time to put together your loan proposal, shop it around. You'll see some surprising differences among the offers.

PROPOSALS THAT CREATE CASH

Now the fun begins. You know what you want for a loan and suddenly you find yourself sitting across the lender's big mahogany desk proposing a $40,000 loan to start your money-maker. You ramble on about what a great deal it is and how much money you're going to make when he politely shows you the door—without the cash. Where did you go wrong? The answer is simple. You acted like an amateur and lenders don't lend money to amateurs. If you have a pile of collateral they may overlook your inadequacies as they glanced at your assets. But not if you're the entrepreneur going on nothing more than a wing and a prayer. That's when you must think like a pro, act like a pro, and sell like a pro.

So how do you become a pro? You don't. You hire one. The plain fact is that business people may be great butchers, bakers, or candlestick makers, but that doesn't make them the financial genius to package a loan proposal that sells.

If you intend to knock on the doors of a few hard money lenders the best advice is to find a consultant who knows how to put the numbers together. Your accountant may be a logical candidate, particularly if he has solid loanmanship experience. Business school professors are another good source. They live in a world of business plans. I was fortunate in finding a retired bank president who enjoys moonlighting by helping entrepreneurs turn ideas into financial logic. Money finders or loan brokers lurk in every newspaper but be cautious, many are con-artists anxious for a fast retainer who never seem to place loans. Give them a close check.

You'll need the pro to be in the trenches with you and field the tough questions:

1. Why do you need the amount requested?
2. What will you do with it?
3. How do you know it's enough?
4. How much less can you live with?
5. Who else will you borrow from?
6. How do you propose to repay it?
7. How can you prove you can?
8. What collateral can you offer?

No matter what lender you approach the questions are always the same. What's important to one may be less important to another but you'll still need answers to them all. And each question is likely to give rise to five more, probing the legitimacy of your answer.

Martin Stone, a Cleveland money broker, objectively says, "Novice entrepreneurs don't anticipate the questions, and when they do they can't come up with puncture-proof data. They rely on overblown words—rosy adjectives, and adverbs. It doesn't inspire lender confidence."

No two loan proposals are identical in form, but they all answer the essential questions and have the financial projections to back it up.

You have your own spade work to do before a loan proposal can take shape:

1. Calculate your start-up costs and document them with cost quotes and written estimates. Lenders are always interested in how the business will come together.
2. Show how the loan will be used, breaking it down by expenditure. If the loan will be used for working capital, tie it in to a carefully prepared cash flow statement.
3. Don't overlook your lease. If location is a factor, your financial projections are based on the location. Without a location in mind you can only talk in generalities.
4. If you plan to collateralize the loan, then define the business or personal collateral you'll offer. Go further. Have appraisals ready so the lender knows what the security is worth.

Concentrate on the three "Cs" of all lending—character, collateral, and cash flow. Lenders, unlike partners you'll meet in the next chapter, aren't as interested in the phenomenal growth you plan for your business as they are the likelihood of being re-paid.

Harry Nickolaow, who specializes in loan placements for leveraged ventures, says it best. "The chances for obtaining a loan go up by 70% when an applicant shows up with a well-thought and well-presented proposal. Lenders who may know very little about the proposed business usually can't challenge the numbers, but they can certainly detect an amateur at the game."

OPEN THE RIGHT DOORS

What's the best source of start-up capital? In truth there is no one best source. As common sense will tell you the best source is the one who'll give you the most money on the best terms. And that, in turn, depends on the venture and what you can offer in return.

Banks and the SBA are best for the larger long-term loans if you can offer collateral. They typically form the base of your financial pyramid.

Private lenders, and even friends and relatives, may be best once collateral is exhausted; however, they usually offer intermediate term (one to three year) loans.

Suppliers, customers, and business affiliates may help you out with short-term unsecured loans to get you started, and are natural candidates to form the peak of your financial pyramid.

Since you will probably go after several sources—and layers—of financing it pays to know the specific strategies for approaching every type lender.

BANKS CAN SAY "YES"

Even though you can find them on just about any street corner, banks still remain the most misunderstood and intimidating of businesses.

Why all the mystery? It's a rare person who hasn't dealt with a bank. You have a checking account and chances are a savings account or two. And you may be one of the bank's favorite people, lending them your money at 7% while they loan it back to you at 16%. How do you think they pay for their fancy buildings?

Business loans are another ball game. Lending to a start-up venture is quite unlike borrowing for a home or auto. It can become so complicated even bankers can become confused.

To begin with, banks offer a menu list of loans. That's one advantage of banks over other lenders—banks have the flexibility to shape the loan to your needs. For example, if you're a direct-mail firm you may be in the market for an accounts receivable loan. A cyclical business will shoot for an open line of credit. An inventory or equipment intensive business may select a five-year secured loan. For working capital you may need a revolving short-term loan. The combinations or possibilities are countless, and to add fuel to the fire, each bank has its own menu board to offer.

So keep an open mind as to the loan package that's right for you. You aren't an amateur if you ask the bank to help design the right loan package for you, provided you have the information needed. Even the most sophisticated businesses rely on their banker to be a financial architect.

The wide range of loans should qualify you for some money. As asset-based lenders, banks typically won't lend long-term funds in excess of pledged collateral. Suppose your business will have $40,000 in equipment, inventory, or receivables. A bank will probably advance 60–75% of the collateral value. But this isn't a fixed rule. If you have a strong track record, a bank may lend in excess of collateral values. For example, in my first Discount City store the best I could land from a bank was $35,000 against $100,000 in collateral.For my second store I was able to finance $90,000, even though my second store only offered the same $100,000 in collateral. The difference was in the bank's perception of risk.

When you're at the idea stage, it's best to confine your loan request to the collateral you can offer. Because collateral is the bank's primary concern, you might as well retain credibility by starting out on the same wavelength. But don't hesitate to knock on the banker's door a year or two later for more money, even though the collateral may be unchanged. You too will have a track record to sell and that's collateral in itself.

Banks do make unsecured loans and your signature alone may be worth more than you think. Here the bank is relying on your personal credit rather than the business finances. But many times this dribble of cash is enough to start a small business. Lay the foundation to build your personal credit rating before you apply. If you have credit blemishes, then straighten out your accounts and try to have the black marks removed from your credit report. Build your credit standing. If you don't have a credit history, you won't have borrowing power. Take out a small loan well in advance of starting out and repay it on time. Now repeat the process, borrowing more each time. You may start out with a $3000 credit line and gradually build it to $15,000 in a year or two through a series of consecutive loans. And many a successful business has been started on less than $15,000.

Multiple bank loans are another possibility. Your signature may be worth $5000 to a bank, but that means it's worth $20,000 to four banks. The way to handle it is to apply for the four loans simultaneously. In that way you legitimately can ignore the other loans on the application since the loans have yet to be granted.

CHARGE YOUR BUSINESS TO MASTERCARD

Ambition has no bounds. I didn't believe it either at first, but I know one gutsy individual who actually started a business on his MasterCard. Now I know we usually think of MasterCard as a convenient way to charge a fancy meal, a new pair of slacks, or even a vacation, but who ever heard of charging an entire business to MasterCard? My friend Bob Kuzara did, and was proud enough to have it written up in the *Boston Globe* as a featured story in the business section. Bob calculated he would need $20,000 to launch his furniture factory, and within 30 days had five MasterCards from five different banks, each with a $5000 credit line. As Bob tells it, "Plastic credit is the easiest credit to get, and when you have enough 'plastic' in your wallet you have your start-up capital."

It makes you wonder. How many ways are there to make a bank say "yes"?

PRESS THE RIGHT BUTTONS

The right bank—and the right banker—can make a whopping difference in your chances for success. No two banks or bankers are alike. Watch where you shop.

To start with, you want commercial banks rather than savings banks or cooperatives who specialize in home mortgages or consumer loans. If you're pledging your home as security, these banks may be interested, but they're still the wrong choice because they can't offer you the loan flexibility your business will need.

Bank size is another factor. Stay with the small banks, and the smaller the better. As a small start-up you mean very little to the large metropolitan banks catering to the Fortune-500 firms. They may have slick ad campaigns to lure small businesses, but few will give you the service or consideration of a smaller bank whose lifeline is the small business.

Consider location next. Banks do give preference to businesses in their immediate area. One reason is that they want you as a depositor.

Timing is also important in shopping banks. Money is a bank's inventory. You want to hit the bank when it has the money to lend and will be most lenient. One way to find out who has the money to spare is to check with the financial community. Heavy ad campaigns are another clue.

Of all the considerations, the philosophy of the bank is most important. Some banks, particularly newer banks, have a reputation as "high flyers," abandoning strict asset-based formulas in favor of a "gut" reaction to a business that will make it. At least five Boston banks have been known to cast big dollars on big ideas and little collateral. And these were loans the conservative pinstripes wouldn't touch. Your city has its share of high rollers. Ask around.

The banker within the bank is your next target. And contrary to popular belief, bankers are people and that gives them their own philosophies, personalities, and prejudices. The chemistry between you and the banker can add points to the win column.

I won't do business with a banker I'm uncomfortable with. I want more from him than a loan. I want candid advice. I expect him to be my financial consultant and one of the architects of my success. When business is slow or takes a wrong turn I want to be able to approach him and work it out over a cup of coffee. If I need expansion capital or money for yet another venture I look forward to my banker throwing his feet on the desk and sharing my entrepreneurial dreams—or calling me a stupid S.O.B. for even thinking about it. In short, he's part of your team. If you don't think you can develop the right chemistry with your pinstriper behind the mahogany desk, then move on. You want more than money.

One last pointer in finding the right banker: try to locate one with experience in your type business. It's a big plus. My own banker has years of experience as a comptroller for several large retail chains. He knows retailing, and his advice means something to me. Make yours work for you.

WHEN THE BANK SAYS "NO"

Rejection can be beneficial. It can pinpoint a weakness in your loan proposal or a fatal flaw in your business idea.

Don't take a loan turndown and stroll on to the next bank until you find out why the loan was declined. Some banks hedge on a candid answer because they neither want to offend or engage in long conversation.But push for an honest answer. I can tell you about plenty of loan turndowns that saved me a bundle on half-baked ideas. Sometimes it takes some fatherly advice from a banker to set you straight.

Problem proposals are easy to cure. You may apply for a $70,000 loan only to be turned down. Will the bank consider $50,000? Counteroffer. It may trigger a compromise.

Your banker isn't an adversary, but an ally in evaluating the soundness of your plans. He may see weaknesses you overlooked or questions other lenders will raise. Listen closely. Pick his brain. If he raises some doubts in your own mind then move on and pick a few more brains. There are thousands of success stories thumbing their noses at bankers who said "no."

A HELPING HAND FROM UNCLE SAM

One advantage in being turned down by banks is that it qualifies you as a candidate for SBA money.

The SBA offers two types of loan arrangements for start-ups. A local bank participates in most of the loans. The bank lends the money, but the SBA protects the bank with a 90% guarantee. If you borrow $30,000 from the bank under an SBA loan, the most the bank can lose is $3000. Still, an SBA guarantee doesn't mean you'll find a willing bank. I know many entrepreneurs who have an SBA commitment but they're still finding it hard to line up a bank. Banks are reluctant to get involved in a "problem" loan, even with the SBA behind them. Typically banks use the same criteria for evaluating SBA guaranteed loans as they do a "straight" loan and the SBA makes a difference only when collateral is the missing ingredient.

What can you do if you can't find a bank to help you under an SBA guaranteed loan? In rare cases the SBA may lend you the money directly. Usually the SBA reserves the "direct" loans for minority groups or business ventures in depressed areas.

Before you go shopping for an SBA loan consider the pros and cons. On the positive side:

1. The SBA will consider loans in distressed areas, whereas most banks won't.
2. Your credit rating doesn't have to be as strong for an SBA loan as it must be for a bank loan. The SBA favors applicants whose credit cannot meet bank requirements.
3. The SBA favors minorities and women, who have historically had problems qualifying for bank loans. That doesn't suggest the non-minority applicant doesn't stand a chance to win SBA financing. Many of my non-minority clients were started with SBA funds, but contrary to what the SBA says, preference does go to minority groups.
4. The major SBA advantage is the length of the loan. Most banks limit loans to five years, but the SBA sponsors 7–10-year loans. This can help your cash flow in the beginning years.

It's not all roses. Look closely and you'll see some thorns:

1. A liberal SBA policy is the one big disadvantage. Since the SBA will only consider you if two or more banks turn you down, it stands to reason the SBA specializes in the weaker or even illogical deal. Though we all know business people who started with SBA financing. I know almost as many who grabbed the money when they had no chance of succeeding, only to fail and end up in bankruptcy. When the SBA loses, they lose only a few tax dollars but you lose everything. A sound start-up plan should attract bank financing. If it can't you should probably redesign it. A nod from the SBA is no assurance you have a sensible start-up.
2. The SBA is collateral hungry. If you own it they want it. With a bank you have a strong possibility of avoiding a mortgage on your home, but not with the SBA. Think carefully about what you're prepared to lose if the start-up doesn't work out.
3. Expect to pay higher interest for an SBA loan. You'll be paying up to 2% more than what a bank would charge on a "straight" loan. The surcharge is used to reimburse the SBA for its guarantee.
4. Here's the big problem. The SBA expects its applicants to contribute 50% of the start-up capital from their own funds. It discourages shoestring start-ups from entrepreneurs hoping to win 100% financing. But there are exceptions to the rule, and the SBA routinely modifies the policy, particularly to minority groups who may have limited capital.

No doubt about it. SBA loans are a mixed bag of advantages and disadvantages. To learn more about SBA loans available to you, stop by your nearest SBA office. Tell them about your business plans and ask them to show you the specific loan arrangement best suited for you. Bring with you letters from two banks showing you've been turned down. And plan ahead. The SBA moves slowly. It can take two or three months to process a loan.

Your venture may do even better in another bureaucratic office. Considering a manufacturing enterprise in an industry hit hard by foreign competition? Turn to the Economic Development Administration, a branch of the U.S. Department of Commerce. They've sponsored many start-ups in such industries as footwear, consumer electronics, and clothing. Farmers have several agencies to help them with financing. If the SBA isn't the right agency for you they can point you in the right direction, or better still call the nearest Federal Information Center.

A FRANCHISE CAN MEAN FINANCING

Thinking of a fast food business, retail shop, or even a motel? Name it and you'll find it franchised. And one benefit of a franchise is the financing. That may come with the package.

Many franchisors will finance 60–70% of the total start-up cost. Generally they'll guarantee your bank loan, charging you few extra percentage points on interest, but in some cases they'll make a direct loan.

One reason franchisors can offer generous finance terms is because the collateral has a high value to the franchisor if you default and he has to step in and foreclose. A franchisor of donut shops explains it this way, "Our franchise package costs $130,000. This covers the equipment, opening inventory, and the franchise fee of $40,000. We require our franchisees to put down $30,000 and we finance $100,000 at six points above prime. It's usually better than a franchisee can get from a bank, since most banks won't lend more than $30,000–40,000 against fast food equipment. However, the equipment can always be resold by us for the same $100,000."

Watch the economics of the deal. In many cases you may have high built-in financing because the franchise package allocates a large part of the price to the name rather than equipment or inventory.

If financing is the controlling factor, evaluate a franchise in this light. Could you start an independent business with less of your own capital than what a franchisor wants as a down payment for a franchised unit? In many instances you can. Besides the fact, you're no longer financing the franchise fee. You also have nobody to answer to but yourself, which gives you a clear field to bootstrap the operation with used equipment and other cost-cutting techniques. Weigh the alternatives by checking out several franchises.

SUPPLIER FINANCING: YOURS FOR THE ASKING

Suppliers can be a generous bunch. In Chapter 9 in this book I show you how to tap suppliers for an opening inventory on 100% credit terms. Perhaps you don't need much of their inventory, but can use a few dollars of their cash instead. They'll be equally generous and for the very same reasons—they want your business.

Who will your suppliers be once you're in business? Concentrate on the two or three largest suppliers. Forget the secondary suppliers. You don't offer enough profit potential to win their financing. But let's assume you project buying $100,000 annually from a primary supplier. Why shouldn't this justify a $10,000–15,000 start-up loan?

Your best bet in attempting supplier loans is to go after suppliers most anxious for your business. You may not mean much to a conglomerate but a local privately owned firm may consider your account vital to its own growth. Another reason. Publicly owned firms have rigid policies and although they grant credit they don't lend money. These constraints don't tie the hands of smaller privately owned firms.

How do you sell the proposition? Use the same selling points and safeguards for obtaining credit in Chapter 9. The strategy is precisely the same.

I've used supplier loans to terrific advantage in many of my own deals. They're right up there on my shopping list. Discount City, for example, was helped along by a $5000 working capital loan from its photofinishing supplier and $3000 from its tobacco jobber. Why be embarrassed to ask? These suppliers now sell over $350,000 a year to Discount City stores. Your supplier may see it the same way.

BIG MONEY FOR BIG DEALS

In the market for $500,000 or more in start-up capital? Welcome to the big leagues of financing—venture capital.

A word of caution before you whip up your enthusiasm. Venture capital isn't for every business. These high risk, high stakes money lenders are on the lookout for capital-intensive businesses with rapid growth potential. And in a tight money economy where capital is in short supply, the frontrunners are the more exotic fields of high technology, computers, and biological engineering.

Who are these venture capitalists? Usually they're a group of investors who capitalize their venture capital firms in part with their own money and in part with government loans. In turn, they help capitalize start-ups with a combination loan and partnership interest.

Venture capital is a financing science unto itself, and I doubt whether many bootstrap entrepreneurs reading this book envision themselves in a one- or two-million-dollar operation on opening day. But if you do and think you can attract venture capital funds then read A. David Silver's *Upfront Financing* (John Wiley & Sons, 1982). It's the best book on a timely and complicated subject.

A FINAL WORD

Will you find your money? Whether it be a dribble of dollars or several million in start-up funds, you'll have a few hurdles. Despite small business financing cutbacks, high interest rates, and an uncertain economic picture for the years ahead, lenders can still be induced to make the old risk—and reward calculation—and place their bets on an attractive deal.

Old Casey Stengel was a perennial optimist. When his New York Yankees returned from a disastrous road trip he simply announced, "You can't win them all."

That message should ring loud and clear in this chapter. You may not find the cash on your first try. You may have to beat the pavement and accept terms that will make life somewhat harder. But regardless of how you borrow—or whom you borrow from—it will put you in your own business. The best part is that someday the loans will be paid off and the business is yours free and clear. And it may have started without a dime of your own.

KEY POINTS TO REMEMBER

1. There's no magical formula to finding money. It takes the right sources, the right terms, and the perseverance to put it together.
2. Pinpoint the loan you want before you go shopping.
3. Structure the loan so you get the best protection and tax benefits.
4. Banks are like snowflakes. No two are alike. Match your deal to the right bank.
5. Draft your loan proposal so lenders know you're a professional.
6. Watch the pitfalls as well as benefits before signing up for government loans.
7. Can you clear the financing hurdle with a franchise?
8. Suppliers will lend money and can be the easiest source of start-up capital.
9. If you strike out on financing, ask yourself the important question—do you really have a solid plan?

7

PARTNERS FOR PROFIT: YOUR BRAINS, THEIR CASH

Yes, Virginia, there are investors out there—cash-toting partners anxious to lend an ear to a proposition to earn them even more money. You'll find them in all shapes and sizes. Some want to be "silent" partners watching their money work, others want to roll up their sleeves and work beside you. Some look for existing businesses on their way to the next plateau, others like nothing better than to take a flyer on an exciting idea. Some can offer you only a few scrimped dollars, while others are an endless river of gold. Some will work with you to create wealth, and some will work against you to create ulcers and headaches. So, Virginia, whatever you find, you'll find it an interesting relationship. It's either paradise or purgatory. Seldom is it in between.

WHO NEEDS PARTNERS?

According to the SBA, the guru of business statistics, 70% of all small business start-ups do. That's just about the percentage of businesses started with "friendly" partnership money coming from friends and relatives all the way up to sophisticated venture capital firms.

Why are partnerships so popular? There's no one reason. Overestimating start-up capital needs is probably the most common. A hesitancy to go after *less costly* but harder to come by loans is another. Some of the myths we exploded in the first chapter help explain it. What it boils down to is a willingness to trade a piece of the pie for a few start-up dollars to complete the financing package. And it's usually faulty thinking. Why? Two reasons:

1. Partnership money is the *most* expensive money you can buy. And it's particularly expensive when you usually don't need it in the first place.
2. Partnerships have the highest failure rate because success depends not only on the success of the venture, but the success of the relationship as well.

The idea of a partner *should* make you think twice. Here's a closer look.

HOW FRIENDLY IS "FRIENDLY" MONEY?

"Not very friendly," if you ask Nancy and Bill Tyler. In 1979 the Tylers signed a franchise to open a videotape sales and rental shop in a Philadelphia suburb. The franchisor was willing to finance $25,000, but the Tylers needed another $15,000 to complete the financing package. "We could have easily taken out a second mortgage on our home to raise it," remarked Bill Tyler, "however, a neighbor agreed to invest the $15,000 for a 50% partnership interest. Looking at it as a terrific alternative to borrowing we grabbed it. We discovered it was like taking money from the philistines. Three years later we had expanded to four stores grossing close to $2 million dollars and it cost us $200,000 to buy back our partner's interest. It was a foolish decision to take on a partner when we could have achieved our goal by paying a few thousand dollars interest."

When you talk about faulty economics, the Tylers don't stand alone. One of my closest friends tells an even more bizarre story of how he took on a 30% partner to start a computer software journal. All the partner invested was $30,000, and now his interest is worth over $300,000. "The crazy part is that I didn't even need his $30,000 to start," my friend admits. "I had enough of my own money into the deal to effectively launch the journal, and advance subscription payments always gave me a healthy positive cash flow for growth."

So the point is made. From a financial angle a partner may be an expensive idea. It is for most start-ups who reach for a partner's helping hand. But it's also easy to understand why it happens.

It's always tempting to reach for a few partnership dollars when you start without asking what it will cost later.

Dig deep. If you want a partner for his money alone, you also want to move slow. If you can raise most of the start-up capital without a partner, then beg or borrow the rest from wherever you can, or pare down costs to match what you have. You may start with less, but at least it's all yours.

Do you still need a partner?

MORE THAN MONEY

It's an interesting fact of life that money is not the motivator behind most small business partnerships. People join together, believing two heads are better than one. Sometimes they're right and sometimes they're wrong. It always depends on the heads in question.

Let's look at the bleak side first. Once you have a partner on board you no longer work for yourself. You're suddenly accountable to your partners as well. They can influence or even control every decision you want to make. Say goodbye to being a loner.

It's difficult for some people to accept. Many a maverick has welcomed a silent partner or two—and their money—only to discover the silent partners weren't so silent. The Tylers of videotape fame learned that bitter lesson too. That's why they finally bought back the partner's interest. The Tylers wanted to expand into a videotape wholesale distributorship instead of more retail outlets. "No way," screamed the partner. Who was right doesn't matter. The Tylers couldn't move without the partner's blessing, and the partner wasn't about to give it. Two heads rarely think alike.

I discovered the same thing in a few of my ventures. Years ago I believed the best formula for success was to make a manager a "working partner" by giving him a 20–30% partnership interest. I figured as a co-owner he'd work harder and steal less while I still enjoyed control. It didn't work that way. When I ordered a new Cadillac through the business my "partner" gave me the jaundiced eye. Another "partner" took a tantrum when I took a "business trip" to New Orleans. It taught me a lesson, forcing me to buy back their shares for a healthy price, but I too was learning what you'll learn. Either it's your own business or it's not. And when you have partners it's never quite your own business.

Is this anti-partner talk? Absolutely not. There are thousands of strong successful partnerships at work proving two heads can indeed be better than one. A synergy is created while the partners achieve what they could never accomplish individually.

Confidence is what a partnership means to Mildred Pendergast of Amy's Fashions, a Providence-based chain of ladies apparel shops. Mildred is the first to admit she could never muster the confidence to go it alone, and neither could her equally timid partner whom she met at work. But the ladies did meet, struck up a friendship, and built on their common goal while feeding confidence and courage to each other. I constantly see it. Two prospective partners will tell me about their plans, each buoyed by the support of the other. The partners may be wrong for each other, or it may be a nonsense idea, or a foolish financial arrangement. What does it matter? The venture may fold or the partnership may break up, but the partners have been in business. They know what it's about and are no longer afraid to go it alone. Sometimes it takes a partner to make you an entrepreneur.

Management? It was the key ingredient for John Miller at Southland Food Commissary of Dedham, Massachusetts. John knew he was a great "outside" man able to hustle accounts for his start-up catering service, but needed an "inside" partner to handle internal operations. Along came Ken Berman with years of experience in food service management to fill the bill. Today Southland grosses over $3 million dollars a year.

Looking to augment skills is only part of the equation. Sometimes it pays to assess your own personality weaknesses and take on a partner with a corresponding strength. It creates terrific partnership marriages. I call them "Mutt and Jeff" operations. One partner may be the idea man while the other puts the plan into play. One may be the resident good guy while the other is the resident S.O.B. One may be the perennial optimist while the other is the realist with both feet on the ground. It's more than management. It's chemistry. And the right partner can be a powerful ingredient in your business formula.

"Just plain old-fashioned fun" is how Becky Gavitas and Sarah Talini describe their gift shop partnership. Close friends for years, they decided to flap their entrepreneurial wings in a small venture to extend their social relationship into a business relationship. "We don't make a heck of a lot of money," confesses Becky, "and from a financial viewpoint the business should really be a one-owner operation," adds Sarah. "But money alone isn't our reason for being in business. We make fewer dollars, but have many more laughs working together." Who can call them wrong?

Several years ago the *Boston Globe* ran a series of business columns along the Dear Abby lines. Someone wrote asking whether he should take in a partner for a proposed car dealership. The reply said it all. "It's like getting married. If you have to ask, you've answered your own question." It's food for thought.

WHERE THE MONEY LURKS

A solid business idea will attract potential investors like bears to honey. Would you believe more people are looking for good investments than there are good opportunities? The trick is to plant your honey pot of an idea outside the right bear caves.

Where do you begin?

1. If you're looking for a "working partner" with capital, the emphasis will be on the career opportunity rather than the financial return. Precisely define the skills you need and seek out prospects just as you would an employee.
2. "Silent partners" kicking in small money in the \$5000–50,000 range are generally high-income individuals in the over-40 age bracket with spare investment dollars. They are

constantly on the prowl for small business deals that can create enormous long-term gains not offered by conventional investments, hedged by the reality that the IRS will share their losses if the business doesn't make it. Professionals, executives, and business owners fall into this category.

3. Hunt candidates who have been in your type business, succeeded, and are now retired. They are quicker to invest because they know your business, have more confidence in it, and often enjoy "re-living" their career through your venture.
4. Don't overlook people who can not only benefit from the profits of the business, but can equally benefit from doing business with you. Suppliers come under this category as I explain in Chapter 6, and so do distributors or potential customers.
5. Put your accountant, banker, and lawyer to work. They have plenty of clients with investment money and can oftentimes sell a deal on the basis of favorable tax angles alone.
6. Advertise. Partnership money is "bought and sold" like any other commodity. Place a simple ad in the classified section of your newspaper, describing your deal and the cash needed. *The New York Times* prints an entire column of "capital needed" listings every Sunday. So will your Metropolitan newspaper. While you're at it, scan the bulging columns marked "Capital Available." It shows just how many people are anxious to exchange money for a partnership interest.
7. Promote your deal. Mention it to your barber and you may end up with his father-in-law as a partner. Many marriages come about through word of mouth.

Don't limit yourself. Set up an active campaign to "network" your deal. The objective is to have 20–30 interested partners. That's the only way to keep the upper hand, bid one against the other for the best deal, and find the right partner.

Beware! Hiding in some caves sniffing your honey pot are some creatures you *don't* want as partners.

1. Avoid close relatives. They're the easiest people to tap for money and that's precisely why it's a mistake. Business is business. It's difficult for relatives to say "no" and they seldom bring objectivity to the deal. Lose $50,000 for a stranger and you lost an investor. Lose it for your mother and you become the black sheep of the family. Don't risk family relationships over money. The same goes for anyone else whose relationship with you means more than dollars.

   Money is a peculiar commodity. I have seen soured business deals turn brother against brother and father against son. Keep them out of it. Should your business go bust you can still show up with the clan to enjoy Easter Sunday.
2. Avoid little old ladies in tennis shoes. Sometimes you'll spot them wearing Gucci's instead while clipping AT&T dividend coupons. Plenty of people have loads of investment capital but are programmed toward the safe, predictable blue chip investments. Your idea for a pizza chain may excite them, but rarely do their investment objectives or expectations match those of an entrepreneur.
3. Run away from crybabies. Unless your business becomes another IBM, they'll be nipping at your heels. First-time investors who only remember the bright rosy picture but never contemplated the risk fall within this category. So too are investors who can't afford the loss or expect a quick cash payoff. You need a seasoned partner who understands what business is all about, and can both afford to risk capital and is practical about what it can accomplish.
4. How about friends? They seem to be a logical choice but seldom are—particularly when you're scouting for a "working partner." What you prize in a social friend is far different from what you may need in a working partner. This is probably the most common error in selecting partners. In my younger days I ventured into a partnership with my closest friend. Why not? We had a ball, playing poker

and chasing the girls together, so why wasn't he the perfect candidate to connive with me for a quick fortune? I found out why when I saw his sub-zero management mentality at work. Fortunately we are still good friends and poker partners, but it's never easy to find out that your best friends can be your worst business partners.

PUT YOUR PARTNER TO THE ACID-TEST

Pull out your magnifying glass and give your potential partner a thorough working over. I don't care how much money he's about to hand you, your job is to make certain you're marrying a "swan" and not an "ugly duckling."

It's easy to act in haste and repent in leisure. Mr. M. spent less time screening partners then he did a minimum-wage stock boy. Mr. M. operates a retail and wholesale bakery business. He had a simple set of standards for a partner—$20,000 and the willingness to spend eight hours a day at the oven. His first partner physically ousted Mr. M. from the premises, and it took six months of expensive litigation to finally throw the partner out. His second partner walked away with $18,000 and was last seen heading west. Undaunted by his first two defeats he now has partner number three, who spends half his time drinking bourbon and the rest of his waking hours at Alcoholics Anonymous. Partnerships are a people game. Finding them is the easy part. Picking them is a bit tougher.

Marty Colburne, a successful entrepreneur with several partnership start-ups under his belt in the Miami area, claims he can spot the "right" partner in one hour. "In the first 30 minutes I know how smart he is, and in the final 30 minutes I know what he knows about the business. And while he's talking I can tell whether he's someone I can work with and build with," says Marty.

Try Marty's checklist.

1. *Check the track record:* With a working partner you want a "doer" not a "drifter." Past performance counts. Education, experience, career growth, and success in other ventures are all tallied on the scorecard.

2. *Investigate personal history:* Chronic illness, gambling, alcoholism or other personal problems have their telltale signs and can be fatal to a working relationship.
3. *Probe prior partnerships:* How did they work out? What do prior partners say about him? This is important even with "silent" partners, to test if they worked cooperatively or are chronic troublemakers.
4. *Meet the spouse:* He or she may be the real power behind the throne. You can never quite tell unless you see them together. And the last thing your business needs is a partner with a meddling spouse.
5. *Examine the lifestyle:* A shoestring start-up needs every penny it can get, and that means profits being plowed back rather than being harvested by a high-roller living for today.
6. *Talk about the business:* What does he know about it? Let him give you his ideas. Listen carefully. It won't take long to find out whether a partner can match your management mentality—or you his.
7. *Do you think alike?* This is the key. Check whether his ideas are compatible with you on important issues such as growth, operations, responsibility, and financial planning. The blending of ideas is indeed the key to every successful partnership.

Above all a good partnership is still chemistry. And to test that chemistry demands more than a pleasant chat. It needs a courtship. It's the ultimate acid-test as you constantly meet to discuss plans, check out competitive businesses, get together socially, and really get to know him or her as a person. As with any courtship, you want to know whether you have the foundation to build a future.

"HAVE I GOT A DEAL FOR YOU"

Money, money, money. It always comes down to money—how much you need and what you're prepared to give up in return.

Let's say your grand idea is a pizza parlor which will hopefully expand to dot the land as Happy Harry's Pizza Emporiums. All you need is $50,000 to launch your first. Since you can't swing any more loans and since your cash is nil, you approach an old college chum who made it big in plastics saying, "Have I got a deal for you!"

Standing there in his smoking jacket is your buddy patiently mixing his first martini. "So what's your deal?"

Maybe you'll tell him that for $50,000 he gets a piece of the action. Of course, he does. But what's fair? 20%? 40%? 50%? 51%? Maybe you haven't thought about it.

Plasticman may like your idea, but as he stirs his second martini he suggests his own proposal. He'll loan the business $40,000, secured by assets of the business payable over five years at three points over prime, and also backed up by a mortgage on your home. For the other $10,000 he wants 1000 shares of preferred stock at $5 par value and 51% of the common stock with a right to convert $10,000 in debt to an additional 20% of the common stock. "Oh yes, " he adds munching on the martini olive, "my attorneys will insist on a simultaneous registration of my shares so I can sell out if you go public." Plasticman concludes by spitting out his olive pit.

It's all so depressing. All you wanted was $50,000 to start Happy Harry's Pizza Emporium and now you're thoroughly confused while you suddenly realize how your buddy made his millions.

Look at it logically.

1. You need your accountant and lawyer to decipher the legal mumbo jumbo. Better still, you want your accountant and attorney to prepare a proposal *before* you call on prospective partners. Don't show up as a rank amateur begging for a handout. That's not business—it's charity. You want to look like a pro as you toast plasticman with your own martini.
2. You have to think about the deal from the investor's viewpoint. And he has plenty of questions going through his mind. How can I reduce my risk? What control do I have? How does my investment evolve over time? How soon can I get my money out? How can I increase my return? When

can I cash out? What are the tax angles? If you find a prospective partner overlooking these and perhaps 101 other interesting questions, you don't want him. He's too dumb to be your partner.

3. Here's the most important point. There's no such thing as a fair deal. Don't look through books or expect a computer to punch out the formula. Your partner will fight for as much as he can get while you jockey to give up as little as you can. The final deal will depend on many variables. The most important being whether you need his money more than he needs Happy Harry's Pizza Emporium. So while your buddy is shopping other deals to bury his money in, you'll be out shopping other investors. The reality of the marketplace will eventually show you the right deal.

PACKAGE YOUR PROPOSAL TO SELL

Everything to be sold is packaged to sell. You have to make it attractive. That's why new cars in a showroom are buffed to a shining gleam each morning and why my publisher will hopefully spend a fortune designing an appealing jacket for this book. It's no different when it comes to selling a piece of your business. You want the most for the least and you must package it to sell. How do you do it? Put on a prospective investor's eyeglasses and look at your idea the way he would.

1. *Sell Your Business Idea:*

Make it come alive. Paint the picture so the investor can visualize it. Why will it be successful? That's the key question. Explain the market, the competition, and precisely how your business plan will turn projections into profits. Show how you plan to operate the business in as much detail as possible, backing it up with costs, financial projections, and plans.

It doesn't have to be an exotic business idea to be a winner. Common, everyday businesses can show exciting profits. In my first Discount City store I sold a 20% interest for $30,000 to an industrialist. Now there's nothing particularly interesting about a discount store. America needed it like it needed another recession. But the town I had my sights on needed it and I could prove the business would show an $800,000 gross and $50,000 profit. A three-inch-thick file packed with facts and figures backed it up. We weren't far wrong. Investors are buying profits. Your job is to prove that the profits will be there.

2. *Sell Yourself:*

Investors don't really buy a piece of a business. What they do buy is a piece of its management. That's you. So you have to sell yourself. Once you've convinced investors you know what you're talking about they'll have the confidence to buy whatever business idea you're selling. Watch a shrewd investor in action. He'll ask plenty of questions and try to punch holes in every answer. He will if he's a shrewd investor, and frankly I haven't come across any with that perfect combination of stupidity and money.

Blow your own horn. Play up your education, special skills, experience, and your own track record. Your first start-up will be the toughest sell and you'll probably end up on the short end of the deal. Once you have a success or two behind you, start mixing your own martinis. You'll have a pack of investors at your door crooning, "Have I got a deal for you!"

3. *Sell the Deal:*

This is the tricky part. Don't suggest the proposed split. Let that come from the investor. Simply provide the basic information he needs to frame an investment offer. What will he want to know?

The amount of capital needed.
How it will be used.
The other sources of capital.
If and when additional funds will be needed.
How profits will be utilized.

Your investor will be able to put it all together in his mind, and glancing over his shoulder at potential gain versus possible risk, make an opening offer. And it may be a far better offer than you imagined. It will be if you packaged your proposal to sell.

BEWARE THE BOOBY TRAPS

There are plenty of them out there. But three deals are particularly dangerous. Here's what to watch out for.

"The Glorified Employee Deal" What's a "glorified employee"? Someone who thinks he's an owner but is in reality only an employee. And that's just what you are if you settle for less than an equal 50/50 partnership interest. A minority stockholder (owning less than 50% of the company) is powerless and in control of nothing. Your partners with the majority interest control the business because they control the votes. They decide who sits on the Board of Directors, who the officers will be, and whether you keep your job. And if they boot you out, you can decorate your walls with the stock certificates.

Check around. You'll find plenty of fuzzy-thinking founders who trade away a majority share of the business for the start-up dollars. Somewhere down the line there's a fork in the road on how the business should be run and guess who's out?

Make it the one *non*-negotiable point in your partnership deal. Never, never accept *less* than an equal partnership and an equal say. It may be your partner's money at stake, but it's still your deal. If you're not worth as much as their money, head the other way.

"The More is Better Deal" If one partner is good, two or three is *not* better. It's worse. You want a business not a political club, and a political "back biting" club is just what you're likely to have when you have more than one partner. Finding two people who can think alike and get along is difficult enough without compounding it by bringing in more.

Not long ago a client picked up a four-store hobby shop chain started by three working partners and a wealthy angel who bankrolled it with $140,000. Within a year, two working partners ganged up on the third, and the third ran to the investor to put the squeeze on the other two. It wasn't a business. It was a battlefield. What they lost in sales they made up for in combat ribbons. It's a rarity when it doesn't happen. Usually it starts with each partner trying to call the shots and ends when they shoot each other. Who needs it? Keep it simple. Go with a maximum of one partner per deal. Make it a fair fight.

"The Tourniquet Treatment Deal" A wealthy partner can be a dangerous foe once the business is churning out profits and looks like a proven money-maker. Some partners will reward you for a job well done and give you more money to expand with, while others will decide it's the perfect moment to dump you and take over your share of the business for a song. That's when they turn their financial one-upmanship into a variety of squeeze plays. It may be refusal to help with any additional financing the business may need. A common squeeze play is to call in loans the company may owe him. Armed with the staying power of cash he may even start expensive but frivolous litigation to get rid of you. Whatever the tactic, the tourniquet treatment is money man's way of proving that in the battle between your brains and his money the money always wins.

Be patient. It may not happen until that perfect moment when the business is well off the ground. But that's just when your money partners get greedy—when there's something to get greedy about. And like any other poker game you want a pile of chips to match theirs when the bluff is called.

It can also work in reverse. Without even realizing it you may be walking your own less financially endowed working partner into a tourniquet treatment. Let's suppose you team up with a partner, each throwing in $10,000 to start the business. Two years later the business is expanding and needs another $30,000. You don't want to mortgage your house while your penniless partner whistles. A mismatch in your financial resources will inevitably lead to either stagnant growth, uneven contributions, or the reality that the financially stronger partner should take over.

Watch out for these three booby-trap deals. They spell trouble with a capital "T."

SEVEN TIPS ON THE CARE AND FEEDING OF PARTNERS

Why is it that some partnerships are whopping successes while others are miserable failures? It's always the case of people knowing how to handle people. And you don't have to be a master politician to keep a smile on your partner's face. A few common sense tips will do:

1. Don't overestimate potential profits. A novice may sell an investor on the promise the business will show a $40,000 first-year profit, and then faces a lot of explaining when he comes in with a $2000 loss. Be realistic and stay on the conservative side. Always underestimate the good and overestimate the bad to look like a genius.
2. Keep your partners involved. Make them co-conspirators in the success—or failure of the business by having them join in the decision-making process. You are looking for trouble to keep silent partners in the dark and then hit them with major problems. Regular meetings to track the progress of the business are a must.
3. Don't rely on standard corporate books and bylaws to document your deal. Supplement it with a written agreement on all major points, including salaries, bonuses, expenses, and division of responsibility. Remember, once you're a partner you're also an employee. Know what you're entitled to. It can avoid plenty of arguments later.
4. Don't make up your own report card on how the business is going. All financial information on the business should come only from your accountant, and let him verify your figures. As part of the reporting process you may be inclined to put together your own financial data to show silent partners. A year or two later when the business fails your partner begins to wonder about the accuracy of your numbers. It can create some nasty lawsuits.
5. Watch out for side deals, hidden profits, or conflict of interest situations. Nothing can turn a partnership into a vendetta faster than a partner who thinks you double-timed your obligation to make money for him. If you're involved in deals that can even remotely impact on your partnership arrangement bring it out into the open and square it away before you start.

6. Don't let minor feuds or irritations mushroom into major battles. If you have areas of disagreement then meet and resolve them before they get out of hand. If you check many of the failed partnerships you'll find it was the small annoyances rather than a substantial disagreement on policy that caused defeat.
7. Listen, listen, listen. It's not just *your* business. Your partners have a say and many times what they have to say makes a lot of sense. It comes back to what I said at the beginning of the chapter. If you want to be the "loner" or the entrepreneurial maverick and call all the shots, then forget partners.

"DIVORCE"—PARTNERSHIP STYLE

Strive for the best, but prepare for the worst. The pessimistic facts are that 70% of all partnerships do break up within two years of formation. And don't look for any one reason. It may be the inability to get along, disagreement on the future direction of the business, or simply an alternate career opportunity for a partner. Whatever the reasons, the dismal statistics prove it's difficult to keep two or more on the same track to build a long-term business future. It's even more difficult with a shoestring start-up with its embryonic problems of poor capitalization and a "touch and go" daily operation.

If "divorce fever" sets in, it may be too late. You must set up the deal so you control it and maintain the upper hand. Otherwise you may find yourself on the outside looking in as your partner walks away with the business.

The best way to handle it is to structure the arrangement so you have the option to buy your partner out. For example, you may need a partner's investment of $20,000 to launch your business. In return, you agree to give him 50% ownership. Perhaps your partner would sign an option to acquire his interest for $35,000 within two years? A silent partner may go along with it, considering it a far better investment than a safer but low yielding savings account.

I have successfully used this technique in several of my own start-ups. Silent partners realize a stalemate can only lead to dissolution of the business and perhaps loss of investment. Conversely, if the partnership isn't working out he's certainly entitled to his share of the net worth of the business and a healthy bonus for risking his capital to start it. So the buy-out figure is both speculative and negotiable. Sometimes it's difficult to precisely fix a fair value in advance. In a few deals I have reserved the "buy-out" option for five years and agreed to let an arbitrator set the buy-out price if and when the option is exercised. But throw an additional ingredient into the deal. When it comes time to buy out your partner, have him finance the buy-out price rather than expect cash. For example, the agreement may provide that 20% of the buy-out price will be in cash and the balance paid over a defined number of years with specified interest and security.

A "buy-out" option will:

1. Allow you to dissolve the partnership should disagreement arise. Having a fixed, predetermined (or arbitrated) buy-out figure puts a ceiling on what it will take to dissolve the partnership while retaining complete ownership.
2. Provide you time to work down existing loans and/or build the business so you can borrow to buy out your partner.
3. Insure that you will not have to share long-term profits or gains with a partner.

Essentially, a partnership structured along these lines has the characteristics of both equity and debt financing. Your partner has an ownership interest in the business, but you have the right to pay his investment back with a deserved profit to regain sole ownership. It may be a steep price, but it's seldom as steep as what this same partner would walk away with many years later. Shake your partner's hand when you say goodbye. Don't forget it was his money that got you started.

KEY POINTS TO REMEMBER

1. Partnership money is the most expensive money you can buy. If you want a partner for his money alone—consider it your last resort.

2. Partnerships are not for everyone. Do you really want to answer to someone else?
3. Look for the *right* partner. And the right partner will bring more than money.
4. Put your partner to the acid-test: Does he have what it takes to succeed?
5. Package your proposal to sell. No one will invest if he can't see the benefit of the deal.
6. A "fair" partnership deal is the best deal you can derive. Forget magic formulas, they don't exist.
7. Avoid nonsense booby-trap deals that can only cause you problems.
8. Plan for the worst. Cover the contingency by cementing a "buy-out" agreement.
9. A partnership is only another form of "marriage." It's the joining of your brains with their money to start on a shoestring. It can work if you know what you're getting into.

8

SETTING UP SHOP

Setting up shop for Hal and Mindy Oreste is a ten-minute affair. Owners of a unique roadside business, the Orestes operate under the name of "The Teepee." Using a nomadic approach to retailing, the Orestes tote their Indian-style tent to various locations alongside interstate highways slicing through New Mexico and Arizona. Within a few minutes of spotting a likely location the tent is up, and several tables loaded with Indian handicrafts are beckoning tourists to stop. "Our objective is to take in $200–300 a day before the sheriff has us packing and on to the next county," smiles Hal Oreste. "And we usually succeed."

Chances are setting up your show will be quite a bit more complicated. Facing you are two considerable investment decisions:

1. Where to locate.
2. How to find—and buy—the necessary fixtures and equipment.

This chapter will show you several techniques for setting up shop on a shoestring, saving you a bundle of cash in the process.

The place to begin is by explaining that it makes sense to consider location and equipment as a package. The two items are very closely related with the location—and what comes with it—part of the strategy to reduce equipment costs. In the following chapter you'll see how to hunt your inventory to bring the business to life. So let's take first things first and give your business a home and some fixtures and equipment to go with it.

DEVELOPING THE MISER'S TOUCH

Businesses started with the miser's touch usually have what it takes to turn it into a pot of gold. It comes down to *underspending* on rent and fancy frills equipment to build and applying the cash where it will do the most good—on inventory and promotion. It's always a balancing of needs and what you probably need least for a successful start is an expensive overhead or costly equipment to chew up cash faster than you can generate it.

So you have to think cheap and be cheap to get in cheap. For some people with champagne tastes it's more than an objective—it's an impossibility. With a few it's not knowing how to put together a business for less than top dollar. This chapter will help. Others simply overestimate what their business needs, throwing away valuable dollars while they find out. Other big spenders just can't bring themselves to think in Spartan terms when their personal lifestyle is on a high note.

Are you likely to be a big spender? MBA students at Suffolk University Business School think so. In 1975 they surveyed start-ups to determine the relationship of rent and equipment costs to profits and success. They checked out comparable retail, service, and manufacturing firms with conclusive findings. The most successful businesses had the lowest rent and capital equipment costs. The study went further: 92% of the businesses examined could have started on an appreciably less expensive scale, with no anticipated drop in sales but with a healthy jump in profits. The big spenders were everywhere. With a tighter purse string they would now have a fatter purse.

A few examples. One Italian-style restaurant in the study spent $90,000 on fixtures, equipment, and renovation costs. A restaurant supply firm estimated the same business could be put together for less than $25,000 with comparable used equipment, competitive bidding on renovations, and eliminating some renovations that actually reduced sales potential. You have to sell quite a few spaghetti dinners to recoup the overspent $65,000.

Another big spender was a small journal publisher found in a $15-per-sq.-ft. plush office building overseeing his increasingly shaky 4000-sq.-ft. empire. The "B" students had a ball with this one while they tallied up $50,000 a year in wasted rent and $16,000 a year to finance plush office furnishings. That's big spending to the tune of $66,000 a year from a business that couldn't afford it. Today you'll find the business where it belongs—in a $10,000-a-year low-rent building with the office furnished in modern K-Mart. But the business is now making money.

That's what it's all about—making money. And you don't make money when you're foolishly spending money. And the most foolish money you're likely to spend is in setting up your shop. So forget grandiose ideas or castles in the sky. You need the miser's touch.

HANGING YOUR HAT FOR A DOLLAR A DAY

At what point are you spending too much on rent? The answer is simple. When there's alternative space available to house your business for less. And for service, mail-order, and small manufacturing firms that cheaper alternative space is your own home. It's where most start-ups in these businesses start and it's the logical starting place.

I recently read an interesting article on some of today's flourishing businesses started in garages. It told fascinating tales of everything from printing plants to mail-order firms whose beginning was a common, everyday home garage—and a rent at less than $1.00 a day to cover the light bill and a gallon of kerosene fuel for the space heater. Others move the clutter out of their basement to hang their hat, and others ascend skyward to the attic or a converted bedroom. Wherever you find them, you won't find them paying rent if they can avoid it.

Shrewd investors are always on the lookout for these "start-at-home" ventures, waiting for them to outgrow the corner of a basement and take the important step into larger outside quarters. It signals a pragmatist at the helm of a growth enterprise.

Is it smart for you to start at home? Here are some pros and cons to consider:

The pros are:

1. You avoid rent costs.
2. You avoid lease commitments. It's important when you don't know how successful your business will be—and can't really assess short-term space needs.
3. It's ideal for a space-time venture.
4. It's tax deductible. The portion of your home used for business purposes can be deducted from your household costs. Uncle Sam can be generous here and oftentimes the tax savings actually net you several hundred dollars a year to help your business along.

Why think twice about it?

1. The principal reason is that it's tough to work and concentrate at home. Many household entrepreneurs report the distractions, family interruptions, and the tendency to sneak away for a few moments of creature comforts reduce efficiency to the point where it's false economy. An "at home" venture may be considered more of a hobby than a business. Whether this is an obstacle for you depends again on your own discipline and the ground rules for your family.
2. Space limitations must also be considered. Many household start-ups have such confined space that "set-up" and "break-down" time eat into efficiency.

These reasons aside, many people reject the idea based on imagery—"what customers will think." It's a factor if you have a steady stream of customers knocking on your door, but with most businesses in this category the customers don't come knocking and have no idea the business is a desk in the attic. Prestige mail drop and telephone answering services and communal office space are answers for those that do. For $10–15 a month you can have the plushest address and telephone number in town, and for $50–75 a month you can pop into a swank—but shared—office to meet your occasional key customer. Look in your metropolitan paper for listings.

When the patter of approaching customers increases, a split operation may make sense. Typically a start-up will rent a presentable office for sales purposes, while confining production to a bargain basement facility. The merger of the two locations comes about when the two functions must be housed together for operating efficiency and control.

Once the business is beyond the survival stage, a rent ceiling should be based on a percentage of sales rather than dollars per sq. ft. "It's better expense control," reports Jack Manoog, a Cape Cod based real estate consultant. "Too often business people figure that if they find bargain-priced space it's a bargain for them. It's only true when the total rent is in line with sales."

What are some of the hottest low-rent bargains around?

Retail basement space leads the list and is plentiful. Many of my clients wisely rented space in a supermarket or other retail basement for rents as low as $2 a sq. ft. while comparable space elsewhere fetches $4–6 a foot. You may have to spend a few dollars to build a separate entrance but it's nothing compared to the rent savings.

Older and larger homes can be an ideal rent saver for "paperwork" or light production businesses. A large home may have 3000–4000 sq. ft. of usable space and rent for $12,000 a year—depending on the local real estate market. Still, residential homes can cut rent by 50% compared to commercial space. One caution: check the zoning before you sign the lease.

Boarded-up service stations can be another bargain. Fix-up costs are small, and stations can be adapted to a wide range of businesses needing up to 2000 feet to operate.

Rental agents and commercial brokers don't usually lead you to the best deals. They're networked into conventional space and conventional space means conventional rent. Since you want cheap rent it means going after it yourself. You may spend more than a dollar a day, but you'll also save more than a dollar a day.

GOING WHERE THE CUSTOMERS ARE

Retail start-ups are another story. Cheap is out and expensive is in. You need a high-traffic location to make it today in retailing, and high-traffic locations bring fancy rents. A high-traffic location is perhaps even more important for a shoestring start-up than for a well-capitalized business because the shoestring operation must start at a profitable level and that only happens with a prime location.

Not all shoestring start-ups agree and to an extent they're right. You can start in a low-rent, low-traffic location and bolster traffic with a high-cost advertising program to pull the people to you. But don't delude yourself. When you spend money to draw customers it's only another form of rent.

The best example of the two methods at work is the Factory Sweater Outlet near my home. Its first location was an abandoned factory building on a secondary road with light vehicle traffic. "The rent was only $7000 a year so we couldn't pass it up," recounts Al Tagerman its merchandise manager. "But it costs us over $20,000 a year in billboard ads to let people know we're around—so it really costs us $27,000 a year to pull our $650,000 in sales." Two years ago the Factory Sweater Outlet opened its second location in an enclosed shopping mall, paying $25,000 a year for 1600 sq. ft. This location is pulling the same $600,000–700,000 a year without advertising, so with mark-ups and other expenses equal, the choice of locations is a toss-up.

Given the choice, the preference should be to the high-rent, high-traffic location. Three reasons: first, is that many retail operations offer convenience or impulse goods. People won't travel for everyday inexpensive items even with heavy promotion. The pulling power of ads will work with clothing, shoes, furniture, or unusual items that fall into the demand category, but most merchandise needs the steady flow of traffic. The second reason is that a good advertising program takes "know-how," too many start-ups think they can whip together a high-powered campaign and fall on their faces. The last reason is timing. Even with heavy advertising, it takes weeks or months to create a traffic-building reputation. Usually you don't have the time.

Can you land a prime location? It's not easy. The very best locations are enclosed malls. Just as suburban strip centers crippled downtown stores, the enclosed malls now dominate the strip centers. If a mall is the type location for your business you'll have plenty of competition for space. Most developers prefer chain tenants with their recognized name and strong credit rating. In many instances a mall will be locked up by chain tenants a year or two before it's even built. The few remaining spaces usually go to strong independents. So how do you land space in a mall?

1. Consider a co-signer for your lease. Many developers will consider you if you can back up your lease with a strong signature.
2. Lease insurance is another possibility. Some insurance firms will guarantee your lease for a premium, taking you over the credit hurdle. A commercial broker can lead you to them.
3. Kiosk or "island" space is always a possibility if you need only 100–200 sq. ft. It's usually idle space for a landlord anxious to make it an income producer. Check some malls in your area and you'll see plenty of shoestring entrepreneurs peddling everything from soft-serve ice cream to stuffed animals in their thriving island locations.
4. Sublets are another possibility. Many tenants want to cut back on the size of their store and will sublet a portion to a related business. Concessioned space is an excellent space vehicle for a shoestring start-up, working equally well in discount stores and supermarkets. Don't overlook the idea.

Some of the most successful start-ups happily pay exorbitant rents to achieve equally exorbitant sales. The Quincy Marketplace in Boston's revitalized waterfront is one example. Rents topple the $30-per-sq.-ft. mark, or triple what you'd pay for suburban space, but the tenants aren't complaining. Most report sales are at least twice what another location would offer. It's difficult to find a city without similar opportunities.

Convenience type businesses—food stores, dry cleaners, appliances, drugs—each have their own logical location. Site analysis is beyond the scope of this book, but remember the key point. A low rent isn't necessarily a bargain. You want a location to give you the customers.

TWO MONEY-SAVING POINTS TO NEGOTIATE

Your attorney can walk you through the typical boiler plate on your twelve-page lease. Your job is to negotiate two critical points that can save you a bundle in start-up costs.

1. Deferred rents.
2. Landlord renovations.

Consider the economics.

1. *Deferred Rent:* Your rent will probably be set at a fixed amount for the first several years, increasing in later years to adjust for inflation. And a heavy cash outlay in the beginning months when sales are lowest can positively put a crimp in your cash flow. The strategy? Bargain for lower beginning rent and add the difference to the later months (or years) when you can better afford it. "It's not an insignificant point," suggests Russ Stockwell, who started the now locally famous Stockwell Chicken Ranch, a family-style restaurant in Southeastern Massachusetts. "Our landlord wanted $2000 a month rent which was a fair enough figure—except we couldn't afford it until the business got off the ground," adds Stockwell. "So we proposed starting at $1000 a month for six months to catch our breath, tacking the $6000 savings on to the next 30 months. Keeping the $6000 in our checkbook saw us through a tough start-up period when survival was nip and tuck."

Security deposits are another negotiable item to be deferred or eliminated altogether. With landlords increasingly having the upper hand, the three- or even six-month security deposit can lock you out of some attractive locations. The cure? One is to pledge personal collateral—a car or house mortgage for an equal amount. Another is to find a guarantor whose liability is limited to the deposit amount.

The same strategy can even save you from the first month's rent. One of my clients pulled just that ploy deferring $7500 in three months' initial rent. The landlord was satisfied, holding a mortgage on my client's computer, to secure the later payment of $7500, while my client had the money to use for other start-up costs.

Can you get the keys to a prime location without upfront rent? In large measure it depends on your respective bargaining position. A desperate landlord with a desperate location may give you six months free rent if you're smart enough to push for it. And you always push when you're working on a shoestring.

2. *Pass Renovation Costs on to Your Landlord:* Negotiate this point for all it's worth for it's worth plenty. What renovation costs are we talking about? You name it. A new store front, ceilings, tiled or carpeted floors, air conditioning, lighting, panelled walls—or whatever else it takes to turn a concrete box into a furnished store. And whatever it takes it costs plenty. Betty Tamer, an executive with a leading shopping center development firm, tells it straight when she says, "Cash-poor independents can't afford to take new space in most shopping centers. And it's not the rent that keeps them out, it's the renovation costs—like most developers we provide only a 'shell,' wall-to-wall cinder block. It stops most start-ups cold when they realize it will cost them $50,000–100,000 to complete it as a 'turn-key.' "

Worse still, renovation costs can't readily be financed by the tenant. Banks can't repossess wall panelling or a new store front now belonging to a landlord. But a landlord can, often incorporating the improvement costs into his mortgage financing. Of course, you'll pay higher rent for a "turn-key" space compared to a "shell" since the landlord must recoup the costs, but it will save you some serious upfront money.

Negotiating landlord improvements is no game for the amateur. Consider these three tips:

1. List what you absolutely need to make the location suitable for occupancy. Avoid the frills and needless high-cost improvements. Don't forget you eventually pay for the improvements in a stepped-up lease.

2. Obtain bids. An architect or contractor can help. Make sure you know the lowest price so you know what it's worth in a higher rent.
3. Negotiate to split the costs, with your share being tacked on to the rent. One advantage with landlord-furnished improvements is their ability to do it at less cost. And don't forget, the improvements are to the landlord's property.

THE MILLION-DOLLAR LOOK ON HUMBLE PENNIES

"Cardiac arrest" is what Barry Adler called it when he received a $48,000 quote to renovate a dilapidated interior into a modern seafood restaurant on the Cape Cod waterfront. "And that didn't include the equipment—just the ceiling, floors, and four walls. With $2600 budgeted I had to be creative—and damn creative to give it the million-dollar look," Barry quickly adds.

"I decided to go with a nautical theme, figuring I could pull together plenty of sea-faring memorabilia to give it the right feeling. Instead of a $3000 drop ceiling I paid $200 for used fishing nets, fireproofing them to get by the fire code. Creating my own 'fishnet' ceiling, complete with used $10 spotlights peeking through, gave it the right touch. Would-be walnut panelling was replaced by four high-school kids giving the walls a fresh coat of blue paint, hurriedly adorned with twenty seascapes for sale on consignment by local Rembrandts. It not only produced a few bucks profit but saved me $8000 on panelling. The architect recommended a $12,000 marble foyer. I had a better idea lining the foyer with floor to ceiling crates featuring fine wines from every corner of the world, adorning it with a $20 sign—'Sea Shanty Winery.' Customers loved it, and while lingering for a seat, would select their choice, boosting wine sales by 40%. Discarding the $24-a-sq.-yd. carpeting samples, a rental floor sander returned the floor to its original high-gloss state. It looked like a seafood restaurant and a mighty classy restaurant at that," Barry proudly will tell you. With humble pennies, Barry achieved his own million-dollar look.

Restaurants aren't the only ugly ducklings to be turned into swans on a few creative ideas. Walk through clothing stores, gift shops, and even the corner drug store and you'll see cost-saving renovation techniques at work. Consumer Value Stores, a 500-store pharmacy chain, knows how to cut corners while building image. Walk into any one of their stores and you'll see manufacturer-furnished wall murals surrounding the store. Coppertone, Alka-Seltzer, etc., form a continuous billboard boosting their sales while brightening the walls. It's a clever idea. And there are thousands of equally good ideas you can use to go first class on a shoestring budget.

If you don't have the creative touch, then borrow it. The best advice is to pick up ideas from others. Observe. Walk through businesses and keep your eyes open. What cost-saving treatments can you borrow for your ceiling? What inexpensive lighting suggestions do you see? How do walls come alive? What's happening under your feet? What are the small touches that can work for your operation? You too will learn how paint, mirrors, and accessories create optical illusions and attractive businesses at a paltry price.

Interior decorators can help. For a $200 fee you can save thousands. Why not? They know what works in a home and the same formulas can work in sprucing up a business. I guarantee it's a wise investment and can save you a fortune in the process.

THE BARGAINLAND OF EQUIPMENT DEALS

The biggest bargains of all are to be found when it's time to buy fixtures and equipment. In fact, you can usually pick up what you need with absolutely no cash outlay.

This is another area where you want to underspend. Never pay top dollar to buy the best or the newest. It pays small dividends. Many small business bankruptcies can be traced to a top-heavy investment in capital assets. Needed cash is gobbled up to buy and more cash is gobbled to pay hefty carrying costs. "High rollers who buy new are making a big mistake," says Ralph DiFonzo of Boston's Central Restaurant Equipment & Supply Company. "A restaurant, for example, can easily cost $100,000 to equip at showroom prices, while the same equipment slightly used may be available for $20,000. And you don't sell fewer steaks from a two-year-old broiler than from a new one."

So where do you find the bargains?

1. The auction pages are your best bet. Paul Saperstein, the largest commercial auctioneer in New England will tell you that he has 20 to 30 businesses lined up for auction at any given time. "Everything from variety stores to manufacturing plants, with good, serviceable equipment going for 10–40% of their original cost." Auctioneers in your city have the same bargains. Here's added information. Don't wait for the ads in the paper. Many auctioneers bid on their own for auction equipment and warehouse it to sell later at a better price. Make a list of what you need and make some phone calls. And don't hesitate to go to auctioneers in other cities. It's well worth $500 in travel and moving costs to save several thousand.
2. Contact chain stores if you want retail fixtures. Here's why. Oftentimes chains remodel and warehouse older fixtures, hoping to sell them piecemeal to start-up firms. In many instances they'll buy out a store and remodel to their own specifications. I outfitted two of my drug stores just that way, buying gondolas, wall cases, show cases, and just about everything else I needed for about 20% of new fixtures cost.
3. Equipment-supply firms are another stopover. The yellow pages list fixture and equipment firms in every type business. There are some tricks of the trade here too. They may only advertise new fixtures—and they'll certainly push you to buy new because they make a better profit. Stand firm. They'll lead you to their own warehouse jam packed with bargains. And if they don't have it they can get it. The businesses they're selling new equipment to have their used items which may be perfect for you.
4. The classified ads offer some bargains. Every metropolitan newspaper features columns of businesses looking to sell

used equipment. From my experiences you tend to pay slightly more when buying from a private party than at a distress sale, but it does offer convenience. Place a few of your own ads. Many business people have equipment they want to unload but haven't actively looked for buyers.

5. Trade journals and associations are frequently overlooked. They lead you to the equipment you're likely to need, and advertising costs are low.

By checking out these five valuable sources you'll have your pick of bargains, and if you play your cards right you may be able to buy without upfront cash and outlay. It only takes leg work.

Charlie Nardozzi, the proud owner of Charlie's Pizza, a bustling shop for the teenage crowd in Boston's North Shore, used dimes instead of leg work. To equip his start-up, new tables and chairs would cost $2500. Two spanking-new Blodgett ovens another $7500, and a new NCR cash register $2100. "Ten thousand dollars was $10,000 too much, I couldn't afford more than $2500 and thought I was forever stuck in my job as a stitcher in a shoe factory," moaned Charlie.

Seven phone calls proved Charlie wrong. The first call was to an auctioneer who led Charlie to two Blodgett ovens only three years old. The price was an unbeatable $2700, financed by the seller who reluctantly agreed to finance with $500 down and the balance over two years at 18% interest secured by the ovens. Charlie was learning. Sellers will finance. Three more phone calls hooked Charlie up with a terrific bargain in tables and chairs. A restaurant under renovation had just what Charlie needed and for $500 Charlie carted them away. Two more phone calls and Charlie had a five-year-old cash register for $250, picked up through the classifieds. "All it had to do was ring up a sale and hold the money. When I'm as large as Pizza Hut I'll upgrade to the fancy computerized registers." So for $1250 Charlie was in business. The final phone call? It was to Charlie's foreman at the shoe factory telling him to look for a new stitcher.

You won't read about Charlie in the *Wall Street Journal,* but success can be a tasty pizza topped with trimmings made in a used oven, devoured on a secondhand table, and tallied on a slightly tired cash register.

100% TERMS ANYONE CAN GET

Buy low, finance high, and keep your cash intact. It's a winning formula for shrewd start-ups. So how do you finance high—very high—with 100% loans?

Banks and finance companies are prime candidates. One reason they'll consider 100% financing on bargain-priced equipment is because the collateral value is there. "New equipment only justifies a 50–60% loan," comments one banker. "If we have a loan against a new $10,000 printing press, for example, we can only recoup $4000–5000 if foreclosure is necessary. But if it's worth $5000 at liquidation, why shouldn't we lend $5000 against it?"

Seller financing is another possibility. Sellers typically aren't as interested in immediate cash as they are in disposing of what's no longer needed. One of my clients even managed to buy a six-seat, $75,000 airplane for his growing commuter airline from a larger airline upgrading to larger aircraft. With the plane as collateral, the seller financed the full $75,000 over five years at 15% interest.

Leveraged financing of new equipment is typically the game of manufacturers or dealers selling the equipment at a sizable profit. Many "so-called" franchise systems are nothing more than a scheme to sell equipment—often at an inflated price. For example, one poorer but wiser franchisee of a $140,000 car wash franchise now realizes that he bought $40,000 worth of equipment and a worthless name for $100,000. Why shouldn't the franchisor happily finance the equipment? Similar stories come from the dry cleaning, printing, and even the soft-serve ice cream industries. There are good and bad actors in every field, but the point is a small down payment doesn't make a good deal when you're paying an excessive price for the privilege.

Increased competition in the equipment fields makes manufacturer financing almost mandatory to their own survival. Store fixture manufacturers routinely have arrangements with banks who will finance 70–80% of the purchase price. Since the manufacturer factors the note, the bank has recourse against the manufacturer. Your credit rating is only important to the manufacturer who has considerably more lenient standards. Computers are another good example. You can't find a major computer firm who doesn't offer a generous financing package, and today you can buy a computer with 5–10% down, reminiscent of automobile financing.

Manufacturer financing has its downside. Even if you do buy at a fair price, the finance charges are usually 2–3% higher than a bank's, although lower than many finance companies. The upside is the manufacturer or dealer is more inclined to honor its warranties or service contracts while you still owe them money.

The greatest danger with manufacturer financing on new equipment is that it's *too* easy to get. A start-up entrepreneur will perhaps call in a store fixture firm and buy $40,000 in new fixtures with $6000 down, and six months later strangle on the $34,000 note. With a few phone calls you may find a slightly used version for $10,000 and perhaps win 100% financing in the bargain.

THE MAGIC OF LEASING

Since 1960 the number of firms leasing—instead of owning—has tripled. Tax savings is one reason, since you can deduct the entire lease costs, while only deducting the depreciated value of owned equipment. It's not the selling point with shoestring start-ups with a different set of priorities.

Why should you consider leasing?

1. Needed cash is low: most firms lease equipment upon payment of only the first month's rent and a one- or two-month security deposit. Buying may require several thousand dollars more in up front cash even with leveraged financing.
2. Obsolescence is another factor: in some industries equipment becomes obsolete overnight. Computers again serve as a good example. With leasing you have increased flexibility to upgrade to newer items. Try to negotiate the clause into the agreement giving you the option to trade up to newer models.

3. Maintenance is a key advantage in leasing. Usually a leasing firm will give you the option to include a maintenance or service policy. Sometimes it's overpriced, but many start-ups prefer it because it does fix costs avoiding large unexpected repair bills on a fragile cash flow.

Is leasing for you? It may be with motor vehicles and high cost equipment with rapid obsolescence, and even cash registers and store carpeting. It's generally not the way to go with store fixtures or other capital assets expected to last more than five years.

HOW TO MAKE THE MOST OF MANUFACTURER'S FREE TRIALS

You can get a trial run on many types of equipment needed for your business—particularly office equipment.

Let's say you need several typewriters, a copy machine and a small computer to start a service business. To buy the equipment in advance may drain your small cash, so instead you ask for a 30–60 day trial run at which point you will either buy, lease, or return the items. The advantage is obvious: you have the needed equipment to get started without spending a dime, buying once the cash flow is rolling. It's a common practice, and most dealers have demonstrator office equipment and even cash registers for just this purpose.

Don't try to play one dealer against the other with a never-ending cycle of trial runs; word gets around.

A HELPING HAND FROM BIG SUPPLIERS

If you're a manufacturer your equipment problems may be solved with the helping hand of raw material suppliers. It's not unusual to buy $100,000 a year of chemicals, plastics, pharmaceuticals, or a host of other raw material and feed it through $20,000 worth of equipment to mold the finished product. So the proposition is this. Since your suppliers are making a healthy profit on your purchases why shouldn't they subsidize the cost of the equipment? Negotiated properly, it has money-saving possibilities.

This one technique virtually capitalized a small baked goods manufacturer. The entrepreneurial baker projected buying over $200,000 a year from his flour supplier. So he drove a hard bargain, demanding the supplier buy the $40,000 in baking equipment for him. The supplier would hold title to the equipment leasing it to the baker for a nominal $2000 a year until the baker purchased $800,000 in flour at which time the supplier would hand the baker a free bill of sale. It made sense to the supplier who looked at it as a 5% discount and made even more sense to the baker who bootstrapped his company with his supplier's money.

SHARING TIME IS SAVING DOLLARS

Idle equipment is idle dollars and you need your few dollars working 120% of the time. When you can't fully utilize equipment, tap into a time-sharing arrangement, borrowing the equipment only when you need it.

I can show you hundreds of examples where time-sharing made a new business possible, or at the least helped it along. A few will do.

The Healthmark Corporation, a temporary help firm specializing in nurse placement, needed a desk, telephone, and access to a high capacity computer to start. The desk and telephone came easy. The price tag on an IBM-360 computer came high. So Healthmark rented six hours a week of computer time from a nearby firm with time to share, defraying its own costs.

The Round Table Press turns out specialized newsletters for several industries. Rather than subcontract printing, it time-shares a full printing plant on weekends from a commercial printer operating weekdays.

A 50/50 time-share on a cash wash? "Why not?" asks Herb Stolte, who originated a novel business picking up and cleaning autos for car dealers and car rental agencies. Within a month Stolte had 25 dealers and agencies signed up and the promise of

200 cars a week to clean. All that was missing was the car wash. Noticing a car wash in the next town suffered from low weekday activity, Stolte bargained to rent the weekday mornings for 20% of the total operating costs. "That's all I needed," suggests Stolte, "so why spend more?"

Time-sharing can make as much sense for costly equipment as it does in the vacation resort field. Not only does it keep beginning costs down, but it may provide access to even more efficient equipment than you could afford to buy.

Define your equipment needs. Circle equipment you may only need on a part-time basis. Those are the perfect candidates for a time-share arrangement.

PROMISE A PIECE OF THE ACTION

Many of the best partnerships are marriages between businesses with equipment and start-ups with ideas.

"It worked for us," says Jerry Hillman, referring to his joint venture with Mystic Plastics, a high-powered plastic extruding firm capable of churning out Hillman's innovative disposable clinical thermometers. "No sooner did I receive the patent than I discovered it would cost me $750,000 to buy the specialized equipment. Venture capital was a possibility, but I didn't want to give up my controlling interest as the venture capitalists demanded. Another alternative was to subcontract production, but that too would put me at the mercy of the production people." The ideal formula for Hillman was the formation of a new corporation, with Mystic Plastics owning 40% while Hillman retained 60% ownership. Mystic, in turn, contracted to produce the thermometers for the new corporation at a very low price.

How common are these joint ventures involving companies with equipment and those that need it? Not as common as they could be. Start-up entrepreneurs facing the hurdle of putting together an intensive equipment business usually look for the money to buy the equipment, or following Hillman's path, seek out venture capital funds trading part ownership. Offering a piece of the action to a company who can provide the equipment is a means to the same end. And frequently it's a better alternative, because you can strike a more favorable bargain with a partner who's only making his equipment work a bit harder.

PRODUCING PROFITS WITHOUT PRODUCTION

The most important message in this chapter is perhaps this last message. You may not need a physical plant to put yourself in business. In fact, you may be better off without it by buying or subcontracting what you plan to sell.

Many start-ups look at their business idea as essentially a production activity, overlooking the common reality that it's more of a marketing activity with production better left to someone else. And when you begin to think this way you'll find it easier—and safer to start.

I learned that lesson in one of my first start-ups. Two acquaintances of mine were fast developing a reputation as store renovation specialists. So we started a fixture and store remodelling firm, complete with a plant turning out customer fixtures built to order, while my partners and a few hired tradesmen began to rack up sales with their creative approach to store renovations. A year later the report card was in and we found we were making money on renovations, but losing our shirt on fixture production. We quickly closed down the factory, subcontracting production to a much larger firm who could turn out the fixtures at half our cost. It was faulty thinking right from the start. We should have realized our strength was in sales and renovations. We didn't need ten people on the payroll turning out fixtures to go along with the remodelling jobs—not when we could buy cheaper.

If your business involves manufacturing as well as marketing consider a two-step start-up. Subcontract manufacturing, and concentrate on marketing during the initial stages. It offers several advantages.

1. You can test the market for your product without extensive plant start-up costs.

2. You'll concentrate on sales and marketing—which your business most needs—instead of diluting your efforts on production.
3. You'll save plenty of money. Few start-ups can generate sufficient sales to keep a production facility humming while sales are building.

Do you really need more than an order book to start? Maybe not.

KEY POINTS TO REMEMBER

1. Avoid the most common and costly start-up error—*overspending* on rent and equipment.
2. Your own home may be the best place to start.
3. Don't scrimp on a retail location. Go first-class for first-class sales.
4. Equipment bargains are everywhere—and will help you save 60–90% of your start-up costs.
5. You can 100% finance fixtures and equipment—if you know how.
6. Leasing can make sense. Check it out and save a cash outlay.
7. Renovations are much cheaper when you use creativity instead of hard cash.
8. Let your suppliers help you buy equipment if the equipment will make money for them.
9. Time-share what you need. Don't let idle equipment drain needed capital.
10. A partner can provide equipment instead of money—and equipment can be as valuable.
11. Do you really need to produce what you plan to sell?

9

FULL SHELVES FROM EMPTY POCKETS

When Peter Hassan had to borrow quarters from the Coke machine to buy lunch a few years ago, he had his doubts about the American dream.

Now he talks as though he invented it. And anybody who can start a company in 1977 with less than $6500 and turn it into a $600,000-a-year enterprise by 1979 has the right to talk.

Hassan, 39, owns the Henrick Interior Studio, selling fashionable tables, lamps, wall decorations, and giftware for the home. "It was an interesting beginning," says Hassan. "I had the carpet down, lights up, fixtures in place, and sign over the front door. What I didn't have was inventory—or the money or credit to buy it. I thought I could instead sell from catalogs, but that didn't work. Customers wanted to see and feel the merchandise. The business was almost closed before it started."

Wisely, Hassan didn't close up shop. What he did do was lace up his hunting boots and scout out merchandise from any source he could. "I discovered there were 2300 manufacturers whose products I could sell, and another 1700 wholesalers and distributors selling the same and other lines I could move. That gave me 4000 chances to succeed. By pounding the beat I could sell myself. Gradually a patchwork of goods were shipped on a patchwork of negotiated credit terms. Two months later we had close to $100,000 worth of inventory on display, and with it we showed a profit in our second month. The rest is history."

Peter Hassan calls it history. But it is more. It is a success story. And there are thousands of shoestring merchants who start each year facing bare shelves, but with the know-how to get those shelves filled with profitable inventory—the lifeblood of their business. They too succeed. Others don't. With near-empty shelves they watch their business die on the installment plan.

If you're planning a retail or merchandise-oriented business, read this chapter several times. You've met Peter Hassan, and you'll meet several other interesting people who started just the way you'll start—with no money and no credit, but plenty of profitable inventory on their shelves. They'll show you how it's done.

YOU CAN'T DO BUSINESS FROM AN EMPTY WAGON

The secret of a successful merchandising start-up is never to look like you started on a shoestring. It's more than imagery. It's economics. You can't do business from an empty wagon. On opening day you not only need the merchandise to sell—but you need *enough* inventory to start at a profitable level.

Common sense? Of course. However, many retail start-ups overlook the importance of starting with the right inventory levels or size operation, believing that somehow the business will build inventory and as a result build sales and profits.

That's what makes retail start-ups so very different from non-merchandising start-ups. While you can start a service or manufacturing operation at "ground-zero" and gradually build it, it doesn't work with the retail venture. The retail business must be financially viable from the first day. You can't start too small and expect something better to evolve.

It's a common mistake. Retail business attracts the majority of shoestring operations. Of course, retail businesses statistically dominate the business scene, but what makes it particularly attractive to the novice is the belief you can rent a tiny storefront, throw a few pieces of merchandise on the shelf, and anticipate success. Three months later you walk by and all you see is a boarded-up storefront, or perhaps another cockeyed optimist about to learn the same lesson.

Let's define our terms. What do I mean by too small? A beginning operation that doesn't have sufficient merchandise to generate profitable sales. The actual store size has little to do with it, except when it restricts merchandising to an unprofitable level.

Harriet Blackman understands the point. Harriet scraped together $8000 in 1979 to open a designer jean shop in the Massachusetts Berkshires, the home of eight leading colleges and thousands of student derrières advertising the latest names in blue jean fashions. Of that total $3500 went for fixtures and other start-up costs. Inventory? "That was my mistake," admits Harriet. "My opening order was $6000, and since I didn't have established credit I paid 50% upon order with the balance due in 30 days. All it gave me was 300 pair of jeans and a store that still looked like an empty airplane hangar. The kids would walk by, look in and keep walking. Those that strolled in usually walked out without buying. Whatever they wanted I didn't have. The business needed $600 a day in sales to make it, and on its best day sales were only $260. Before I knew it I had worked the stock down to nothing to cover rent and my own $300 a week salary and the business was gone."

Harriet's story didn't end there. When her store was auctioned, the assets were picked up by two enterprising students from one of the local colleges ambitious enough to send it on its second launch. Within a month they had it stocked with over $32,000 in jeans, blouses, belts, and related casual wear apparel. Spare space at the front of the store was concessioned to another student who set up showcases with handcrafted belt buckles, jade jewelry, and Indian artifacts. It looked like a business and *was* a solid business, ringing up over $1000 a day. The interesting point is that the young partners found the inventory to create their viable business without spending upfront money.

Dr. Barry Bleidt, a professor of retailing management at Northeastern University, claims that most retail start-ups fail for the very reason Harriet Blackman stumbled. "Entrepreneurs merchandise the business based on what they have to spend, rather than on what the business needs to succeed," counsels Professor Bleidt. "Usually there's a considerable difference between the two."

A walk down any Main Street confirms his message. We recently helped a young chap set up a liquor store in a 2400-sq.-ft. downtown location. The accountant ran the numbers and calculated the business needed sales in the $500,000 range to break even. To support the sales the business needed a $50,000 opening inventory. That's not how our young client saw it, and defying the odds tried to bootstrap it with a $12,000 merchandise level. The store collapsed two months later from poor sales.

It's far safer to *over*-merchandise a start-up rather than to *under*-merchandise it. You'll start out with considerable trade debt, but it's counterbalanced by a business launched on its strongest foot. If the sales are there, the business will eventually work down the debt to a manageable level. Conversely, if it's *under*-merchandised it won't have the profitable beginning, and without profits you can't logically build.

How much inventory do you need for a successful start? It's all in the numbers, so pull out your pocket calculator.

1. Define your break-even point. Your accountant can quickly recap your expenses and margins to figure the magical point at which you begin to make money.
2. Aim for a higher figure considering that you'll need *profitable* sales to work down beginning trade credit.
3. Calculate the inventory needed to generate the required sales. Every business has average inventory turnover figures. Follow industry guidelines. Don't delude yourself by thinking you can turn inventory faster than industry standards. It seldom happens.
4. How do you find out what the average turnover is for your type business? There are plenty of available sources. The Bank of America, San Francisco, California, has operating data available for every type business and you can obtain a copy of the data by writing Bank of America. But here's a word of added advice. If you don't know the turnover ratios for your business, you probably don't know enough about the business to give it the shoestring try.

Let's pull it all together. When I started my first Discount City Store, I aimed for a $120,000 starting inventory. It wasn't by accident but by design. Operating expenses for the store amounted to $140,000, and we figured we'd be working on a 25% gross margin. Therefore, we would need about $560,000 in sales just to break even. But we had to do better than break even to stay in business. Virtually all our inventory and most of our fixtures and start-up costs were financed for a grand total of $200,000. Figuring that we would have to repay at least $60,000 a year to keep the creditors pacified, the business would actually have to generate that much in profits. So with our numbers honed fine, Discount City would have to do about $900,000 to cover expenses and pay back debt. Since cost-of-goods on $900,000 in sales would be about $675,000 (for a 25% gross profit), and since we correctly anticipated turning our inventory 5.5 times a year, our slide rule pointed to $120,000 in needed merchandise. It's all in the numbers.

Play with your own numbers. We might have been able to set our sights lower and shoot for sales in the $400,000 range, but it wouldn't make sense in our 4000-sq.-ft. store with its fixed overhead. With a smaller store—and smaller overhead—the lower sales and inventory may have been a start-up alternative, but in our case we deliberately set our sights higher.

Carl Shumrak, owner of Possessions, Inc., a successful greeting card and gift shop in a Boston suburb, followed the same technique but on a considerably smaller scale. As Carl would say, "At my stage of life I don't want to get rich, I just want a business that can give me a comfortable $30,000–35,000 income without killing myself." Carl's answer was a 1800-sq.-ft. location in a high-traffic strip center. Pouring over the numbers, Carl found that operating expenses (including his own salary) would be about $85,000. Since his type business operates on a "keystone margin" (50% gross profit), Possessions needed $170,000 in sales to break-even. "My target was $220,000–240,000 to give me a comfortable edge and the cash flow to pay financing costs. And to generate $240,000 in sales, I knew I needed $45,000–50,000 in inventory. A smaller inventory would mean smaller sales and the numbers wouldn't work.

"But for us the numbers did work. We borrowed $10,000 to buy some giftware lines that would only sell COD, and captured $38,000 in merchandise from other suppliers willing to go on extended credit. With a few sharp promotions we hit $262,000 in our first year, and within two years we were out of the woods and didn't owe a dime. You can't do business from an empty wagon—or a half-empty wagon for that matter. When you open the doors it must look like they're open to stay."

A CLOSED CHECKBOOK NEEDS AN OPEN MIND

No matter how much inventory you need for a successful start, you never get it. Not if you're starting with a closed checkbook and no credit rating as the typical shoestring merchant. That brings us to what I call "concentric merchandising." Don't look it up in a business dictionary, for I coined the term myself. What it amounts to is merchandising based on what you can *get* rather than what you *want*. Eventually, and with some profitable sales behind you, you'll be able to mold your inventory to what you wanted in the first place. But for now let's see if you can master the art of concentric merchandising.

A classic example is Highland Jewelry, a now thriving Long Island jewelry store grossing $600,000 annually. But when it started ten years ago, its sign read "Highland Jewelry and Giftware." "The giftware tag was out of necessity not desire," says Evelyn Morton who operates the store with her son Bob. "We conceived the business as a high-quality jewelry operation and never wanted the giftware lines. However, we only had $12,000 to invest and the banks wouldn't touch us. Jewelry suppliers wouldn't touch us either with a ten-foot pole. We called Seiko, Longines, Rolex, Benrus, and a dozen Providence and New York jewelry firms but they were reluctant to even open us on COD, and virtually laughed us out of their offices when we asked for credit. We discovered that when you talk jewelry, it's either cash or an impeccable credit history going back to the Civil War. So we invested $6000 to bring in a few select lines, but it was hardly enough to start a healthy business. We needed other lines—lines compatible with jewelry—that could be obtained on credit. Giftware was the answer and we even tacked on a luggage department. Giftware and luggage inventory was easier to come by on credit, and it didn't take long to locate $20,000 from gift and luggage suppliers anxious to do business with us. The merchandise mix was enough for a start. For the first year or two we did most of our business with giftware, but gradually we built up our jewelry line while working down giftwares. Within five years we were out of the giftware business (except for some high-priced lines) and concentrating on jewelry. Sometimes you have to use a 'back-door' approach to build the business you want."

And it can take many forms. While Highland Jewelry did it by dabbling with trade credit in the easier giftware and luggage lines, R. L. Stearns Company, another bangles and beads purveyor, got its foot into the jewelry field by starting with the credit-easy low-priced lines, upgrading as it went. "We only had a 400-sq.-ft.-mall store so we were limited for space, forcing us to stay with jewelry alone," says Henry Kominski, 32, its bushy-haired president. Without cash or credit we couldn't go for the top lines so we started somewhere halfway down the scale where there are hundreds of suppliers and manufacturers looking for retail accounts. They're never as fussy, and we were able to hustle together a $19,000 inventory on workable terms." Concentric merchandising is knowing how to go *for the easier credit lines within your field*.

"Synergistic diversification" is a fancy name for what Helen Cryten calls her "mish-mush" merchandising emporium hiding under the name Helen's Leisure Time, located in a Detroit shopping center. "The business started out as a bookstore and ended up a collection of whatever I could get on credit. The only other criterion was that the goods had to relate in some way to leisure time," Helen confesses. "The twelve top book publishers turned me down cold for an opening order on credit so I bought their best-sellers for cash, cutting the book department down to 25% of the store space, then I went after paperbacks, greeting cards, adult toys and games, party goods, and anything that looked, tasted, or smelled like leisure—including a gourmet cookware department. What I ended up with was nine mini-departments connected only by the common thread of leisure and the ability to get it on credit." Helen smiles when she calls it her "mish-mush," but it's a profitable "mish-mush," generating $290,000 a year in sales. Concentric merchandising is knowing how to *branch out into related lines*.

Unusual stories? Hardly. It's only the science of merchandising borne out of necessity. The stories continue:

Helen Olgar's Slacks, a five-store New England chain was started when lingerie suppliers said "no" to Jerome Kelm's request for opening credit. "I wanted to compete with 'Frederick's of Hollywood,' but it didn't take long to find out lingerie manufacturers are as stingy on credit as they are on G-string lace," laughs Jerry. "Two days later I was introduced to a New York ladies' slacks manufacturer looking to break into the New England market—and willing to back me with a $25,000 credit line for the privilege. A phone call to my sign painter and he replaced the still wet paint announcing "Jerry's Naughty Nightime Shop" to Helen Olgar's which sounded like a safe enough name. I'm not sure I'm having as much fun selling slacks, but it's a damn profitable line. Profitable enough to grow to four more stores. My next store, however," adds Jerry, "will be Jerry's Naughty Nightime Shop. Now I can afford it." Concentric merchandising is knowing how to *start with different lines*.

If concentric merchandising is borne of necessity, it sometimes leads to an even more successful business than originally planned. The "add-on" or "substitute" lines oftentimes prove more profitable than the intended line. And in many instances it leads you to a winning format for your business.

That's what happened to me and Discount City. As an entrepreneurial pup, I planned a typical discount department store—a miniaturized version of K-Mart with orderly, logical departments and the usual neat array of products within each department. The only problem was that to bring the necessary products together would require credit from 236 different suppliers. I tried and 197 turned me down. My inventory would have more holes than a slice of Swiss cheese. So I switched gears and changed the format to a "close-out" store, in reality closer to a Turkish bazaar or a rubbish dump with neon lights. Now any merchandise was fair game provided I could get it cheap, sell it cheap, and of course not pay my supplier until long after I sold it. So in came the $3.98 garbage cans, and the 49-cent six-fingered back scratchers from Taiwan, and $120,000 in assorted bargains from around the world. But I was no longer "locked in to specific needs and every possible supplier I could find became my happy hunting ground. Taking the theory of concentric merchandising to its outermost limits I discovered a more successful merchandising plan. Perhaps you won't have to bend your initial plans quite as much, but you too will find an open mind is needed when you have a closed checkbook.

Plan ahead with this step-by-step guide:

1. Define the merchandise you expect to carry—and its sources of supply. Now expand on it concentrically.
2. What related or "tie-in" lines can you *add*?
3. What similar lines with easier credit can you *substitute*?
4. What alternate sources are *available*?

Use your imagination. For every line—or supplier—you add, you increase your own chances for finding start-up inventory by one.

CREDIT MANAGERS CAN SAY "YES"

That doesn't mean they will. In fact, it's usually in the credit manager's best interest to say "no." After all, credit managers are programmed to avoid losses, not bend over backwards to create risky sales. So your job is to re-program the credit manager and get his nod with a few convincing reasons why you deserve credit.

It's never an easy sell. The woods are full of "bust-out artists," bankruptcy frauds, deadbeats, and ne'er do wells who are trying to pry their own share of merchandise from under the cynical eye of the ever-watchful credit manager. Now you come along with a company that is little more than a name on a piece of paper, a few bucks in your checking account, and a business that Dun and Bradstreet never heard of. It's hardly enough to inspire confidence. So how do you get around credit managers who dislike would-be businesses with no sales, profits, credit history, or cash register?

The place to start is by realizing that credit terms, although uniformly stated, are never universally applied. The credit terms you can wrangle from a given supplier will depend on a combination of factors, including demand for the line, competition, the profit potential of your account, the risk-assessment, and even the chemistry between you and the credit manager. Some suppliers are notoriously rigid and live by an unbendable credit policy—usually tied to a Dun and Bradstreet rating. Others have their own policy, but will still listen.

There are proven strategies to get around both types.

1. Build a credit rating before you go credit hunting. Call in Dun and Bradstreet as soon as your corporation is organized. Tell them about your plans, your personal background, and anything else that's favorable. Somewhere along the way the D & B representative will ask you how the business is capitalized. What a nosy question. Just tell him you're still interviewing prospective partners and several bankers. As a new start-up, D & B won't assign you a credit rating, but will publish what you tell them. Even that much of a listing is enough for some suppliers.
2. Line up a few credit references. Make it legitimate. Don't trump up phonies. But chances are that you do have three or four people you've already done business with—perhaps they're equipment suppliers—who'll vouch for you. Check with them first before giving their name as a reference.
3. Work through sales people. If it's a large order try to work directly with the sales manager. Go as high up the ladder as you can. Sales people, unlike credit managers, are sales oriented. They want to sell you, and if you're halfway credible, will try to sell you to the credit manager. On orders under a $1000 it may not be practical. Oftentimes these small orders are automatically cleared without any credit check. But on larger orders a credit check will be done. That's when you want the sales department walking your order through.
4. How you submit an order counts. Print up purchase orders with your name engraved. It gives you the appearance of an

established business instead of a "fly-by-night" operation. Use your own purchase order even when a supplier's order form is available. It's a good idea to enclose a sheet listing your references.

5. Don't forget your bank as a credit reference. And here's a strategy to put you a few points ahead. Maintain at least a \$1000 balance in the business account. Banks never disclose your exact balance but will report an average "three digit" (\$100–\$999), "four digit" (\$1000–\$9999), or "five digit" (\$10,000–\$99,999) balance. With a "four digit" \$1000 balance, you have the same bank rating as a customer with \$9999 on account. If you can swing a \$10,000 balance during the credit hunting period, so much the better. It puts you in the big leagues. Check with your banker to make certain he's reporting it out the way you want.
6. Watch your timing. You'll have the best chance to push an order through during peak selling seasons. September through November are the best months, for example, if you're going after merchandise that can move for Christmas, while March and April are hectic for summer seasonal goods. Credit departments are too busy to be as thorough as they might be. Also be on the lookout for new lines, hot promotional campaigns, or heavy competition from new competitors. That's when suppliers dramatically relax credit in favor of sales.

Play the odds. You may need merchandise from 20 to 30 small secondary suppliers, placing a \$300–\$2000 order with each. Don't expect to win credit from them all. It won't happen. What will happen is that perhaps 40–60% will extend credit (usually automatically) and ship. Another 20% will outright refuse and invite you to buy COD or cash-in-advance. The remainder may try a "split-approach" by either asking COD for part of the order, with the balance on credit, or suggest you cut your order size. The point is that you may need "backup" or alternate suppliers when credit is declined. Have their orders ready for submission so you don't lose time when a primary source declines.

It may seem elementary, but even experienced business people often overlook the common sense approaches to credit success.

BUY NOW—PAY LATER

Buying inventory on credit terms is the easy part. Any schemer with a pen and a pile of purchase orders can load up a warehouse with inventory if he wants to work hard enough at it. Thirty days after the goods arrive it's another story. That's when it's time to pay the piper.

Everything I said so far in this chapter pre-supposes normal trade credit. What you buy today is due and payable 30 days hence. The harsh economic reality, however, tells you that what you buy today can't be paid for in 30 days because as an initial stocking order most of it is still on your shelf when the bill falls due.

Now if you're in the game to play it crooked, load up, sell out, and skip to Guatemala, there's no problem—unless you someday wish to return to the U.S. and the waiting arms of the Federal Marshal. But that's not what you or this book is about. You want to build a solid respectable business, and between that reality and the reality that you won't be able to timely pay for your opening inventory lies our problem. So how do you handle it? The options are few.

One approach is the buy now—pay later (much later) strategy. Essentially, what you do is buy on 30-day credit terms, and then dribble your suppliers as much as you can afford—and as little as they'll patiently wait for until your bill is paid. Without initially realizing it your suppliers provided you with long-term inventory financing. That's precisely how most shoestring start-ups go about it. Generally, replacement orders are paid COD and as long as the initial order is being systematically—albeit slowly—reduced, creditors usually do wait for their money. The morality of it all aside—shoestring entrepreneurs accurately say that if they requested a two- or three-year payout on the initial order they'd never obtain credit clearance. When you're talking about secondary suppliers and a $1000–2000 order they're usually right. Small suppliers aren't inclined to grant generous credit terms and they certainly don't see themselves financing your bootstrap operation.

The problem with this rob-Peter-to-pay-Paul approach is its impact on credit rating. You have to build your business for the long haul and that means building supplier confidence right from the start. In short, suppliers can understand bootstrap financing and will even live with it, but you have to bring an even-handed honesty to the situation.

Here's a tempered approach that does work.

1. Try to negotiate extended credit terms for the initial order. Don't ask for two years. As I stated before, you won't get it. However, many secondary suppliers will give you three to six months "dating" if you push for it. They understand why you need it and when they grant it they're acknowledging their willingness to help you get started. When you can't pay on time there's no surprise or resentment. The supplier has been programmed to think in extended terms and it's not difficult to extend the terms a bit more.
2. Always communicate with your supplier when the bill falls due. This is the key point. Don't let them come chasing you. In my first Discount City venture I had $96,000 in payables fall due one month after I opened. What money I had, I needed for operating expenses and to replenish what was sold during that first month. But I did have about $6000 I could pay on my opening stock and it was even more money than I expected to have available. Spending three days on the phone I contacted each of the 47 creditors owed the $96,000, proposing future orders be on COD and so much per month on the back bill. Some blustered, some threatened, but most went along with it. Surprisingly, of the 47 creditors, 38 gave me no trouble at all. The big reason was that I was now buying COD. I may have owed a given supplier $3000 on the opening order, but in the course of a year I may buy—and pay for—another $15,000 in replacement goods. The monies due on the initial order suddenly become a small part of the total equation.

I've discovered another strategy that can work for you. Don't break the bad news all at once. Work it in gently. For example, a supplier owed $3000 would be told that I'd pay $100 for each of the next three months and by then I hoped to bank finance (I knew it was futile). To the creditor it began to look like a three-month problem, although I knew it would be a two- or three-year "problem." But in the intervening three months I faithfully bought and faithfully paid. When I called again three months later to say bank financing was bleak, but why not continue for another six months it was all anticlimactic. The resistance was gone.

3. I mentioned bank financing to replace short-term trade debt, and it is an excellent idea. Some people will look for bank financing to buy inventory and be turned down for lack of collateral. It's a "Catch-22." You don't have the money so you can't buy the collateral (inventory). But once you have the inventory for collateral, some banks will be interested. In any event, you do owe it to your suppliers—and your credit reputation and cash flow—to try.
4. Return goods help pacify creditors. Your opening inventory may consist of thousands of dollars in slow movers that aren't working for you. Send it back for credit, but when you do it, simultaneously push for extended terms on any balance owed. You're in a better bargaining position before you return the goods than after. Creditors always look at return goods as a sign of good faith. Once you do it your creditor realizes it's only a cash flow "workout" rather than dealing with a crook or con artist with larceny in his heart.

What will it take to make it through the first year or two while you do a juggling act with your creditors? Everyone seems to have an answer based on personal experiences. Elliot Galahow, an accountant and consultant to leveraged start-up firms, says, "Realistic cash flow projections are the most important item. If the business starts on a profitable level, and continues to turn over its payables, suppliers will wait it out through the survival stage. All the suppliers want is the light at the end of the tunnel." Jeff Kosberg, an attorney involved in small business bankruptcies, claims the decisive factor is communication and developing a supplier relationship. "A retailer, for example, will start with too much short-term debt and panic. Rather than work up a payment plan and sell it to his suppliers he hides while the creditors gang up on him and push him out of business. The smartest thing a businessman in this position can do is hire a bookkeeper or comptroller for a few hours a week to deal with the suppliers," adds Kosberg.

It's good advice. However, success goes beyond tactics. When it's your suppliers' money on the shelf, you can't afford a false start. Show your suppliers a winning business and they'll work and build with you.

TACKLING THE ONE BIG SUPPLIER

Most businesses rely on one principal supplier to bankroll anywhere from 40–80% of the opening inventory. It's as common as corn in Kansas. Drug wholesalers provide about 70% of the merchandise for fledgling pharmacies. Hardware wholesalers do about the same for hardware stores. Liquor wholesalers score higher, oftentimes providing 80% of the stock for their retail liquor customers and small food stores frequently buy all their merchandise from one wholesale source. Even clothing stores, noted for their diverse lines, may end up buying the bulk of their inventory from one supplier. Chances are your business will lean on one principal supplier for most of the beginning inventory. That's the supplier who requires very special handling. Unlike your small secondary suppliers, your primary supplier is a breed apart and will take a much harder look at your business.

Can you convince a primary supplier to gamble and ship an opening inventory on credit? Absolutely. But let me qualify it. You'll need a proposition that makes sense and a proposition that makes sense is one with a big benefit and a small risk.

"Wholesalers are in business to sell goods," says Sam Roseman, 57, a newborn entrepreneur with his six-month-old convenience store in a Nashua, New Hampshire, suburb. "If they won't work with you on an opening inventory there has to be a good reason."

Sam knows what he's talking about. In fact, he had three wholesalers bidding for the privilege to stock his store.

Sam's story unfolded when he was laid off for the third time in five years from his position as a cost analyst for an engineering firm. He selected food retailing because it was a business he knew something about, enjoyed, and could get his family involved in. "Besides," adds Sam, "a food store is one of the easier and safer businesses to enter." At first Sam considered several franchised food stores including "7–11" and some offered by local supermarket chains. Although the franchises offered financing, Sam decided he didn't want to put up with franchisor control.

"Money was my problem," Sam recalls. "I had $10,000 and it was only enough to buy used fixtures and refrigerated units, with a few thousand left for rent and other start-up costs. But what I did have was a lease for an excellent location and the drive to make it work. Turning to several food wholesalers I found they were interested in stocking the store on 100% credit. I finally negotiated a deal with a Rhode Island wholesaler who makes weekly deliveries to New Hampshire. He agreed to stock me with an opening $35,000 inventory, financed over four years at 16%, secured by a mortgage on the inventory and my personal guarantee. The only other proviso is that I buy at least 70% of my products from him and pay current. But that's no problem. My only other vendors are paperback books, newspapers, a tobacco jobber, and my milk supplier. It was a great deal for me because it put me in business. It was not a bad one for my wholesaler either. He's selling me $300,000 a year in merchandise and can't really lose on his $35,000 investment."

I have seen hundreds of businesses in virtually every merchandising line sponsored by a principal supplier anxious to "buy" a new customer. Many of my own businesses depended on one or two suppliers for their start. And as Sam Roseman found out, there is always the right way to put their goods on your shelf. Try these tips:

1. Negotiate with every major wholesaler who could qualify as your primary supplier. Don't limit yourself. You never know which one will give you the best deal until you knock

all their doors. It's no different than shopping for a new car. Shop!

2. The best time to shop is *after* you have the location lined up. Don't sign the lease until your merchandise is committed, but the location still comes first. Reason? Suppliers base credit largely on their assessment of the location and the sales and profits it can produce.
3. Put your proposal together *before* you shop for merchandise. Your business plan should be as detailed as what an investor or banker would expect. Your supplier's investment is no smaller so why should you tell him less? Your plan should include a proposed layout, description of operations (hours, staffing, pricing, promotion), and financial projections and budget for two years. This is an important step. It not only shows what your business is about, but shows what you know about the business. The reason goes deeper. Your supplier also knows something about the business. He can offer plenty of ideas and criticisms. Pick his brain and make him your free consultant.
4. Meet with the top man. An opening inventory of $30,000–50,000 is not an everyday credit decision, and credit managers may not have the clout to make the decision or want the risk of the decision. Sometimes they lack the initiative to check with someone who can decide. It only takes a phone call to briefly explain why you're calling and to invite the president of the firm to dinner. A word of caution. If you know the sales manager or credit manager, try to work through them. Protocol is important.
5. Define what you need in opening inventory. Reduce it to dollar amounts and a description of the lines or type merchandise you need. Be prepared to defend the quantity as it's also a test of your managerial know-how. The lines are important because the profit margins vary from line to line. A supplier doesn't want you to "sharpshoot" by using him only for the low-profit lines while you shop the "gravy" items elsewhere.
6. Start selling the benefit—and the benefit is your future

buying. For example, if you project $400,000 in sales, a supplier may translate that into $200,000 a year in purchases. While he's enjoying his Steak Diane, he's focusing on the $200,000-a-year account you represent. That's the carrot. Now back it up. Commit yourself to future buying. Reduce it to a committed percentage of what you would buy from a wholesaler. For example, if you know that you'll buy 70% of your stock from a wholesaler you may agree to give him all your wholesale purchases except for 10% which may go to back up suppliers. How does your wholesaler know you'll live up to it? He doesn't. And your wholesaler can't force you to buy from him once you have his opening inventory. What you can do is put it in writing and if you default on your buying agreement he can immediately call for full payment on the opening inventory. It's an important point. Your wholesaler isn't in the finance business. He's giving you credit for your opening stock to "buy" your future business. Convince him he'll get it.

7. Don't be a "captive" customer. You'll agree to buy most of your product from the supplier, but you expect the same prices, allowances, advertising rebates, and promotional concessions as any other "cash" customer buying in comparable quantity. Some suppliers will "lock you in" and take away discounts, etc. It's not only unfair, but you can't afford it. Make sure you're buying right.
8. The payback period is a negotiable item. Two to four years is the average, but the economics of your business and its cash flow is the determining factor. Have your accountant decide this item and work it out with the supplier.
9. Interest? Most suppliers charge 18–24% on overdue accounts. Although this too is a negotiable item, you should be charged a lower rate because it's a financed inventory rather than an overdue account. Most suppliers borrow at prime rate, considering their size, and a fair compromise is to pay 2–3% above what your supplier pays to borrow.
10. Security. This is the key to reduced risk. Your supplier should be offered a mortgage on all inventory. If you

default he has first claim on the inventory to recoup what's owed. His central concern will be a depleted inventory if foreclosure is necessary. An effective safeguard is to suggest a written provision that you'll maintain a defined minimum inventory. A shrewd supplier may enhance the value of the collateral by taking an assignment of lease besides. Upon foreclosure he not only gets the inventory but the location as well. It's not unreasonable, but as with all legal documents, have your counsel check it out. Should you guarantee the account? If it's your first business venture, you probably will have to. After you have a track record it's a bargaining point.

Study these points. How can the supplier lose? George Maloof, President of New England Wholesale Drug Company, admits that it's difficult to say "no" to such a proposal. "Many times a young pharmacist will come to us to stock him for a new drug store. We evaluate it in terms of our own profits from the account. If we see him buying $200,000 a year from us, we may make $20,000–25,000 a year profit. We'll almost always grant an opening inventory of $30,000–40,000 on the strength of its profit potential if it does make it, and the strength of our security if it doesn't. Sure, the business may fail a year or two later but we invariably recoup what's owed. If we don't, it's a small loss compared to the potential it initially offered."

That's what they all say once you show them how to look at your winning idea.

CONSIGNMENTS ARE AS GOOD AS CASH

Many businesses don't start by buying goods. What they do is look for merchandise they can sell on consignment. It's a natural for a shoestring start-up and works well in a large number of businesses. It particularly flourishes in the clothing, shoe, furniture, housewares, appliance, and stereo industries and can work in any field with high unit sales and is competitive at the manufacturers' level.

What makes consignment sales so attractive is the fact that the supplier takes no risk. As you sell the goods you take your percentage and remit the difference to the supplier. Until the goods are sold, the seller retains title. If you fail or close up shop the supplier only has to step in and remove his goods. And it's that lack of risk that induces a supplier to provide goods to any logical retailer who can move the goods, bypassing the nasty concerns of credit or cash.

Lancaster Dress used consignment merchandise for its start, and now that it can afford to buy, it still adheres to its successful consignment merchandising program. Started in 1979, Lancaster could hardly buy the inexpensive racks for its first Phoenix, Arizona, location. Inventory was a bigger problem. Without cash or credit the New York houses would only ship token orders. It wasn't enough for a successful start. That's when Lancaster's owners, Scott and Mary Hempstead, grabbed a plane to New York and spotted a dress manufacturer with a bulging warehouse. "We convinced the manufacturer the dresses had a better chance of selling in our store than in his dusty warehouse," says Scott Hempstead, "and the manufacturer agreed. We didn't want to buy the dresses outright, as we didn't know how well they'd sell. It equally suited the manufacturer who didn't want a long-term financing arrangement. So he shipped $40,000 worth of dresses on a strict consignment basis. We discount the dresses by 20% and once a week remit the cost on what we sell together with an accounting. This year our sales are up to $2,400,000, and we now buy on consignment from 20 manufacturers in the ladies apparel lines. It's a great feeling to know you can build a multi-million dollar business without investing a dime of your own money or credit on merchandise."

The only way to find consignment merchandise is with an active search. Invariably it will lead you to the doors of manufacturers with excess inventory that for a variety of reasons can't be quickly sold for cash through normal channels. You have to put them in the consignment business by showing the benefits—and how it will turn their excess inventory into cash. Frequently a supplier will ask you to take a smaller markup, considering you aren't buying the merchandise outright, but a slightly higher price shouldn't stop you. You're still working on 100% of his money.

Art galleries are masters at consignment deals. The typical art gallery may have 60–100% of the pictures on the walls placed there by hungry artists willing to be paid when the painting is sold. A friend of mine opened a retail store that I can't even describe. It sells Near-Eastern "anything." It started with about $2000 in Mediterranean-style clothes and since expanded to feature oriental rugs, brass accessories, jewelry, and even art works depicting the Middle East. Some came from suppliers and some from artists or individuals cleaning out their attic. But it's all there—$60,000 worth—and it's all there on consignment.

A burgeoning retail industry is the "consignment shop" itself, where people bring used clothing, toys, or "what-have-you" for whatever it will fetch. It's the entrepreneurs' way of moving the garage sale out of the garage and into their own store.

Big or small, hard goods or soft goods, if it can be sold it can be sold on consignment. It's high on the list for every shoestring merchant.

HOW TO FIND MERCHANDISE AT ROCK-BOTTOM PRICES

I love auctions. Where else can you pick up good salable inventory for as little as a dime on the dollar? It's the next best thing to stealing it.

How many start-up ventures actually start when an entrepreneur with a few dollars in his pocket shows up at somebody else's broken dream and walks away with a truckload of inventory to nourish his own dream? Plenty.

That's how I got into my first greeting card and gift shop business. Spotting the bankruptcy ad in the newspaper, I showed up on a snowy winter day more out of curiosity than interest. My interest peaked when I realized that I'd be the high bidder for $40,000 in good merchandise for $6300. So I bought, negotiated a new lease, sold a half interest to a working partner for $15,000, and considered it one of my best investments.

It's particularly smart to look for auction merchandise as your "merchandise core." You may find $10,000–15,000 in good merchandise as your foundation and build from there with trade credit. And it will help you get trade credit because you have a healthy percentage of what you need to begin with.

Here's a useful tip to consider. You don't actually have to attend an auction to buy for a dime on the dollar. Auctions are conducted for bankruptcy trustees, receivers, and foreclosing banks. If you know a business is going up for auction in the near future, you can negotiate to buy the inventory at private sale without an auction, but at the appraised auction value. It will give you first crack at some very good buys once you let auctioneers know what you're interested in.

Other sources of good merchandise at the right price?

Try manufacturers' closeouts. New York is the mecca for this type merchandise and you may need contacts. Allied Buying Service and Affiliated Buying Service are two recommended buying agents who can put you in touch with the right companies.

Twice a year the merchandising "show of shows" is held at the Chicago Navy Pier. Over 5000 manufacturers, peddling everything for any line business (except clothing), offer merchandise at 20–40% less than you can buy through a middleman. All the chain buyers are there but you don't need a chain to buy. They'll sell in small quantities to a one-store owner. Considering the great deals it's amazing more independents don't take advantage of it.

There are several publications listing closeout, distress, and liquidation merchandise. The one I recommend is published by the American Entrepreneurs' Association. Write them at:

AEA Research
2311 Pontius Avenue
Los Angeles, CA 90064

SOME IMAGINATION PLEASE!

How many ways are there for landing merchandise with little or no cash or credit? Countless ways. This chapter only scratched the surface. The opportunities extend only to the limits of your imagination. And some people have great imaginations, and with it start some very unusual businesses.

Ron Humphrey built a $400,000-a-year toy business with his

own stroke of imagination. Hundreds of woodworking hobbyists turn out wooden planes, ships, trains, and assorted delights for the kiddie set following Ron's specifications. Ron buys their output on 90-day terms, assured that the merchandise will sell long before then.

When IBM turned Hank Jensen down for credit to open a typewriter sales store, the undaunted Jensen opened a used typewriter and office equipment business. Sending out 20,000 flyers to office firms, Hank soon had $160,000 in used typewriters to sell on consignment.

My favorite story involves two young chaps who never did quite make it as shoestring merchants. But they're not complaining. The Winslow brothers took over the lease on an abandoned 20,000-sq.-ft. supermarket spending their last dime in the process. All that came with the lease was an assortment of abandoned fixtures. The business needed $200,000 in merchandise, and that was $200,000 more than what the Winslow boys had to spend. Bypassing the credit approach, the Winslows shrewdly decided to let others do the merchandising while they collected rent. So they concessioned the meat department to a local butcher, the bakery department to a bakery firm, groceries to a grocery wholesaler, and one by one the tenants—and their merchandise—began to fill the place. The Winslows operated the checkout, crediting sales to the various concessionaires while keeping 10% to cover rent and advertising costs. Last year the Winslows showed a net profit of $70,000 for themselves—and never sold a nickel's worth of their own merchandise.

What I remember most about the Winslows was not what they did, but what Jack Winslow once said. "If someone isn't clever or imaginative enough to get the merchandise, they won't be imaginative enough to sell it."

There's a bit of truth to it.

KEY POINTS TO REMEMBER

1. A healthy start-up needs the merchandise to give it the successful start.

2. Expand your sights to include lines from suppliers who will give you credit, rather than limit yourself to suppliers who may not.
3. The easiest credit sources are your small secondary suppliers, provided you follow some basic rules.
4. Design a winning proposal for your one primary supplier. Sell the big benefit and low risk, and he'll soon sell you your opening inventory.
5. Don't overlook consignment goods. It's one of the most popular ways to give your start-up the products to sell.
6. If you have cash to spend then spend it wisely. Bargain-priced merchandise is everywhere—if you know where to look.
7. Use your imagination. You'll need it to sell what you do buy.

10

A BLUEPRINT FOR BUYING A BUSINESS

Name your business. Whether it's an accounting service or a zipper factory, you have the inevitable decision to make. You can start from scratch as you may be planning—or take a short cut and buy an existing business. And many bootstrap entrepreneurs are discovering the fastest, easiest path to becoming their own boss is through acquisition instead of the tortured route of building from the ground up.

Flirting with the idea of a buyout isn't switching gears or chilling your creative spirits. You have one objective—to get into your own business with as little cash as possible. Buying a business *can* be a strategic alternative to starting, and as Barry Levine, an acquisition consultant counsels: "Buying may be even wiser than creating when you consider the dozens of businesses available in every field begging for a fast takeover. It's indeed a bootstrap entrepreneur's playground."

BUY OR CREATE?

The debate continues. Which is better—to buy or create a business? There's no one right answer as the decision rests on the facts of a given situation. I have started nine businesses and purchased ten. I now know that I should have bought some of the former and started some of the latter. However, you should expect an acquisition to offer these advantages:

1. *Less Risk:* This may be the most important reason why so many people prefer to buy. The established business has a track record. You know its sales and profits and you can reasonably predict what the business will do for you. A start-up is guesswork at best and you never know how it will perform until after it's in operation. The statistics prove the point. Businesses in operation for five years fail at the rate of 20% within the following five years, while new companies face an 80% failure rate.

   Many entrepreneurs take a split approach, buying their first venture and expanding through start-ups. With an established business behind them they have the base to support a start-up gamble. And as so many report, it's safer to learn the ropes with a going concern that can absorb managerial error. Consider the possibilities.
2. *Faster Cash:* The going concern has its sales base and cash flow working for you from the first day. Even if the business is operating at a loss you do have a sales threshold to build from. In contrast, the start-up may have sizable losses until sales do reach the break-even point. This can be a key consideration in many lines of businesses with a predictably slow sales curve. As you've seen in Chapter 3, the most common start-up error is inability to gauge the losses until profitable sales can be reached with the resultant inability to fund the losses. "Everyone's an optimist," says Ray Johnson, who in 1981 opened his Strathmore Press, a small printing plant serving the large printing plants for short-run subcontract work. "We needed $20,000 a month to break even and thought we'd hit it within two months. We were wrong. Nine months later we folded with our best month at $8000." Ray adds this pointer, "Don't start unless you can realistically assess how long it will take to reach profitability and can keep the business afloat until you do. If you're shaky on the projections you're smarter to buy a

business and pay the premium for the privilege of solid sales."

3. *Easier Entry:* It takes a very special breed of entrepreneur to put together a start-up venture. Whipping together a physical plant, employees, suppliers, and customers may look easy but many entrepreneurs go through several false starts before realizing their best approach is to take over a going concern. "You have to understand your creative level," recounts Bob Kuzara who started several firms. "While some people enjoy the challenge of piecing together an enterprise, many others consider it too burdensome an obstacle, and will only venture into business if they're handed the keys."

   In a very real sense the decision to buy or create is not based on the numbers but on the personality of the individual. For every entrepreneur who enjoys the innovation, planning and maneuvering to put together a business, there are three others who lack the self-confidence and momentum. Perhaps only one person in ten is equally comfortable with either approach.
4. *Lower Cost:* You may be able to buy an existing business for even less than it would cost to duplicate the tangible assets under a start-up. One reason so many people avoid considering an acquisition is because they erroneously believe buying is more expensive. In many cases it's true as sellers of a profitable company will want a premium for good will. But there are the exceptions, particularly with the troubled firm with turnaround potential that can oftentimes be picked up for a fraction of the value of the tangible assets. One of my best buys was a large discount store with a $150,000 inventory and $30,000 worth of fixtures picked up for the bargain price of $120,000. It would have cost me substantially more to buy these assets on the open market. You can save money with the *right* acquisition.
5. *Better Financing:* You can win better financing with an existing business. Banks and other lenders have more con-

fidence lending to the established business and you have many more sources of "built in" financing available with an acquisition. I consider financing one of the most favorable advantages of buying, and later in this chapter you'll see how and why you can bootstrap yourself into an existing business with little or no cash of your own.

When should you discard the idea of buying a business in favor of starting from scratch? When you have a very unique or different business format in mind and can't find a matching business for sale. Traditional businesses are always a candidate for a takeover and even if you plan operational changes it usually doesn't take much to alter the format of the business to match what you want the business to be. And the advantages that came with buying can still make it your best move.

Years ago I faced the "buy or create" dilemma for my first pharmacy. If I wanted a traditional drugstore I probably would have preferred to buy, but what I had in mind was anything but traditional. My plan was to set up a prescription shop without the typical front store merchandise and sell prescriptions at wholesale cost plus a $1.00 dispensing fee. I had the plan down to a science and even had the name "Cost-Plus Pharmacies" trademarked. Buying an existing pharmacy and converting it to what I wanted would have been a waste of money since we'd have to tear out fixtures, discard most of the inventory, and renovate to our own specifications. Obviously, it made more sense to start with a clean slate.

Essentially the buy or create decision is a competitive process as you weigh the benefits of each against the realities of what the marketplace has to offer. It's not unusual to find entrepreneurs intending to create only to come across an attractive acquisition, just as it's not unusual to find a corresponding number who consider themselves buyers until they see the price tags sellers place on their business.

I will, however, offer this advice. Don't make the decision to start from scratch until you have thoroughly checked out available businesses. It's the only way you can compare the trade-offs and decide your right path.

PROFITABLE BUSINESS FOR SALE: NO CASH DOWN

Ask 100 shoestring entrepreneurs why they decided to create rather than buy a business and 95 will tell you, "I couldn't afford the down payment to buy. The only way I could get into business was to set up shop from scratch." Would you give the same answer? If so, this may be your most important chapter because the buy or create decision can only be intelligently made when you have all the facts. And the facts are:

1. You *can* buy any size or type business with absolutely no cash of your own.
2. You *will* find it considerably easier to *buy* without cash than to *start* without cash.

Admittedly it's difficult to sell that message to people who have been conditioned to think it takes more money to buy than to create from scratch. And why shouldn't people be conditioned to think that way? Have you ever seen a business advertised for sale on no cash down terms? Ever hear of such a deal from a business broker? Of course not. But ask yourself one more question. How many business acquisitions are you familiar with?

I can tell you from firsthand experience of at least 240 no cash down transactions and thousands more where very little money exchanged hands. I've acquired ten of my own businesses, and my largest personal investment was $1000. And several of my acquisitions had price tags in excess of $100,000. How many others share my experience? I estimate that 50% of all small businesses could be rapidly sold with absolutely no cash investment from the buyer and still satisfy all the seller's objectives.

It's too common a story. A seller will put his business on the market for $50,000 and ask for a $25,000 down payment. They don't ask the important question: "Will buyers with $25,000 be interested in my business? Can a qualified buyer with little or no cash satisfy my objectives and help me sell quicker?"

For their part, buyers who listen to such demands reason that they can't qualify for the business with only $5000 in available cash and never ask: "Could I both satisfy the seller and buy the business with only $5000? Do I really need $25,000?"

And so it goes, sellers want to sell and buyers want to buy but few know how to swing the no cash down deal.

YOU CAN BUY ON 100% TERMS

How many ways are there to achieve 100% leverage in a business acquisition? I can tell you at least 200 proven techniques you can use to close the gap between price and your meager bank account. Used in combination the possibilities of a cashless takeover are endless. In my own book *Own Your Own/The No Cash Down Business Guide* (Prentice-Hall, 1983) I uncover the strategies in detail and show how others bought their profitable business with little or no cash down. I'll highlight a few of the more common methods in this chapter to give you the broad picture, but if you do have a strong interest in buying a business as an alternative to starting one, then *Own Your Own* should be on your reading list.

In *Own Your Own* I advise readers that it is far easier to buy on short cash than create a new business. I offer two reasons: (1) The existing business typically provides its own built-in financing for 70% to 100% of the purchase price. (2) And when you do have to scout the few final dollars to complete the financing package you have many more sources and alternatives than you do with a new venture.

Jim Corcoran can show you the anatomy of a cashless takeover. Jim is one entrepreneur who didn't back away when he came across a Steak and Ale restaurant selling for $100,000 in Frisco's Bay area. The seller refused to assist in financing, leaving Jim with a $100,000 problem considering he had no cash of his own to invest. Rolling up his sleeves, Jim designed his own 100% financing plan.

"The large dollars come easiest," says Jim, who quickly found a bank sufficiently impressed with the history of the business to lend $60,000 payable over five years. That chipped the balance down to $40,000.

The next strategy was for Jim to inquire about existing liabilities owed by the business. The seller acknowledged that the business owed $20,000 to creditors which the seller would be obligated to pay at the time of closing. Jim had a better idea. Jim would assume the liabilities and deduct it from the purchase price. Why shouldn't the seller agree? It was only money he'd otherwise have to part with when the business was sold. Now Jim only needed $20,000 to close.

The last dollars to put together a deal are always the hardest, but Jim gradually whittled away at the elusive $20,000 to close the gap. The business broker, due to a $10,000 commission on the deal, helped by lending $5000 from his commission to save the sale.

Knocking on the doors of several suppliers found some additional money. A meat supplier selling over $100,000 a year to the business considered a $5000 cash loan a good investment to maintain good will, followed by another $5000 loan from the cigarette vending machine firm anxious to maintain its machines at the profitable location. Now Jim had $95,000 in financing locked up and needed only $5000 to close. The solution was found in some used kitchen equipment that would be Jim's when he purchased the business. With a few phone calls Jim found a buyer to take out the excess equipment at the time of sale in return for $5000. The final scorecard:

$ 60,000	bank financing
20,000	assumed liabilities
5,000	broker loan
10,000	supplier loans
5,000	sale of excess assets
$100,000	

The results?

The seller enjoyed the same net cash he would have received had Jim walked in with $100,000 of his own money.

The broker salvaged his commission.

The creditors don't care who pays them.

The supplier loans guaranteed the suppliers strong profits for many years to come.

These strategies do work, and many of my own leveraged acquisitions come together in much the same way. The important points to review are:

1. Buying a business on no cash down terms does not necessarily mean that the seller ends up with no cash at the closing. As you can see from this case, the seller cashed out with all his money and with seller financing the process of achieving 100% leverage can be even easier.
2. With an acquisition you can readily find 60–80% of the purchase price with bank, SBA, or seller financing. The focus is always on the remaining 20–40%—that portion of the acquisition price typically represented by the down payment.
3. There are countless ways to find and use sources of capital other than your own to achieve 100% financing.

FINDING THE LARGEST DOLLARS

Your first objective is to cement 60–70% of the financing with the large dollars that can be routinely financed with bank and/or seller financing.

Earlier in this book we discussed bank financing in terms of funding a shoestring start-up, and I pointed out that although bank financing is always a possibility with a start-up, it's seldom a priority source because both collateral and a track record are missing.

An existing business will catch a banker's eye and it's particularly so with a business with collateral to offer. A survey of 100 recent acquisitions in our area shows that bank financing represented on average 58% of the purchase price, and in several transactions the banks financed over 80% for buyers with apparently few assets of their own to pledge as collateral.

Your one best source of financing on an acquisition is the seller himself. In the vast majority of the leveraged takeovers I've been involved in, the seller agrees to finance anywhere from 30–80% of the purchase price and I've had several deals where we convinced a seller to go the whole route and provide 100% financing. Sellers, of course, usually resist self-financing preferring to cash out, leaving you to scurry to outside sources for financing. It's always a pipe dream for a seller anxious to unload a business pitted against a buyer wise enough to call their bluff.

Why do you want to negotiate for seller financing?

1. Sellers will finance more of the purchase price. While a bank may stop at 60%, you may be able to push a seller for 70–80% financing.
2. You'll win better terms from a seller. Banks may charge 16–18% for a small business loan (based on a current 11% prime rate), but many sellers will agree to a 10–12% interest rate. Don't forget the seller's motive in financing is to help sell the business and not make money on the interest. The length of the note is another factor. Banks seldom finance for longer than five years, while sellers may agree to 7–10-year terms. I know of several cases where a seller accepted a 20-year payout, considering it a form of annuity.
3. You'll need less collateral to back up the loan. Banks typically try to obtain personal collateral to add to the collateral the business can offer. However, sellers are content to accept the business assets as security.

A smart strategy is to pyramid seller financing on top of bank financing. A seller, for example, may say, "I'll sell the business for $100,000 and finance $50,000 of the price." Once the seller holds a first mortgage on the business you can no longer go to a bank expecting the same security. The tactic then is to counteroffer that you'll obtain $50,000 in bank financing if the seller will instead accept a second mortgage on the business for $20,000–30,000. While the seller will be in a slightly weaker position coming behind the bank in terms of security, the seller may be sold on the advantage of financing less in return for more upfront cash for himself. But you can see the benefit for yourself in terms of having 70–80% of the financing through the combination of both bank and seller financing. And when you do have 80% of the money can the other 20% be far behind?

LOOK FOR THE LIABILITIES

The one valuable financing block that both sellers and buyers overlook is the debts of the business. In most cases a seller will quote a required down payment sufficient to paydown existing liabilities, and in many cases the lion's share of the down payment is earmarked for creditors. Oftentimes you can substantially slash a down payment by assuming the liabilities and turning the money owed creditors into a source of built-in financing. It's a very common and workable technique. Several of my own deals have been substantially self-financed by taking over the seller's liabilities.

The near-bankrupt business offers its own interesting possibilities. In your travels you'll come across businesses that owe so much money that you can walk in without investing a dime. In fact, companies in trouble can present fabulous opportunities for no cash takeovers. Some the very best deals involve companies just one short step from the auctioneer's hammer. Sellers are usually willing to let you take over the business just to rid themselves of what they see as a problem business or perhaps in exchange for a token payment or even a job.

I'm always on the lookout for troubled companies with turnaround potential and quickly channel them to shoestring entrepreneurs with the skill to straighten them out. And the right owner in the right business can do wonders. One recent example was a client who picked up a grocery superette grossing $400,000 a year, floundering under $120,000 in trade debt. So without a dime to his name he acquired the shares of stock in the near-defunct corporation and threw the business into a Chapter 11 Bankruptcy reorganization settling the debts for $40,000 paid over three years. He now tells me he can sell the same business for over $100,000 and pocket $60,000 in equity. That's not bad when you consider he walked into the deal with neither cash or personal risk. And it's done every day.

Shoestring entrepreneurs are natural candidates for the troubled business because the management skills needed to handle the insolvent firm are very much the same as those needed to walk the financial tightrope of a shoestring start-up. Ken Barron, who has leveraged his way into both start-ups and acquisitions, reasons, "If you're the type who can start from zero and accumulate $100,000 in assets and $100,000 in liabilities to build a business and make it work, then you're the same type to inherit the same shaky business from someone who can't make it work."

Ken's not the only one who knows how to turn a seller's nightmare into a personal fortune. Lurking in every area and line of business are other shrewd entrepreneurs waiting to grab the floundering business they can mold into a money-making machine with no personal investment. It may also be your smart alternative to a shoestring start-up.

A creative buyer and willing seller can always manipulate debt levels to cover a buyer's cash short position. In one of our recent cases a business was selling for $90,000. The seller agreed to finance $60,000 and allow the buyer to assume $15,000 in existing liabilities owed trade suppliers. However, the seller insisted on $15,000 in "walk-away" cash, which was $15,000 more than the buyer had. The solution? The seller agreed to increase the debts by an additional $15,000, taking the money out of the business instead of paying creditors; while the creditors became the unwitting financiers for the cashless buyer.

The technique of using existing liabilities must be looked at from the perspective of the buyer, the seller, and the creditors. The buyer's objective is to use liabilities in place of his own cash. The buyer's corresponding concern is how much short-term debt can the business safely handle?

The seller is primarily concerned with protection from creditor recourse, should the liabilities remain unpaid. The creditors for their part must be willing to both allow the buyer to assume the debts and provide the time for the paydown of anything beyond normal trade debt levels.

While the respective interests can usually be protected by legal agreements and indemnifications, it's the buyer who must take the initiative and ask, "Why not allow the existing business debts to take the place of my own money?"

SQUEEZE CASH FROM CASH FLOW

There are hundreds of ways to squeeze the cash flow of an existing business to take the place of a down payment.

You've seen how increasing liabilities can free up cash for a seller. You can accomplish the same objective by reducing inventories. For example, a business may be selling for $100,000 based on an inventory of $60,000. If the inventory at the time of sale is only $50,000 the price is reduced to $90,000. But couldn't the $10,000 reduction be deducted from the down payment portion of the price? Of course. The strategy then is to negotiate your deal so the seller intentionally liquidates part of the inventory in advance of the sale using the generated cash to replace all or part of your down payment.

Another example. Accounts receivable may be included as part of the price. Whenever I come across a deal involving receivables I negotiate for the seller to retain the receivables and deduct its value from the down payment of its reduced price.

Cash flow can help you in other ways. I can tell you about a buyer who could only raise $260,000 towards a $300,000 price on a supermarket. The buyer candidly told the seller he was short $40,000 and offered to issue four $10,000 post-dated checks, dated one week apart. Until the checks cleared the seller could hold the closing documents in escrow. It was no magic trick to cover the checks from a business grossing $60,000 a week. Many sellers will allow you to tap cash flow *after* you take over the business to squeeze the last few dollars needed to push the sale through.

One advantage of the going business is that it can be shaped in so many ways to create cash for a seller without need for buyers digging into their own pockets.

To show you just how these techniques can come together to satisfy both a seller and buyer I have only to tell you about one of my best acquisitions—a large cosmetic shop in the western suburbs of Connecticut. The seller was asking $120,000 for the business, free of liabilities and with $60,000 down. In addition, the seller guaranteed an inventory at closing of $80,000. With conventional haggling we negotiated the price down to $110,000 and then began to negotiate the deal that would provide 100% financing. Here's how we put our financing blocks together.

1. The seller originally agreed to finance $60,000 for three years at 15% interest. It was a start. Although we managed to negotiate the term to five years at 12%.
2. The business had $15,000 in liabilities and the seller agreed to our assuming the debt; however, we asked him to increase it to $25,000 and take out $10,000 from the business that would otherwise go to maintain liabilities at their current level. With his consent we now had $85,000 in financing.
3. We didn't need a $90,000 inventory to profitably operate the business. We estimated the inventory to be overstated by $20,000 so we bargained for the seller to reduce inventory by the $20,000 and cut the price—and our down payment—by the same amount. So now we had $85,000 toward a reduced price of $90,000.
4. The final $5000 was the easiest part. As part of the deal we would be acquiring the prepaid utility deposits and insurance premiums, which amounted to $7000. Since the business had established credit with the electric and telephone companies, they agreed to return the $5200 in deposits which we turned over to the seller to complete the $90,000 financing.

There was a postscript to the story. Included in the sale was a $9000 Buick sedan. At the closing the seller asked if he could buy the car from the business, which we happily agreed to. We actually walked out of the closing with not only a business grossing $420,000 a year—without spending a dime of our own—but pocketed $9000 in cash besides.

It may all appear a bit too breezy and pie-in-the-sky for you, but believe me deals such as this do exist, and smart buyers know the right buttons to press to shape a business into a no cash down situation.

HIDDEN ASSETS MEAN HIDDEN MONEY

We've only scratched the surface. One of the best ways to find your down payment is to uncover hidden assets within the business that can be turned into instant cash.

It's a four-step strategy:

1. Locate any business asset you can sell, borrow against, exploit, or turn into instant cash.
2. Arrange the sale, lease, or money raising transaction in *advance* of the sale, but make it conditional upon the sale.
3. Coordinate the transaction to closing the sale so you can use the money to fund your acquisition.
4. Make certain it's an asset you will have the legal right to sell, rather than assets mortgaged under the financing plan.

Now with the basic strategy behind us, let's see what assets are the best money-raising candidates. Here's a checklist to consider:

1. Excess equipment.
2. Customer lists.
3. Patent rights.
4. Trademarks or copyrights.
5. Excess motor vehicles.
6. Cash surrender business life insurance.
7. Pension funds.
8. Sublet or concessional space.
9. Advertising space.
10. Credits due from suppliers.

In *Own Your Own* I listed these top ten cash generating assets and several months after the book was published I received a letter from a chap in Illinois who told me he successfully used his own list of 93 potential assets to cannibalize for a down payment. In his letter he tells how he once managed to take over a tire and muffler shop for absolutely no cash of his own by pre-selling 20,000 discarded used tires cluttering the rear yard. The seller wanted $50,000 for the business and to the seller the tires were an eyesore and a liability. Not to this buyer. He heard that electric power plants use rubber as fuel and negotiated the sale of the tires at $1 apiece to come up with the $10,000 down payment. "It was remarkably easy," says this imaginative entrepreneur. "I obtained the contract to sell the tires to become effective upon the closing. In turn I assigned the $10,000 receivable to a bank who loaned me the $10,000. A week after I acquired the business the electric company picked up the tires and paid the bank, while I had my business and an empty rear lot to begin collecting more tires and a down payment on maybe another business."

The stories continue:

A buyer of a tile manufacturing plant prearranged the licensing of its secret process to a Mexican manufacturer for $25,000.

A buyer for a car dealership arranged to lease billboard space on top of its building bordering a high-traffic highway for a $12,000 advance rental.

A buyer for a plastic extrusion plant had a clever accountant who negotiated the purchase of the seller's ownership interest by borrowing against the employee's pension plan funds.

Bill Finneran, a creative buyer with several no cash down acquisitions to his credit, approaches a target business with this philosophy, "I look for assets that can quickly produce cash. And once you start looking you'd be surprised at what can be sold, rented, licensed, or borrowed against. When you have it down to a science you can usually free up more than a down payment." Finneran is quick to add, "One of these days you'll even find me taking the penny out of the fuse box."

Study your target business before you buy. What assets can you turn into cash to make that sale happen?

YOUR TWO BEST MONEY SOURCES

In most cases you can find ways to uncover your down payment from sources within the businesses. Occasionally you need a helping hand from external sources and your two best bets are:

1. Business Brokers.
2. Existing Suppliers.

Never overlook the importance of a broker as a source of cash. Seventy percent of all businesses are sold through a broker, so there's an excellent chance a broker will be involved in your deal. Now here's another interesting statistic to consider. The average conventionally financed small business acquisition requires only a 20% down payment. Conversely, the typical brokers fee is 10% of the sales price. This translates into the inescapable fact that 50% of your down payment is earmarked to pay the brokers fee.

The obvious, but cash-saving, point I'm leading to is that a commission deferred is a down payment saved. The strategy is to convince the broker to loan you a portion of his commission for the privilege of saving the sale and his total commission.

For example, on a $100,000 deal the broker stands to earn a $10,000 commission. While brokers earn their living from commissions and not lending money, any broker will tell you the two inevitably must co-exist. So you ask the broker to loan you perhaps $5000 from the commission, secured by the business, and payable over one or two years with reasonable interest.

Will the broker go for it? Absolutely. There are only two exceptions to the rule. Several of the large firms won't lend or compromise on commissions as a matter of policy and precedent. These same firms also lose plenty of sales. However, every broker will resist if they believe you're bluffing and can raise money from other sources. And that's when they should refuse. Your job is to convince the broker. The only way you can buy the business is with his help. When they think their commission is at risk they seldom refuse.

Suppliers are your second best source. Suppliers are discussed elsewhere in this book as the primary source of credit for a start-up, however, few people think of suppliers as a source of cash for a down payment. I never did see a difference between asking a supplier for $10,000 in credit to merchandise a new business as opposed to $10,000 in cash to buy a business. Money is money and in either case the selling point is the value of your future business to the supplier.

Earlier in this chapter you read about Jim Corcoran, who is now comfortably established in his Frisco restaurant partially financed by a $5000 loan from his meat supplier. Why wouldn't it make sense for the supplier to lend a paltry $5000 for an account that would create $100,000 a year in sales?

Supplier loans would happen quite often if more buyers simply asked. Suppliers seldom turn down a reasonable request. Don't call it charity. An advance loan in only another form of credit.

One leading hardware wholesale firm president says, "A new customer is not shy in asking for $10,000–15,000 in credit *after* they buy the business, but few will ask for the few dollars *before* to make the takeover possible. Many buyers bypassed opportunities because they don't think of their suppliers in terms of writing out a check. Not long ago a young couple asked us for a $10,000 loan to help with a $30,000 down payment for a health and beauty aid store. We were already selling the business over $200,000 a year, and a turndown would only mean a lost account. So we'd be foolish to say 'no,' we charged 18% interest on the loan, but more importantly, we saved a $200,000 a year profit generator for our own business."

Buying power is borrowing power and it underscores all negotiations with suppliers. Existing suppliers will lend for fear of *losing* an account. Prospective suppliers will lend to *win* an account. Both are prime candidates.

Confine your search to the major suppliers. You don't have enough to offer small secondary suppliers. Project the sales of your business and tie the loan into a commitment to buy in the future. A two- to four-year payback on a cash advance loan is reasonable, and so is 15–18% interest and a personal guarantee and/or a business mortgage to secure the loan.

Taverns, restaurants, and other businesses with concessioned juke boxes, cigarettes, and other vending machines are always prime candidates for loans from the vending machine companies. Typically the vending company and the owner split profits 50/50. Two or three high-volume machines can generate $15,000–20,000 in annual profits for the owner. Since the competition for good location is fierce, vending companies routinely will pay anywhere from one-half to a full year's profit as an advance for a concession lease. I once came across a young couple who trading on this advice purchased a bowling alley with no cash of their own. The bowling alley was selling for $180,000 and with bank, seller, and other financing blocks in place, the enterprising buyers were still $20,000 short. Along the rear wall of the bowling alley stood a row of soft drink, cigarette, and candy machines grossing $100,000 a year. The owner's share of the profits from these machines exceeded $20,000 a year and three vending companies engaged in a bidding war to win the choice location. The high bidder agreed to an advance against commissions of $20,000 and an outright cash bonus of $5000 besides.

As the buyer of an existing business you should be able to negotiate anywhere from 10–20% of the total purchase price from suppliers. In itself it may be sufficient to cover a down payment without being overly clever in other areas. Unlike the start-up venture, you can prove what money your suppliers stand to make from you. It's as good as money in the bank.

PLAYING BY THE RULES

Leveraged takeovers have their own set of rules which go contrary to traditional financing strategies. You've seen the financing blocks that can take the place of your down payment, but now let's put it together as a strategy:

Rule 1. *Ignore Down Payment Requirements.* Pretend the words *down payment* don't exist. Whenever a seller tells you what you need for a down payment, he's looking at it in one of two ways. First, it may be the *seller's* perception of what is needed to finance the deal, or *his* perception of what he wants to walk away from the closing with. Now you already know you'll find many more financing sources than the seller ever dreamed of, and still be able to hand the seller all the cash he needs.

Rule 2. *Build from the Ground Up.* Building your no cash down financing pyramid requires one careful step at a time. Start at the bottom with the largest financing blocks, gradually climbing to 100% leverage by adding your layers of financing. The reason most cash shy buyers fail is because they are intimidated by the big picture and never face the financing challenge in small manageable steps.

Rule 3. *Maximize the Borrowing Potential.* Don't leave one level of financing to go on to the next until you've exhausted all the possibilities for more cash. Every extra dollar in bank or seller financing means one less dollar to search for higher on the financial pyramid.

Rule 4. *The Deal Dictates the Financing.* No two leveraged takeovers have precisely the same financial structure. While this chapter shows you the most common techniques, your best sources of financing will depend on the deal, what's most readily available, and what provides the greatest economic benefit.

Rule 5. *Bigger Deals Are Only Bigger Numbers.* While most no cash start-ups do begin on a small scale and grow through a build up of profits, the leveraged takeover can be on a grandiose scale. A leveraged takeover allows an entrepreneur to start on the mezzanine level rather than wallow for several years at the bottom with a cash poor start-up.

Rule 6. *You Don't Need Cash.* Lock up your checkbook. If you can't swing a leveraged takeover on totally borrowed money, you either have the wrong deal or wrong approach. If it's the former, then move on. Eventually you'll find the type business you're after that can be fully financed. If it's the latter, then perfect your technique. While I can only show you the basic strategy, you'll need your own style, persuasiveness, imagination, and perserverance to close your winning deal.

KEY POINTS TO REMEMBER

1. Determine whether you're a business buyer or creator.

2. Buying a business may be a better alternative to starting from scratch.
3. Who needs money? Thousands of businesses are available for little or no cash down.
4. Don't fall victim to a seller's down payment demands. Create your own 100% financing plan.
5. A bad business can be a very good buy.
6. There are hundreds of ways a business can generate its own financing. Look to the internal sources first.
7. Brokers and suppliers are your best sources of external financing.
8. A leveraged takeover can put you into a larger business faster and easier than a shoestring start-up.

11

PYRAMIDING TO THE TOP

You can only wonder whether Ray Kroc, founder of the wildly successful McDonald's fast food chain envisioned 6000 outlets scattered throughout the world when he opened his first hamburger stand in the 1950's. Did the youthful entrepreneurs who toyed with a new computer design in their garage somehow dream that their Atari Corporation would make them multi-millionaires overnight? America is the land of Horatio Alger stories. Where else can you start a business without two nickels to rub together, and cash out with more money than any one person can rationally spend in five lifetimes? That's what makes the game of business so fascinating. No matter how small you are at the starting gate, you never quite know how big you'll be at the finish line.

For every Ray Kroc there are 10,000 names you'll never hear of. But entrepreneurs everywhere in every type business someday reach the point when they have one solid, stable business off and running and sit back and ask, "Where do I go from here?" It's the beginning of the long march to real success. One store becomes two and then four. Before your realize it, you have a small empire of 20 or 30 money-makers. Then you look back and remember where it all began and still wonder where it will all end. It's indeed a fascinating game.

IT'S EASY TO MULTIPLY A WINNER

A successful operating business can give you incredible leverage for fast expansion. As any fast-track entrepreneur can tell you, starting your second business is considerably easier than your first, and once you have the blueprint perfected you can easily propel your way to the top by continuously duplicating what you have.

Winners can be magically multiplied from their own momentum. You have cash flow available to you. Trade credit is yours because suppliers are doing business with you and are being paid. Banks and other lenders know that you have more than an idea—you have the ability to operate a winning venture. Prospective partners begin to focus on growth and not risk. Management and manpower seasoned from their embryonic start are ready to tackle an expanding operation. In short, you've marshalled assets, power, and influence. Expansion is trading on what you *have done* and not on what you *might do*.

That's how it always is when you have a winner behind you. Putting together my first Discount City was a nightmare. I had no cash to work with. Suppliers never heard of me, so why should they sell me on credit? Bankers thought I had leprosy. Who could blame them? Even I had my lingering doubts. It was a different story with the second Discount City. I could tap $30,000–40,000 from my first store for working capital. Stacking the shelf was only a matter of a few phone calls. My banker was now anxious to lend me whatever the business needed. Two prospective partners offered $400,000 for a small piece of the business. Suddenly you find people coming to you with money and you're now turning *them* down. And you can turn them down. You worked to put together your first shoestring deals, and now it's time for your business to work for you as the foundation for more.

BUT WHO NEEDS IT?

That's more than a rhetorical question. Someday your shoestring venture will be flying high and it too will be ready to expand. The chances are you'll be the one holding it back.

About 99% of us fall into the "who needs it" category. You work your butt to the bone to start and build the business until it is successful and reach a comfortable income. Ambition runs out and the business is stalled in a holding pattern. You've heard the rationalizations: "How many steaks a day can you eat?" Or "A Chevrolet will take you anywhere a Mercedes can."

I'm not going to preach on how you should live your life. Plenty of people are very content with one small business and don't want a life of "wheeling and dealing," collecting businesses like squirrels collect nuts.

This chapter is for those who do, or perhaps only want to take their business one notch higher on the ladder of success.

You've heard of the Boston Red Sox, Celtics, and Bruins, but I bet you never heard of the Boston B.U.M.S. It's a very exclusive club of Boston's Unemployed Millionaires. Membership is limited to entrepreneurs who started on a shoestring and cashed out with at least one million dollars. They tell some interesting stories on how they launched and built their business. Most say the decisive point was when their business was ready to expand. "It's easy to sit back, rest on your laurels, and let the business take you where it wants to go," says one member who started with a bicycle rental shop in a local resort town, and ended with 15 businesses ranging from a car dealership to a partnership in a large restaurant. "But it doesn't happen that way. You build not for the money, but for the sheer joy of it. Call it ego trip, power, drive, or satisfaction—something makes you go for one more challenge."

Maybe you're the type who needs it even if it is for the sheer joy of it.

BIGGER CAN BE BETTER

There are many good reasons to set your sights on a larger operation and consider expansion. And expansion doesn't have to change your lifestyle or turn you into a workaholic. In fact, you may find running several businesses not only more profitable, but even easier than operating one. Look at the possibilities:

1. *You Have Management Power:* It's the best reason to expand. Growth can allow you the management team to really

succeed. Running a small one-man show makes you a generalist in an era of specialists. And it does make your life easier when you have specialists aboard. With my first store I had to do everything but the sales and stock work. When I expanded into the second Discount City I could afford a buyer-merchandiser for both stores. The combined operation immediately became sharper. We've since added a full-time ad specialist, a comptroller, another buyer, a personnel manager, and best of all, an operations manager to oversee the 12-store chain while I play golf.

It doesn't take more time to run a larger operation, only more time on the important decisions. With strong subordinates to help manage your business you will probably find that you can take even more time off and stop being married to your one-man show.

2. *You Have Buying Power:* It's critical for many businesses, especially in the retail lines. Unless you're dealing in an exclusive product line you're fair game for all the bigger boys who *can* buy better and sell lower. Many businesses expand because they *must* expand to compete with the chains and discounters in a very competitive jungle. Independent clothing, liquor, drug, food, hardware, and toy stores—to name only a few—have been clobbered by their lack of buying power. You may find a competition-free location so perhaps you can survive with one store, but if you expect to grow you'd better expand fast so you can match the competition on their terms. Your customers are watching your prices.
3. *You Have Advertising Power:* It's as important as buying power. The independent business can't afford saturation advertising. What it can afford is feeble at best. A friend of mine now owns a chain of seven jewelry stores and for the first time can afford large space ads in the metropolitan newspapers. Since he started his ad campaign sales have increased 30%. Can you afford to reach your customers?
4. *You Have Location Power:* In Chapter 8, I explained why retailing is now primarily a real estate game as competitors jockey for high-traffic mall and shopping center locations.

If you're a retailer you need the strength of size to put you into the right money-making spots.

5. *You Have Cash Flow Power:* What do I mean by cash flow power? The ability to cover the slumps in one business by the cash reserves of another. Every business has its ups and downs. When an independent goes into a long sales slump, or suffers an unexpected loss, he has no place to turn. The multiple business operation only has to borrow from a sister business.
6. *You Have Staying Power:* I love staying power because I intend to stay in business for a long, long time. That's why I expanded. "Why put all my eggs in one basket?" I reasoned. When you have one business—even a successful business—1001 things can happen to quickly kill it. A formidable competitor can move in next to you, a landlord can refuse to renew your lease, new technology, or a fatal labor strike, to name a few. So I spread my risk and opportunities by branching out. An owner of a small business has security for as long as he or she is in business, but with thousands of ventures closing every year for one reason or another it isn't that much security. Can you predict how long your shoestring enterprise will last?

Maybe none of these reasons makes much sense for you. Then you may be like Joe Tevald, the only mechanic I know who drives a Rolls-Royce. As Joe explains it he needs a Rolls to comfortably squire leisurely between his 68 gas stations. As Joe says, "The fun is owning them not working in them."

WHERE DO YOU GO FROM HERE?

Suppose you've dived into the water with a business of your own. The hard part was the cold water of doubt wondering whether you'd make it. If you haven't drowned, expansion should be easy. Why not? You not only have your feet wet, but you're already swimming. Now all you have to do is add a few strokes to your repertory.

But before you enter deeper water you have to know where you are, where you want to go, and how you expect to get there. Those are the three essential questions and on the next few pages you may find some answers. For now, put away your crystal ball. Don't worry about five, ten, or fifteen years from now. Long-range planning is fun and can get the adrenalin pumping, but you can only take it one step at a time. The objective is to make each step the right step.

TEST THE TIMING

When do you expand? As with any other management decision, timing is critical. Some moves come too quickly. The existing operation isn't sufficiently strong to support—or gamble on—another start-up. One of the most common reasons for business failure is an eager beaver entrepreneur who expanded too far too fast, and had the whole operation come down around his ears. On the other extreme are the too conservative types whose caution retards the progress their business could safely make with a more aggressive expansion program. So you try to walk the tightrope.

There are some ground rules you should follow. The first is that you're not ready to expand until your existing operation is running profitably and with a surplus cash flow. Cash flow is an important ingredient. You may have a profitable business and still have a negative cash flow, as so many shoestring start-ups do as they try to work down their initial debt.

Expansion, in reality, is only the re-deployment of excess cash or available credit where it will do most good—in another leveraged operation. So you can't intelligently expand if your existing business needs those same dollars or available credit to improve its own performance.

Look at it as a competitive process. Your existing business is competing with the prospective unit for the capital or assets needed to expand. Where will that money give you the best return? Measure it carefully. You should only consider expansion when your money will make more money in yet one more business.

The second step is to assess when a new start-up will reach its own break-even point, and whether your existing operation can support it until it does. Some businesses rapidly reach a level of profitability while others take time to reach it. Not long ago we consulted to a small but rapidly expanding chain of donut shops. It's an incredible business. A donut shop in a good location can hit a profitable sales level one week after it opens. Since each addition isn't a cash drain on the existing operation, expansion is limited only by the owner's ability to find locations, hire competent help,and put the shop together.

I play the "what if" game in making an expansion decision. What I ask is: "What if the new operation doesn't work out? What impact will it have on my existing operation?" Assessing risk is part of the expansion formula. If we have to pledge the assets of our existing operation to finance a new start-up we move slowly—very slowly. One failure could destroy the entire business. Conversely, I've expanded into other businesses that did stand on their own financially and legally. Some made it and others didn't, but as independent units none posed a financial threat to any of my other ventures. I think this is the best way to expand at first. When each business is on its own you have the best of all worlds—opportunity with very little risk.

That brings us to what I call the "push-pull" theory of expansion. Logically you'll "push" towards expansion because you do have a sound base to grow. Sometimes it's equally logical to be "pulled" into expansion to save what you have. The strategy is that the future will somehow bail out the past.

A perfect example of the "push-pull" theory hard at work is one of my best clients who couldn't run one business, but somehow thought he could run three. His stores are losing a bundle and we have only one of two choices—to contract or expand. If we contract to one store, he'll have to contend with a mountain of debts existing from the closed stores which would jeopardize his one remaining store. We decided to expand into a fourth store that would hopefully have high enough sales and profits to stabilize the existing stores. Of course, my client plans to go on an extended vacation while we bring in a real manager to turn the entire operation around, but with a new store ringing up $1 million in sales we have a cash flow to work with.

It's not a unique story. Many chains are losing their shirt, and the more they lose the faster they expand. The chase is on for cash flow to cover up their past managerial sins.

In still other cases expansion is needed to cover fixed overhead—particularly an owner's salary. For example, I know a small computer store trying to support three partners and each partner needs a $500 weekly salary to survive. Simple arithmetic tells you that you can't pay out $75,000 a year in salary when the business only has a $90,000 income. Expansion was the only solution.

THE MANY PATHS TO SUCCESS

Ten years ago the Clausons opened their first "Quick Stop" Automotive Center, with $100,000 in start-up capital borrowed from a bank, a few relatives, and a select partner. Despite heavy competition the business did exceptionally well, paying each of the two Clauson brothers a $35,000 salary and a $50,000 profit besides. Within two years the business was paid to the ground, and two young entrepreneurs who started with nary a penny of their own decided it was time to expand and eventually multiplied their winner into 15 more. By now the Clausons are happy millionaires with 12 more "Quick Stop" centers on the drawing board.

Do you have a winner to multiply? Most chains and franchise systems are nothing more than a nucleus of two or three carefully shaped and profitable prototypes duplicated countless times as the pyramiding process propels the owners to enormous wealth.

Many shrewd entrepreneurs start their first business intending to expand as a chain or through franchising. For the first year or two they carefully tuned the business to a profitable pitch and add several more units following precisely the same formula. The theory is that if five prototypes can make it, 5000 can.

Did you ever hear of Radio Shack? It's now part of the Tandy Corporation with almost 6000 stores. Thirty years ago they opened their first hi-fi shop in a crowded little store in downtown Boston. One of their first employees was a radio buff high-school classmate of mine who in later years told me that when the owners started they foresaw only three or four stores in the Boston area.

Whether it be a fast-growth franchise system or a rapidly expanding chain, somewhere down the line the decision was made that they did have a winner on their hands and the formula for expansion and a fortune.

Franchising is in its heyday. Farsighted entrepreneurs with an attractive business concept to sell are finding they can cash in fastest and easiest by going the franchise route. Many choose franchising because they don't want the headaches or risk of multi-unit management. As franchisors they need only to sell, establish policy, and supervise while availing the problems of daily operations. Expansion speed is another factor. Company-owned stores can only expand at a rate consistent with its financing and manpower. Even with fast concentric growth an emerging chain could hardly dominate a local market within ten years, while many franchise systems started less than five years ago have a national network of thousands of units. And don't ignore the economics. Collecting franchise fees and royalties can produce powerful profits, and you *can* start a franchise program on a shoestring.

And you can franchise just about any type business. VR Business Brokers was a one-office operation several years ago. Today they have 400 franchised offices nationwide. Union Prescription Centers was a four-store midwest chain in 1967. By 1971 they had 135 franchised. Dunkin' Donuts numbers their franchises in the thousands and you can find them in several countries. I remember the founder making donuts in his very first donut shop. These, and many more, have come a long way in a short time and they did it all by starting with a winner others wanted to duplicate.

Manufacturers have their own avenue of cashless expansion. Many owning valuable patents or trademarks are licensing these valuable rights to other firms, preferring to collect royalties to the capital intensive alternative of building more factories or trying to crack important markets.

Not every business is the whopping money-maker that will have lines of prospective franchisees waiting in the wings, or be the first of many in a dynamic chain. Ninety-five percent of all businesses are "me-too" operations generating comfortable profits for its owners in its own non-descript way. Their expansion potential is not in their self-multiplication, but to continue to pump the profits by which other acquisitions can be made.

David Seltzer, an ex-sales representative for a Pittsburgh paper firm, decided on a different path. In 1974 Dave started a printing plant, and with his wife working beside him, sales leaped to $2 million annually. By 1977 Dave was debt-free and with heavy cash on his hands. Expansion was the only way his money could make more money. Another printing plant was out. Why compete with himself, Dave figured. Uncomfortable with businesses he had no experience in, Dave expanded "vertically," opening a business forms distributorship. Now Dave prints the forms through his printing company and sells them through his form company. Dave now has his sights on buying a paper supply firm. When he does he'll control three businesses at different points in the distribution channel.

Imagine starting your day by visiting your appliance stores, journeying into your car dealership for lunch, and checking in at the headquarters of your sporting goods chain in mid-afternoon. Before heading home you check your movie theater to see that everything's shipshape. Now that's an entrepreneur. It's also Ken Volpi, a daredevil type, unafraid to tackle any business provided he can start or buy it on a shoestring, find the right people to operate it, and sit back and have it make money for him. Ken remembers growing up poor and watching his father's garment business wiped out during the Depression. Ken learned from his father's experience and decided the only security was to have different businesses working at the same time. "If one industry is down, another is bound to be up," Ken philosophizes. "Besides, I enjoy the different challenges, problems, and opportunities of a spicy mix of ventures."

You've met several people who travelled their own road to success. You'll have your own path marked "opportunity."

UNLEASH YOUR GROWTH POWER

What is your present business worth? Surprisingly few business people carefully analyze their business' net worth, and fewer still understand how to parlay the net worth into more businesses. And many start-ups—even the highly leveraged shoestring start-up—can quickly build equity and the borrowing power to launch another business or two.

Periodically I conduct "start-up seminars" at local business colleges. About 40% of the participants are already in business and are looking for ways to find expansion capital. I always ask this one question, "What can you squeeze from your existing business?"

One participant, Selma V., showed up the following week with her financial statements to put me to the test. "Show me how to get the money out of my fabric shop to open another," she counter-challenged. Of course I enjoy challenges, particularly when there's a small fee attached. So with our bargain struck I went to work:

1. An inventory reduction program was the first step. The inventory was slashed from an excess $80,000 to $50,000 by discounting the slow-moving overstocks, generating $20,000 in cash.
2. The fabric shop always paid COD for merchandise. Opening the business up on 30-day credit terms gave us another $20,000 to add to the pile.
3. Some spare office furniture and equipment was sold through a used equipment dealer for another $4000.
4. Noticing that 1000 sq. ft. of space stood empty we found another tenant to sublet the space for $2000 on advance rent.

That gave us $46,000 to work with and we hardly started. The big money was yet to come. One trip to Selma's bank and we had a commitment for a $60,000 loan. Now we had $106,000 to work with. But what would it take to open another fabric shop for Selma, our friend and willing student? If you ask Selma she'll tell you it can't be done for less than $100,000. Selma was wrong again. In a month her second store was off and running in a suburban shopping center complete with a $50,000 inventory ($40,000 purchased on lenient credit terms), $12,000 in fixtures and equipment (leased for no cash down with an option to buy), and a big red and white sign proclaiming: "Selma's Sewland Fabrics," designed by a sign painter willing to have his $2000 bill paid in 12 convenient installments. So for $12,000 cash, Selma had her second store, and her business had the growth power to finance eight more. It's not high finance, but only common sense and the ability to see the dollars hiding in your business.

Jeff Kosberg, a consultant to many small growth companies, points out, "Expansion-minded entrepreneurs are always looking for capital, while the money is usually under their feet in the form of excess inventory, old receivables, or other pockets of waste. While they continue to look to external sources they should first concentrate on the internal."

Shake the growth dollars loose from your business:

1. *Test your new borrowing power:* Even if your business if heavily mortgaged it may have plenty of borrowing power. Consider the equity you've built since opening. Assets are up and your loan balance is down. And you have the track record, which is a bankable item. One banker explains that an existing business is the perfect vehicle for "bridge" financing. If a new unit needs $50,000 to start the combined assets of the two businesses is usually sufficient to justify 100% financing. Many businesses decide to expand years after they first opened and as mortgage-free enterprises their equity would produce a better return invested in a second unit rather than lie idle in the first.
2. *Make your inventory work harder:* Show me a business with excess inventory and I'll show you a business with its expansion capital sitting on the shelf. Take the case of Heritage Hobby & Crafts. Heritage was operating one store with a $140,000 inventory. All the business needed was $70,000 to support sales. So Heritage divided itself into two stores with double the income. Operating with a lean inventory can free up enormous amounts of cash. Suppliers may accept overstocks for new merchandise to help launch another unit or you can turn it into cash yourself. But merchandise is money and when you need money you never overlook your merchandise.

3. *Expand with suppliers' money:* Leverage is the name of the game and you don't have leverage unless you're using every dime of credit safely available to you. Many times we'll come across a business with very small accounts payable that can safely be pumped up by $20,000 or more, freeing cash for another start-up. This technique of playing with your suppliers' money for as long as possible certainly helped Discount City along. Stretching payments from 30 days to 60 days gave us the equivalent of one month's purchases for expansion capital. And when you're buying $500,000 a month it's a lot of money to expand with. We lay no claim to inventing the concept. Even Fortune-500 companies are sluggish on payments as they wheel and deal their way to an expanding empire. It has nothing to do with morality, but only with the decision of where the money in your checkbook will do the most good.
4. *Use your credit clout:* In our operation we have a standing rule. If a supplier won't extend us 100% credit on an opening stocking order for a new store it's no longer our supplier. You have that clout once you have one or two businesses in operation and now need inventory for one more. We look at it this way. We may give a supplier $500,000 in business a year. It's a small trade-off to ask for $25,000 in lenient credit to help inventory another store which will give him even more business. Many of the largest chains have been propelled along by suppliers pouring in the needed merchandise and never daring to refuse. Of course, quite a few suppliers have been burnt in the process of succumbing to the charms of their fast-growth customers, but as one poorer but wiser supplier says, "When your customer is growing, you either help them grow or pull out. There's no middle ground."
5. *Check your pockets of waste:* Don't leave stones unturned when shaking the money loose. When Carl Shumway wanted to expand his northern California wholesale book distributorship to a second San Diego operation, he estimated it would take $160,000 in capital. "I was ready to take in a partner to finance the deal but instead I did

some housecleaning. We did everything from liquidating $60,000 in slow inventory to chasing down slow receivables. We borrowed $48,000 from the company's pension fund and even talked the electric company into returning our $4000 deposit. We had more money than we needed and didn't have to go beyond our four walls to find it. Not only do you find money, but you find inefficiency, and you don't expand from a soft, sloppy base."

PROSPECTING FOR THE BIG DOLLARS

Internally funded growth can take you only so far and so fast. Eventually you'll begin to think in terms of prospecting for equity capital to grow even faster and on a safer footing.

If you return to Chapter 7, you'd see a slight bias against partnerships as a way to finance the initial start-up, and for good reason. It's usually not necessary to go after partnership funds to put together a shoestring deal because so many better sources of capital and credit are available.

The expanding venture, on the other hand, may begin to look at partnership money as one of the best sources of financing. While the advantages and disadvantages of taking on partners remain the same, you can strike a considerably more beneficial bargain with partners during the growth stage compared to the idea stage. So the partnership decision is really a matter of timing.

Benefit from the example of Cy Cunningham, enthusiastic over the idea of opening a medical billing firm in Akron, Ohio. Cy saw the need for a service to handle the complicated third-party billings for the area dentists, physicians, and pharmacies, and with fair accuracy estimated it would take $150,000 to properly capitalize it. His best partnership offer was $75,000 for a 50% interest in the business and bank financing for the difference. Cy turned down the deal and instead managed to borrow $100,000 in bank financing and ten of his largest physician accounts agreed to finance another $60,000. It was a heavily leveraged start-up but Cy owned it all. Within three years the business had a $600,000 income, $85,000 profit, and virtually no debt. It was a success story worth repeating and Cy decided to repeat it by opening offices in Cleveland, Cincinnati, and Toledo. To raise the $800,000 in expansion capital Cy now went after partners—convincing a large computer firm to invest the $800,000 for a 30% interest and the commitment to lend the corporation another $1.5 million for further expansion. Cy knew the right time to strike for partnership funds. Had he started with a 50% interest, it would have been diluted to 35% when it came time to go for the big dollars.

Hal Lynch, a finance consultant with a long string of growing clients, admits that timing is the critical factor when considering equity capital. "Too many people sell a piece of the business too soon and give up too much in the process. Others wait too long and either fail because of over-expansion or never reach full potential. There is always that perfect moment to pull in a partner or two, but for each of us it's a different moment." Keep your eye on your perfect moment.

SEVEN GROWTH RULES

Before you leap into an expansion program, take a hard look at some of the most common mistakes and the strategies to avoid them. And people who travelled the road before you offer these words of advice:

Rule 1. ***Evaluate Your Own Strengths.*** Do you have what it takes to manage multiple operations? This requires the ability to set controls, delegate, and motivate. You're no longer a one-man show and that means the ability to work through other people.

"I breached the Peter Principle when I opened my second shoe store," smiles Ben Pike, who engineered his way into business with a $6000 loan from his father-in-law and parlayed it into a $400,000 profit center in Brooklyn's south side. "I could be everywhere and do everything with one business to run, but when my second came along I had to work through my two store managers. I was no longer in the shoe business—I was in the people business. And it's a very different business."

Rule 2. ***Don't Build on Quicksand.*** Make certain your existing operations are solid, smooth running, and in good financial health before you expand.

Connie and John Krasnow, like so many people, stumbled on this point. The Krasnows had two nursing homes in southern New Hampshire when they decided to open their third. "We weren't ready and it was as simple as that," admits Connie. "Our existing homes were too deeply in debt and losing money and we had no blueprint to correct the situation. We were probably running away from our two nightmares by thinking a third would somehow solve our problems," adds Connie.

Rule 3. ***Protect Yourself.*** Set up each business as a separate corporation. If one goes sour it won't take your good businesses with it.

"Legal organization is important when expanding," say Frank Lainer and Keith McCarthy, who once owned a prosperous greeting card and gift shop in a Chicago mall. "We made the mistake of using our original corporation to open our second store in a suburban mall. This mall turned out to be a dud, and we lost $120,000 which our corporation—even with its one healthy store—couldn't absorb. So we filed bankruptcy, losing everything. If we had the foresight we would have used a separate corporation for our second store, protecting our first."

Rule 4. ***Consider Logistics.*** "I thought I was Superman who maybe could don my red cape and fly from Boston to Buffalo to check on the third employment agency we had opened," confesses Blanche Lerner of Lerner Employment Agencies. "At best I could get to the Buffalo office only once every two or three weeks and that's too little supervision for my business, even one with a strong manager. So we sold the Buffalo unit at a loss and learned never to locate beyond our reach. Business people think a business can run by itself. Unless you're constantly on top of it you have problems. And you're never on top of it literally unless you're on top of it physically."

Rule 5. ***Watch Cash Flow.*** Every acquisition or addition has to stand on its own two feet without draining cash from existing operations. If you plan to support a start-up make sure you know what the support payments will be and that you can afford it.

Expanding into a deficit operation can topple an existing company with an insufficient cash surplus to support it. "The best advice I can give is to set limits on the money you'll pour into a new start-up," offers Pat Pellini, who admits to draining his once viable Pellini Bakery of $120,000 to keep his second bakery afloat. "But it floated just long enough to kill both businesses," he adds.

I offer my own postscript on this one. Whenever I set up a new business, I'll set aside a cash reserve from the other businesses. That's it. If it's not enough to see it through the survival stage it doesn't survive. You have to know when to turn off the spigot.

Rule 6. ***Don't Bite Off More than You Can Chew.*** Growth is a gradual deliberative process with each step being logical in context to the existing organization. Each addition is one that must be easily assimilated in terms of management, markets, money, and know-how.

Allen Van Kamp, a management consultant with the firm by the same name, claims that the most common growth error is moving into new ventures the existing organization can't handle. "And what a firm may not be able to handle covers a lot of territory," adds Van Kamp. "The most common error is going outside your field. The Bankruptcy Courts are loaded with companies who, for example, may have successfully operated four or five restaurants and suddenly you find them in the hotel business. But what did they know about hotels? Size is another stumbling block. Plenty of people have the management mentality to run a $300,000-a-year business and they think they can now handle a $3-million operation. It takes considerably different skills. Don't bite off more than you can chew. Stay with what you know."

Rule 7. ***Don't Forget Your Humble Past.*** Growth can dim memories. And when you're growing helter-skelter you tend to look only to the future and forget the past.

Now take my advice. It was the past that gave you the winning formula. You scrounged for pennies and wrung a dollar from each dime. You fought the odds, gambled on the risks, and did it all your own way.

You've changed just as your business has changed, and you'll go through more change before you reach your finish line. But you do have a heritage and a mighty proud heritage. Not everyone can be a shoestring entrepreneur, but once a shoestring entrepreneur, always a shoestring entrepreneur. You wouldn't want it any other way.

KEY POINTS TO REMEMBER

1. Your first business can be the springboard for many more.
2. Everyone will jump on board to help, once you show them what you *have done* rather than what you *might do.*
3. Bigger can be better. Size is power and it all leads to more profit power.
4. Test the timing. There is always a right—and wrong—time to take your next step.
5. Expansion can take many paths. Choose the one that's right for your business—and you.
6. Your business has growth power. The money to expand can be found internally.
7. The best time to consider partnership funds is during the growth stage.
8. Expand by the rules. Take a lesson from others who can show you the right way to success.

12

MAKING IT WORK

What is it really like to take an idea and fashion it into a successful small business? Are the new entrepreneurs like the success stories crowding the pages of the money-making opportunity books with their happy tales of the John Js and Sally Ss waxing rich overnight, or is there something more to it? *Do* the inspiring words match the realities?

Let's separate the wheat from the chaff. Real people create businesses, not words from the pens of creative writers. And these very real people have interesting stories to tell. Meet and talk to these people and you begin to share their experiences, their triumphs, and their tragedies in trying to put together a business—and make it work.

In writing this book I have talked to hundreds of people who have journeyed through the entrepreneurial process, with an abundance of enthusiasm if not an abundance of cash. Like snowflakes, they were joined by this common thread while weaving a story with their own unique pattern. They were found in retail shops, small manufacturing plants, service businesses, and in hundreds of very different enterprises ranging from a deep-sea treasure salvage firm to a manufacturer of telescopic lenses. Seduced by the attractions of a new and better life they come from every background, age group, and educational or work-life level. Some seem to have made it and many others didn't, but for most the final scorecard still isn't in as they struggle one day at a time.

For each of these people, I had plenty of questions to unravel their own experiences. Five were selected for this chapter. They were chosen not as success stories, but because each, in their own way and in their own words, describes what it means to start on a shoestring.

Here's what they have to say.

SOUND STEREO:

The Melody of Millions in Sales from a $2000-Beginning

Bach and Beethoven constantly flood the home of Leo Walsi, who describes himself as a music fanatic. For Leo, the next best thing to listening to fine music is selling top-notch equipment so others can enjoy their own musical delights. Today, you're likely to find the 38-year-old with shirtsleeves rolled, extolling the virtues of his woofers and tweeters in his Fall River, Massachusetts, store. "Every sale has its own sweet melody," Leo smiles. "The cash register chimes like a soothing symphony," he adds with a mischievous grin.

Leo, how did you manage to end up in the stereo business?

Since graduating from Boston University, I taught high school English. After twelve years on the job I was frustrated with the thought of earning only $18,000–20,000 a year. The only way I could see to earn more was to go into business for myself. So I began to tinker with the idea of going into a business that was somehow musically related. One day my wife and I shopped for a new stereo set for our bedroom, and I was astonished to see how little sales clerks knew about stereo equipment, I was always an electronics buff and I figured with my background and interest I could outsell untrained clerks in a department store any day of the week. And I was right.

How does selling stereo equipment relate to your interest in music? It wouldn't appear to provide any more satisfaction than an artist selling painting supplies.

That's where you're wrong. The quality of music is no better than the quality of the equipment it's played on. Superior technical performance is something any music lover can appreciate. I enjoy creating the best sound system so the listener has the best music. It's all part of the fun of music.

How did you intend to beat the competition? After all, every department and discount store sells stereo equipment at "knock-down" discount prices.

I thought about it and it worried me plenty. As a small independent I knew I would need a very different approach to the market—a reason for customers to shop me instead of the discount stores. So I made the decision to build the business on three selling points. First, I stock equipment other stores don't carry. The Scandinavian countries turn out great systems that beat the Japanese and American counterparts found in discount stores. These hard-to-come-by systems are the nucleus of my inventory. Service is another selling point. We'll even go to a customer's home and wire up a system at no extra charge. And we advertise that service. The most important advantage in shopping Sound Stereo is that our clerks are both fully trained and interested in their work. We won't take high school kids and pay them minimum wage. I look for salespeople who know as much about stereo systems as I do and are every bit as interested in it. You never really sell a stereo system, you sell a customer on your knowledge and interest and that gives him the confidence to buy from you.

How well did that approach work for you?

Our growth tells the story. When we opened in 1976, we grossed $80,000. This year we'll gross over $2 million in three stores. In fact, the only reason we didn't grow faster is because we didn't want to lose our personal touch. It's hard to find qualified people to staff additional units.

That's quite a phenomenal growth, Leo, considering you started on a shoestring.

Not really, I can show you half a dozen chains with hundreds of stores, each who started after I did. Part of our momentum is that we're riding the crest of a booming industry. At this point, our small initial capital has little to do with how fast we grow. We're over the hurdle of having too few dollars to expand.

I understand you started your mini-empire on $2000. How did you plan on opening a stereo store with so little cash?

I didn't know any better, and glad of it. I'm not really sure you do plan these things. What I did know was that there were thousands of customers who'd prefer to deal with someone who knew what it was all about and would cater to them. So I cashed in my life insurance, rented a 400-sq.-ft. storefront in the downtown area, bought a dozen stereo systems and some components for cash and credit, and began to promote like hell.

Leo, let's back up and take it a step at a time. What made you so sure so many customers would be service- rather than price-oriented?

If you know your business you know the soft underbelly of the competition. You look for the niche—the differential advantage. I told you about ours. By talking to stereo customers you realize it's all a mystery to them—much like computers are today. I had no doubts there'd be enough customers willing to pay 10–15% more for someone to de-mystify the selection process.

A 400-sq.-ft. storefront and a dozen stereo sets doesn't seem like much of a come-on to attract customers. Did anyone mistake you for a fortune-teller?

We looked like a gypsy store operation, but if someone walked in to have their fortune told he'd still walk out with a stereo system. Seriously, our physical plant may have looked like we'd be around for three weeks, but we didn't intend to pull in traffic from the street. Initially we pulled people through advertising and word of mouth. Once they were in, 70% bought. That's twice the national average and says something about our sales ability.

You use the term "our sales ability." Who else worked the store at the beginning?

Just me. I'm modest. I was the only person on the payroll for the first year. The store wasn't big enough to hold two. In the second year we expanded to 2000 sq. ft., and added one sales clerk and one part-time stock boy.

Was the total capitalization for the business $2000 or did you borrow some additional money to start?

In addition to my own $2000 I had $3000 borrowed from my father. I didn't want to go after serious financing from a bank until the venture proved itself, and I had something to show a bank. It wasn't that I didn't need more money, it was just that I didn't think I could get bank money.

How did you manage to make the business grow from such a small start, especially in the first several months?

There's only one way a tiny business can grow. You take every dime in profits and plow it back into the business. Gradually you begin to build equity, and in turn you match it with bank or trade credit financing. During the first several months I took absolutely no salary—living off my wife's earnings—and because rent was a low $250 a month, I showed a fast profit and could reinvest about $1500 a month into more inventory and advertising. By the end of the year, for example, my inventory was close to $40,000 compared to the $6000 starting inventory.

Obviously, you had some help with trade credit both to start and as you went along?

At first I had my hands full getting merchandise on credit. The lines I wanted were very selective in who they sold to. As a new business with no credit rating I had to sell myself instead of the business and I did. It took a trip to New York and a meeting with the distributor for several lines before two opened me up with a $5000 credit limit. I made it a point to pay within 30 days to solidify my credit rating. When trade credit is important for growth you protect it. As I went along I had the credit to open new lines. Today we do business with 50 suppliers and have credit with all of them.

Did you select the lines because credit was available or were these the lines you primarily wanted?

These were the lines I wanted. It would have been easier to get credit from the distributors of the Japanese and American lines because they had a competitive war going on and were always anxious to see their merchandise on a retailer's shelf. But that's just why I stayed away from them. Everybody in town had these popular brands and I wanted the Scandinavian brands I could honestly tout as the "Cadillacs" of stereo. Now we carry the popular brands as well since many customers are more confident with a recognized name, even if it is an inferior product. But since our start was based on a unique image we wanted the unique lines to go along with it.

That's interesting. I would think that customers want a broad selection instead of limited lines. In this book, for example, I warn retailers not to start with too small or limited a merchandise mix, yet you've gone against this advice and succeeded.

Whether your approach or mine is correct depends very much on the type business in question. If you're talking about a drugstore, for instance, and twelve brands of shampoo are popular, you need all twelve. You can't go with six and expect half your customers to switch because they know what they want when they enter the store. Stereos are another story. Customers seldom walk in with a fixed brand in mind. There's brand recognition but little brand loyalty. Therefore, you can usually sell them from even a limited stock. Looking back though, I admit my own allegiance to only three brands cost me sales. Had I diversified into several of the more popular brands earlier, there are many sales I would have saved. For the retailing start-up it is probably better to quickly diversify by adding lines instead of adding depth to existing lines.

You mentioned advertising as playing a decisive role in your success. What was your advertising strategy?

Everybody has the same strategy: use ads to pull customers. The trouble is, most start-ups don't place enough emphasis on advertising and promotion. And it's these new small ventures who need it most to gain a foothold. When they do advertise, it's haphazard, with neither enough attention to expenditure, message, or media. Before we opened I planned to spend $2000 on an advertising blitz and the greater of $500 a month or 5% of sales thereafter. Strategy was the brainchild of a free-lancer who studied advertising at the NYU School of Retailing. She was an absolute lunatic. Since I was supposedly selling my great brilliance as a stereo design expert, she had me adopt the role of "Professor Walsi," complete with four-cornered hat and tassle. In the ads I looked like Professor Corey, the TV comedian. But that's just the sales pitch she wanted. And we always stuck with that theme to build an institutional image around me. When you have a small ad budget you can't design ads that get lost amidst everyone else's. You have to do something crazy so customers remember your name.

How did you go about setting up and equipping your store?

There's nothing to fixturing a stereo shop. When you start out with a few pieces of merchandise you don't try to look like a mass merchandiser, but instead try to have each piece presented like a jewel. What I did was to buy several hundred yards of gray commercial carpeting and carpeted not only the floor, but the walls also. Floor and wall pedestals to display the stereos had the same carpet covering. It gave a subtle, rich image and it was dirt cheap to accomplish. Spotlights cost only $600 and produced the right lighting. My renovation costs were low because the store had a decent store front, air conditioning, and didn't require structural work.

What form of organization do you use? Is Sound Stereo incorporated or a sole proprietorship?

We've been incorporated from the start. I wouldn't think of going into business without a corporation because otherwise there are too many legal pitfalls. In the first year my accountant set me up as a Subchapter S corporation, anticipating a loss that I could take against my wife's personal income, but it backfired when the business showed a $12,000 profit. That's when we dropped the Subchapter S status.

You say Sound Stereo earned a profit the first year. How long did it take before the business reached the break-even point?

We had a ridiculously low break-even point to begin with because I wasn't taking salary. It's no big trick to reach profitability when your overhead is less than $1000 a month. From that standpoint we made money right away. Had I taken a salary, the business probably wouldn't have shown profits until the second year. Truthfully, had I taken a week's pay from the beginning, I'm not sure the business would have made the second year. I think the key to a successful start for the undercapitalized firm is an owner who can afford to get by on little or no income until the business begins to pay its way. In one way or another you do capitalize the business. If it's not upfront investment, it's through deferred salary.

What about an entrepreneur who has few start-up dollars and still needs a week's pay to support a family. Do you think he can make it?

It depends, of course, on the economics of the situation. To say it accurately, it may be that the owner can take out some money but he better be prepared to sacrifice part of his income so he can build the business. I've seen plenty of people open a business and immediately try to take home a large week's pay. Many of these people came from $250–300 a week jobs and all of a sudden they own a business with a $3000 a week cash flow. Suddenly they have access to more money than ever before and within a month the husband has a new car and the wife a new fur coat. It takes inordinate self-discipline to go from a $300 a week job to a $150–200 a week self-imposed salary when all that money is in front of you.

How many hours a week did you work during your first year?

The store was open from 10:00 a.m. to 9:00 p.m., six days a week. So right off the bat I had a 66-hour schedule. I tried to handle installations on Sundays, and that would tie up another 5–6 hours a week. Bookkeeping and other paperwork could be handled while I was at the store, and I tried never to bring it home with me. I still work over 60 hours a week, but now most of my time is spent on overseeing the managers of my three stores.

You mentioned that you expanded from 400 sq. ft. to 2000 sq. ft. at the end of the first year. What made you decide it was time to expand and how did you go about it?

It was obvious that we needed more space. Our inventory was

up to $40,000, and with sales climbing fast we couldn't stay put with what we had. Fortunately we were able to expand by taking over a recently vacated store adjoining ours. The new store was a quantum leap over what we had, so we borrowed $50,000 from the bank for expansion. Thirty thousand dollars was used to add new inventory and $20,000 was for renovations.

Was it difficult to obtain bank financing for expansion?

Not at all. Lenders look at a going business in a different light than they do a start-up. How could a bank turn down a business doubling sales every few months, and operating with healthy profits constantly plowed back into the business to build collateral? More than the numbers, the lender says to himself, "This guy knows how to operate a shop." It's different than walking in with a so-called business plan to show what you might do. Banks love performance, not projections.

Leo, is it your advice then that a start-up should wait before going after bank financing?

Again, there are no hard and fast rules. If an entrepreneur thinks he can land a few dollars in bank financing to start then he should go for it. I don't think he'll be terribly successful unless he can pledge a house or some other hard collateral. "Friendly" money from relatives and friends, coupled with trade credit, is probably an easier way to obtain start-up capital. Bank financing can come later when the business shows positive signs and needs a spurt of cash to finance faster growth.

How fast did your sales increase? You've been in business only several years and you've climbed from $80,000 to $2 million. Where do you see the sales topping off?

My objective was to double sales every year. In the early years growth came faster because a store reaches a saturation point. Once we expanded to 2000 sq. ft. in our first store we saw a dramatic increase in sales, growing in our second year to $500,000. Now we expect a store to reach $500,000 in sales by the first year and top out somewhere around $1 million within three years.

What kind of profit margin do you expect? I understand the stereo business is a price competitive industry.

What industry isn't? Working on a decent margin is part of our strategy. The industry average is a 20–25% gross profit. Ours is 40–45%. We don't emphasize the popular lines that are price sensitive. By featuring the high-grade more exclusive products we can get our price. The highest margins are not on the stereo units but on accessories, speakers, and amplifiers. Those are the blind items that command a 50–60% margin.

Who are your customers? Is there a particular age or income group?

That's something that surprised even me. I originally thought I'd draw from the over-40 age bracket—older people with disposable income who would want a high-quality sound system. Very few of my customers are from those ranks. The older generations aren't "tuned in," so to speak, to the stereo market. To them a stereo is nothing but a high-priced phonograph. The kids are tuned in. A quality stereo for them is almost a peer group status symbol. Probably 70% of our customers are under 30 and think nothing of dropping $1000 to buy a good unit. We have slanted our advertising to go after the youth market. That's where the action is.

Did expanding from one store to three create many operational problems?

Only in the sense of my own responsibility within the organization. Once you have one successful business you use its format as a prototype—a cookie cutter—for the others. The difference was that I had to divorce myself from selling and hire managers for each of the stores. I was no longer running a store but running the managers, who in turn ran the stores. It's a very different experience. For example, I can walk into a store and see a clerk idle, or see a unit improperly displayed. I can no longer tell the clerk to get to work or re-display the unit. I would be undercutting the manager's authority. So the hardest lesson is to learn how to work through your managers. It takes a very different management style to operate multi-units. Not everyone is comfortable with it.

Do you regret your decision to expand?

I look at it with mixed emotions. I can earn $100,000 a year or more with one store, so sometimes I ask why I need three—or five or six the future may bring. It's probably not the money but the challenge of growing. What I do miss is the opportunity to sell and deal directly with the customers. That's my real strength.

It seems you've been able to start and grow with very few problems. Was it as easy as it sounds?

Of course not. We made plenty of mistakes and they hurt. We also had our cash flow problems. I have a shopping list of fiascos. One was location. I would have been better off starting in an outlying strip center. The downtown area offers no parking and not enough foot traffic to compensate. Another was my inventory. As I said before, we should have expanded our selection much earlier. We also selected some lines that turned out to be "dogs" from a sales standpoint.

What were the cash flow problems?

They weren't severe but they were there. We had two back-to-back months when sales were low and we began to run behind in vendor payments. On balance, our cash flow was easily monitored because we worked only with cash sales, selling a unit and re-ordering a unit. In many cases we had a cash deposit even before we had the merchandise in stock, working from catalogs and advance sales. The key to cash flow is reaching your break-even point and then building inventory as you build profits. You can't let your inventory growth exceed your ability to pay. That's very difficult to control in many businesses, but not in a business dealing with high-ticket items.

How do you set up budgets to control expenses and plan for profits?

It's not complicated. I calculate the fixed expenses and give the manager a budget to control the variable expenses. For example, on a new store I may estimate first-year sales at $500,000. With a 40% gross margin I have $200,000 for expenses, debt service, and profits. The fixed expenses—rent, utilities, insurance, etc.—are pegged at perhaps $75,000 or 15% of sales. My manager is allowed to spend up to 12% of sales on payroll and 5% on advertising. With that control I have 8% reserved for debt service and profit.

Did you use the same approach when starting out?

More or less, except I didn't have the budget refined to the point I do now. When you begin you have a rough idea how the numbers should work, but you still play it by the seat of the pants because you don't have the final fix on what the numbers really are. With a larger organization it becomes sophisticated. The line items on our budgets are down to the penny and monitored weekly by computer printouts.

Do you run the business as a centralized operation or do you let the managers run their own show?

All buying, pricing, and advertising is handled by me. For our operation these are logical functions to be centralized. The managers have full authority over hiring and personnel, within budgetary limits.

Let's go back to your beginning. Did you ever have any doubts whether the business would make it?

Not from the viewpoint of whether it would go bankrupt. We never operated with much debt. It was more a question of whether the business would be worthwhile. As I told you, in the first year I worked close to 70 hours a week without a paycheck and our sales were still soft. It was only when I expanded and sales very rapidly increased that I knew I had a money-maker. For me it was the moment of truth.

If you could offer one point to a prospective start-up, what would it be?

Go out and do it. You can talk to 100 people and read 100 books, but nobody knows what will or will not work until it is tried. If the venture fails you'll either have it out of your system or learned enough to make it succeed the second time around.

That's the downside. The upside?

UNITED FITNESS CENTER:

Building a Business by Building Bodies

With the compassion of a marine drill sergeant, Jerry Shea parades through his Manchester, New Hampshire, health club with his own gruff cadence calls. "Pump that iron faster," he growls at one pudgy neophyte struggling to shed a few spare pounds. For 12 hours a day, Jerry continues the beat, catering to his growing rosters of customers interested in physical fitness.

Jerry does know how to build bodies, but he's still not sure he can build a business. Starting in 1980 with a few borrowed dollars, his United Fitness Center is a "situation very much in doubt," as the lanky 28-year-old entrepreneur would say.

Jerry, when did you first decide to open a fitness center?

The idea came from my ex-partner. We both served together in the Navy, discharged in 1979. When we were handed our discharge papers we, of course, began to think about a career. That's when he suggested opening a health club in our home town of Manchester.

Did you have any prior experience in the business?

No, and neither did my partner. But we both enjoyed "working out" in a gym two or three times a week since our high school days. The Navy had their own way to keep us in shape, since we didn't have any particular experience or training in any other field, I suppose it was only logical we'd end up with a health club.

You mention an "ex-partner." What happened to him?

He sold me his interest in the business a year after we opened, the business couldn't afford to support two partners. It can hardly support one. Another reason he sold out was because he couldn't handle the pressures of the business. He was the cautious methodical type, who belongs in a large corporation. Running a small business is very different. You have a thousand problems to contend with and you have to be the type who enjoys it. That wasn't for my partner and that's why I bought him out instead of my being the one to sell out. We're still good friends.

How much start-up capital did you and your partner invest?

Ten thousand dollars between us. My partner actually invested more than I, $7000 compared to my $3000. But when I bought him out I agreed to pay him $10,000 over two years with 20% interest, so he made out okay.

Can you really start a health club with only $10,000?

You can start any business with $10,000. What you're asking is whether it can last. In my case I'm not sure. That's my problem. We didn't have the money to do the job right to begin with, and the business is paying the price today.

Let's go over that, Jerry. What were your start-up costs?

If you look around you'll see that all we have here is a 3000-sq.-ft. club, carpeting on the floor, panelled walls, lockers, and a shower room. We'll get to the equipment in a moment.

The shower room was installed by the landlord, that's why we rented this particular location. It would have cost $10,000–15,000 if we had to do it ourselves. Five thousand dollars was spent to buy the carpeting and wall panelling, but my partner and I did all the installation work ourselves, saving $10,000 in labor costs.

Equipment you can lease with very low dollars down. We feature Universal-brand equipment that's worth over $25,000 and we pay $650 a month to the leasing company. In two more years we'll own it outright. The lockers and miscellaneous gym equipment were picked up at auction of a New York club that went bankrupt. It helped. We only paid $2500 for equipment with a replacement value of over $20,000.

Did you start the venture with any debt?

Nothing serious. Of course we owed the leasing company close to $25,000, but we look at that as an expense rather than as debt. The landlord agreed to defer two months rent so we owed $4000 to him, and we owed another several thousand dollars to electrical contractors who upgraded the air conditioning and installed lighting.

You commented that your limited starting capital is the cause of your problems. Yet you got the ball rolling with little debt. So why is money still a problem?

Because you can't compete today with a second-rate health club, and when you don't have the money to build a first-class facility you can't attract enough members.

What would a first-class club offer that yours doesn't offer?

Many things. The most important is a steam and sauna room. Members want more than exercise machines. They want to work out, take a steam, and dry out in a sauna. The better clubs have it all—swimming pools, whirlpools, massage rooms, tanning rooms, and even "recovery rooms" to enjoy a drink while watching TV. And they offer better equipment. For example, the two lines in the business are Nautilus and Universal. We only have a few Universal pieces. Nautilus came out this year with a piece of equipment to strengthen lower back muscles. It costs close to $8000 and that's only *one* piece of equipment. How many prospective members will be lost because we don't offer the equipment, while a competing club does?

Are you saying that you underestimated what it would take to open a successful club?

Partly. But you have to look at the situation from when we began. Even a few years ago health clubs were little more than gyms. You could open with what we had because health clubs weren't the total fitness centers they are today. We also looked at it from the viewpoint of location. Manchester is a working town. We figured we could feature ourselves as primarily a gym to work out in and ignore the frills. It didn't work well.

You say it didn't work well. How have sales grown and are you making a profit?

When we opened we offered three plans—a lifetime membership for $1000, a one-year membership for $250, and a pay-as-you-come at $7 a session. We signed up about 100 members for the one-year membership, perhaps 50 for lifetime membership, and have very few who pay as they go. In our first year we grossed $125,000. You sign up more members each succeeding year but lose income from members who paid their lifetime membership in the first or second year, so our gross is stabilized at the same $110,000–125,000 a year.

Can you make money on a $125,000 income?

No. It costs me almost $2000 a week just to keep the doors open. Rent is $24,000 a year, utilities $10,000, payroll—exclusive of mine—$20,000, and $10,000 for equipment leases. Then you have all the small expenses from advertising to insurance eating up another $30,000 or so. I know my costs. At $125,000 a year I can probably earn only $15,000 a year and it's not enough money for a 70–80 hour work week.

What are the prospects for building memberships?

They're not good. Manchester isn't a growing town. But each year I have more competition. In the past few years we've had several hotels open on a nearby highway and they now offer health club memberships—with all the fancy trimmings. Actually, I'm lucky not to lose customers let alone gain ground.

Then what advantages can you offer a member?

Only three. One is that we are located downtown. It's convenient for local businessmen who want to catch a half hour of workout time before heading home. The second is that we are lower priced. Memberships in the hotel clubs are about 50% more. The third is that I spend more time with my members. I'll design a specific exercise program for a member and monitor his progress. It's personal attention the fancier clubs don't offer.

Are all your members male?

Yes. Of course, to run a club for women you need separate facilities. I played with the idea of dividing the week so men have it four days and women three, but I think I'll lose more male members than I'll gain in female members. But that is one big advantage a hotel facility with dual facilities can offer. A husband and wife can go together.

Have you run into cash flow problems since you started?

Cash flow is what kept me going. When a member joins, he pays 25% upfront and the balance over one year. With the upfront payments we've managed to keep our head above water.

Jerry, it's clear that your problem is the inability to increase sales—and profits. What do you intend to do about it?

I'm not sure what my options are. More advertising isn't the answer. Every prospective member has already heard of us. Upgrade the facilities? It would cost me $60,000–100,000 to put in a steam and sauna room. And you can't finance it because it's only an improvement to the landlord's property. Even if I had the money to upgrade, I'm not sure the added memberships would cover the cost. We already have a second-rate image and that's difficult to change.

Do you think relocation of the business to a less competitive area can be an answer?

If an area doesn't have good competitive facilities, it's underpopulated, and if it's underpopulated it can't support my stripped down version of a club. It's not a workable solution.

Have you thought of selling the business?

I made the decision to sell if sales don't substantially increase in the next year or two—which I don't expect to happen. I've already made up my mind not to stick out the long hours for a low pay. I could make the same or better money doing any of 101 jobs without the long hours or headaches.

What makes you so confident you'll find a buyer?

There's always a buyer for a business like this. I can put it on the market for $45,000–50,000 and let someone in for $10,000 down. There are plenty of people with $10,000 in their pocket who think they can double what a seller did for business. Maybe they can.

What would you do, Jerry, if you did sell?

I'd buy a health club. I wouldn't start another from scratch. Many of the hotels and resorts will set up a first-class facility and lease it to an owner-operator, on a percentage of gross basis. Even large manufacturing and hi-tech firms are setting up "on-site" health clubs as a fringe benefit for employees. Rather than operate it themselves, most prefer to lease it. It would give me a first-class facility, a captive trade, and no upfront financing needed. There's no way I can earn less than I'm making now. I'm sorry I didn't do it back in 1979.

You don't sound like a man thrilled by his own business. Do you regret starting the venture?

Not really. It's part of the learning process. Sometimes you do have to go into two or three ventures before you find one that clicks. I'm older now and can look at a business deal with greater objectivity than I could in the past. It's no calamity to take a shot and strike out. You learn a lot about yourself and what running a business is all about. When you do start again you hope you won't make the same mistakes, although you're bound to make new mistakes.

What did you learn about yourself from this one venture?

I was too optimistic. My weakness was enthusiasm rather than checking the demand for what I had to offer. Had I looked realistically at the rapid changes in the health club field, and the competition springing up around me I would have nixed the idea. My strength is the ability to handle daily problems. The next time I'll obtain more help in researching the market.

What's the one word of advice you'd give an entrepreneur planning to start on a shoestring?

The amount of owner investment doesn't mean that much in the total scheme of things. If the business has the right ingredients it will overcome small capital or high debt. If it has a serious flaw, then more money isn't the solution. The business will still fail—it just may take longer. The important question is—do I have something to offer enough customers to produce a profitable company?

ANIMAL HOUSE:

Combining Nature's Wonders and an $8000 Investment into a $350,000-a-Year Money-Maker

The monkeys hang from tree limbs, bears recline outside a paper maché cave, and poodles huddle around a fire hydrant. These and hundreds of other species are up for adoption at Animal House, the stuffed animal zoo ringing up $350,000 in sales at a bustling Pittsburgh mall. The zookeepers, as they like to be called are Ann Kaplan and Wendy Hoffman who started their animal emporium in 1981 with $8000 in borrowed funds. How successful is the venture? As Ann says, "We're making money and having a lot of fun doing it. What else counts?" Here's their story.

Ann, how did you and Wendy team up?

We belonged to several clubs together and shared much in common, including the fact we were both recently divorced and had to go out into the working world. We began to commiserate with each other and compare notes on career opportunities when we realized we each wanted our own business in the retail field. Since we hit it off so well it was only natural to team up.

How did you come up with the idea for a store specializing in stuffed animals?

We knew we wanted a specialty store—a store selling a very limited line of merchandise. Our original idea was to open a facial salon selling our own brand of cosmetics, when we read about a very successful stuffed animal shop in Baltimore. We checked it out and liked what we saw. But we didn't stop there. We found several stores similar to ours and they all seemed to be doing well. *Entrepreneur Magazine* even had a write-up on this type business and gave it high marks as a profitable business that can be started with little cash. I think the article gave us the final confidence we needed.

Did either you or Wendy have prior experience in retailing?

We both had retail experience and I suppose that's why we gravitated towards a retail business. Before and during the early years of my marriage I worked as an assistant buyer for Federated Department Stores. Wendy's experience was as a cosmetic consultant in a smaller store in Philadelphia. However, neither of us had experience with this particular type business or line of merchandise.

Since you knew nothing about the business, how did you go about deciding on such things as suppliers, inventory, and pricing?

Our biggest mistake was to assume it was an easy business to learn. Looking back, we simply figured that all we had to do was stock the store with stuffed animals and create an interesting format for the store. So we learned as we went along and made too many mistakes in the process.

Back to my original question, Ann, how did you select suppliers and decide on a pricing policy and merchandise lines?

We found suppliers by going to the New York Gift Show. Several manufacturers of stuffed animals were there and they gave us the names of others. Once we opened we received catalogs from probably 30 other suppliers. Our merchandising wasn't particularly scientific. Wendy and I would go through the catalog and pick out lines we found attractive and thought would be popular sellers. As for pricing, we started with the manufacturers' suggested retail list, which is usually to double your money. We've since modified our buying, merchandising, and pricing policy.

It sounds like you made some mistakes. Can you tell us about them?

It's never easy to confess your errors, but our major mistake was to order too many of the common lines. Seventy percent of our original lines could be found in stores such as Child World and Toys "R" Us. That's not the way we wanted it. What we wanted was the distinctive lines you couldn't find in most of the other stores. Now we do business only with suppliers of the unusual lines. That's what a specialty store should be all about. And now that we've been able to find the right sources of supply, we can usually triple our money. A $20 item costs us in the vicinity of $6–7. You can work on that kind of markup when you have an unusual product not featured in other stores.

Ann, I've interviewed several other shoestring start-ups in the retail field and they all seem to be saying what you say—

go for the highly specialized lines so you're not fighting larger competitors. Should that be the primary strategy?

Absolutely. Retailing has come full circle in the last 20 years. We're back to the era of the specialty store, and the specialty store is a perfect opportunity for the business person with small capital. They key to the specialty store is to feature merchandise that is distinctive. If you feature what all the other stores carry, there's no reason for your existence. We want people to walk through our store and see our products for the very first time. That's what Animal House is all about.

Animal House seems to have more animals than the San Diego Zoo. How many types of animals do you have?

We stock about 1000 different products, representing about 80 forms of animal life. We have everything from stuffed snakes to a six-foot grizzly bear. Whenever we find a species we don't have in stock we add it.

I can understand stuffed panda bears and poodles being solid sellers, but who wants a stuffed snake?

You'd be surprised. Last year we sold over $25,000 worth of the slithery creatures. The more exotic the species the better it seems to sell, although cuddly bears are still our best-sellers.

I imagine that most of your customers are children?

No. The largest percentage of our customers are grandmothers always looking for a very different gift for their grandchildren. In many cases a child will drag a parent or grandparent into the store because the store does attract children. A week later the parent will come back and buy an item as a surprise gift. Boyfriends are another constant source of business, always picking up gifts for their girlfriends.

Is the business seasonal?

We do about 40% of our business during Christmas. February is our next best month because stuffed animals can make an excellent Valentine Day's gift. We have another spurt for Easter, when we usually sell out on stuffed rabbits.

Do you stock only stuffed animals or are you expanding into other lines?

We're moving away from stuffed animals and into lines that are decorative. For example, we now have an inventory of paper maché parrots and myna birds. They are colorful decorations for a dining room or family room. We have on order several coffee tables with brass elephants as a pedestal, ceramic giraffes, camels, tigers, and leopards are popular decorations for a home and they move as fast as we can get them. We even have a display of jewelry boxes with animal carvings. Our objective is to reduce our stuffed inventory lines to 60% of our mix and increasingly emphasize the decorative products.

You seem to have an interesting way to display the animals. They appear to be in their natural habitat.

It's all part of merchandising. We want the animals to look like they're almost alive. And we try to give them appeal. A monkey with a banana in his hand and a sign saying "I'm lonely, take me home," has a personality. It will outsell a product without the sales pitch by ten to one. We do whatever we can to make our creatures lovable. That's when people buy them.

Let's go back to the beginning. How did you manage all this on an $8000 investment?

That was the hard part. We ran out of money very early in the game. The rent, utility deposits, and sign absorbed our entire investment and we had absolutely no capital for fixtures, inventory, or working capital. We had some anxious moments.

Taking it a point at a time, Ann, how did you happen to land a lease in what appears to be a very successful mall?

We were lucky. Usually the better malls won't rent to an independent. We had two things going for us. We weren't competitive with other tenants, and mall developers do want the widest possible mix of tenants. We were also willing to settle for a 1000-sq.-ft. store. Most tenants need considerably more space so you have a better chance with what developers call "scrap space."

How expensive is the rent in a location like this?

We pay $20 a sq. ft. or $20,000 a year. In addition we pay an override of 5% on sales over $300,000 a year. On top of it all, we pay our share towards the merchants association and common area maintenance. This year our occupancy costs will be about $30,000.

Do you consider the rent excessive, when measured against $350,000 gross sales?

No doubt about it. A rent of 9% of sales is high, but it's not excessive for us because we work on a 60% gross profit and have low expenses. We can still turn a healthy profit and without a mall location, a specialty store such as ours probably wouldn't be successful.

Ann, you said you had no capital for fixtures and inventory. How did you fixture the store with no cash?

Everything you see are make-shift fixtures. It forced us to be creative, and I think we developed a far more intriguing store as a result. A few examples: We varnished an actual tree as a display for the monkeys. Fishnets on the walls are perfect for hanging other stuffed animals. You don't see many fixtures because they distract from the merchandise. Wherever you look we want you to see animals. It's only a matter of displaying them in an interesting way. We did buy two used showcases for $100 and painted them ourselves. A used cash register cost us $300, picked up from a used equipment dealer for $25 a month.

Inventory must have been a different story. How did you initially stock the store?

It was all done with trade credit. We found that trade credit isn't much of a problem in this field because it is so competitive. But we were probably naive. Wendy would go through the catalogs and write out purchase orders. For our opening stock we mailed out 30 purchase orders for $27,000 worth of merchandise. The merchandise didn't flow in as we expected. We finally received about $15,000 in merchandise, but other suppliers held back because we didn't have a credit rating.

Does that mean you started with about 50% of the inventory you planned on?

No. We talked several of the holdout suppliers into shipping. A few agreed to ship smaller quantities and a few others shipped on the strength of our personal guarantees. Eventually we opened our doors with about $20,000 in merchandise. But we did have to shop around to get that credit.

Did you consider bank financing to obtain the inventory?

Wendy mentioned it but I was against it. I didn't think we needed it and didn't want to go through the red tape to obtain a bank loan. I just didn't think we were talking about enough money to make it worthwhile.

Assuming the suppliers sold you on 30-day terms, I imagine you had a problem paying the bills on time?

We opened September 1, 1981, and found that at that time of the year many manufacturers will give you "Christmas dating." For this reason, many of our bills weren't due until January, 1982. This gave us four months to turn the inventory so we were able to minimize the cash flow problem. In the fourth-month period we grossed $80,000, so we turned the merchandise several times. The difficulty with trade credit financing is that you want to take the profits and sink it into added lines, but you can't because you're obligated to work down payables.

How fast did your inventory grow? You started with $20,000. What is it now?

In the two years since we opened, the inventory has grown from $20,000 to about $40,000. As you can see, we have a space limitation, so we're trying to upgrade lines and produce more sales per square foot. That takes higher ticket items.

How did you finance this growth in inventory? Did it come from profits, trade credit, or outside financing?

It came totally from profits. We started with a $20,000 inventory and $20,000 in payables. Our payables are down to about $8000, which means our net worth increased by $32,000 since we opened. But it's not totally fair to say we showed that much profit.

For the first six months Wendy and I took a very small salary and that really helped the business along.

Did you have any moments when you thought the business might not make it?

Not since we've opened our doors. We estimated $15,000 a month as our break-even point. In our first month we grossed $18,000. Of course, a business like ours reaches its maximum sales very quickly because it depends on a high-traffic count and impulse shoppers.

How much sales growth are you experiencing?

In our first year we grossed $270,000 and $352,000 in our second. This growth came about because we had more merchandise and better quality lines from when we opened. Our average sale in the first year was $12.40 and now it's close to $19. We are picking up some business from referrals, but our strategy is still to increase sales by expanding into decorative lines and higher ticket items.

Do you do any advertising for the store?

We're not sure it's cost justified. Plush animals are primarily an impulse item. We don't think people will go out of their way to find us. Most of our customers are people who never intended to buy until they walked by our store. Once we move into decorative items we may try some advertising in local homeowner magazines. A housewife looking for an unusual item may travel to a mall, but plush animals don't fall into that category.

Promotion is a different story. We've tried many promotional gimmicks within the mall itself. Each Saturday during November and December we have a college student walk around the mall dressed as a large grizzly bear. He's the same kind of creature you're likely to meet at Disney World. The kids enjoy it and it lets them know we're in the mall.

How many people do you have on your payroll?

The store is open 9:00 a.m.–9:00 p.m., six days a week. Wendy and I split the shifts, alternating 9–5 and 1–9 shifts. We overlap the afternoon hours because those are our busiest hours and it gives one of us time to catch up on ordering and bookkeeping. In addition, we have another sales clerk always on the floor. This year we intend to hire a stock clerk to come in for 3–4 hours a day because merchandise must be uncrated and displayed as soon as it's received. We don't have storage facilities and now we receive merchandise almost on a daily basis.

Ann, do you and Wendy have separate responsibilities or do you equally share all the work?

Wendy and I share the buying decision since buying is the most important activity in our business. Wendy does all the bookkeeping and bill paying because she's better at it than I. We always believed one person should handle the books so it's totally coordinated. Wendy was the logical candidate because she's extremely tough on vendors and is quite good at orchestrating our cash flow. I was never good at numbers and I can't even get my own checkbook to balance.

Do you operate as a corporation or as a partnership?

As a corporation. Wendy and I each own 50% of the shares. I'm President and Wendy is Treasurer and Secretary. We thought it would be safer to operate as a corporation and our accountant and attorney agreed.

Animal House is a great name for your business. Did you pirate it from the movie by the same name?

I wouldn't say we pirated it, but what else would you call a store featuring nothing but animals? It was the best name we could come up with.

What were your biggest problems since you opened? You don't build a $350,000-a-year business without hitting a few potholes.

Buying the wrong merchandise was our number one problem. At the beginning we misjudged what would sell and overstocked on slow movers. We still have merchandise that's been with us since we opened. Now we have much tighter control. We experiment with one or two pieces of an item and re-order only in proportion to sales. Inventory control and tying merchandise to sales is critical when you operate with little cash.

How profitable can a business like yours be?

Once we got by the first year, Wendy and I each started to draw $300 a week in salary. We are now up to $400 a week and in another year expect to up it again to $500 a week. After salary, profits should be about 7%, so in total we should each earn about $35,000 a year from the business.

Do you intend to take the profits out of the business or reinvest it back into the venture?

We'll probably reinvest another $10,000–15,000 to expand our lines. Once our inventory reaches $50,000 we can begin to take profits out of the business. We don't think the business can justify more than a $50,000 inventory level in terms of space or sales.

What about expansion? Do you have any plans to enlarge the store?

It's not in the cards. The two tenants on either side of us are here to stay. Our only option would be to take over a larger store in the mall if it became available. We would be interested in doubling our size because merchandising is limited with a small 1000-sq.-ft. store. We could bring in many more lines if we had the extra space and the only expense that would go up would be rent, so we would have a much better profit picture.

Wouldn't another option be to expand by opening a second store in another mall?

We definitely do not want a multiple unit operation. The strength of our operation is the fact that a boss is always present. Once we expand into a second store we'd have to depend on outsiders to staff the stores for one shift a day. We don't want that.

Why not? You'd only be relying on your personnel to sell. You would still control buying and merchandising.

It's a question of trust. When you leave a store to help you never know what's going into the cash register and what's going into their pocket. Wendy and I talked about it and we prefer to have total control by working together in one store. We can make enough from one store without worrying about two.

Do you and Wendy agree on all decisions? It seems that when you talk I hear one voice representing two minds.

We agree on the major decisions and that's why it has been a successful partnership. But we worked out our business philosophy before we agreed to team up, and that's why we probably have so few disagreements today. Fortunately, a business like ours is rather smooth, we don't have many earthshaking decisions to make. About the only thing we do disagree on is the selection of new lines. Typically we resolve it by letting our sales clerk break a stalemate. You can't take it too seriously.

Of all the start-ups I've interviewed, yours is one of the smoothest and most successful. What do you see as they key points in your success?

There are several factors. The timing was right. By opening at the start of the peak sales we're able to dovetail high initial sales and extended credit terms. The main point is still the numbers. Our business survived because it had a combination of strong sales, very high profit margins, and exceptionally low overhead. The business could rapidly generate cash flow and profit. And that's just the kind of business you need when you start with limited capital. You can't go for a business with only long-term potential. You need something that can take off very rapidly. A specialty shop in a good location, such as ours, is a perfect example.

How carefully did you plan your venture before you started? It sounds like your success came about through trial and error.

I think every business does. You can only plan so much. Once you're in business you have to quickly adjust to all the "zigs and zags" in the road. You don't know what the problems and opportunities are until you get your feet wet. Our own planning was limited to the type location, approximate size, and of course, the name and merchandising approach. We had no detailed financial projections and I don't think it would have helped if we did. All we knew was that we were willing to work without pay for awhile and give it our best shot. Our management approach was far from scientific.

You're obviously happy running your own business. Any regrets?

None. I thoroughly enjoy it. The business is fascinating, especially searching out new and interesting lines. Next year we plan to go to Europe to see what lines we can import. You don't get that kind of satisfaction from a job. I'm so spoiled that I couldn't work for anybody else. There's something about taking an idea and actually making it work. Had this business failed I probably would have just started again.

HEALTH CARE PERSONNEL:

Bootstrapping Their Way into the Exploding Home Health Care Field

"Finding a special duty nurse to care for patients confined to their home has been no easy chore for Miami area shut-ins," say Pat and Mary McCullock, a husband-and-wife team whose objective is to cure the problem with their three-year-old Health Care Personnel Agency.

The McCullocks make no claim to instant success. The demand for their services is there, but so are the constant problems of juggling cash flow to keep the business on an even keel. Their success or failure is as speculative as finding their next check in the mailbox.

Pat, tell us more about your business. Exactly what does it do?

We have one function. We provide private-duty nurses to patients confined to their home.

Are these nurses on your staff or do they work on an "on-call" basis?

They're all independent contractors who work on an "on-call" basis. Essentially we're like Kelly Girl who provides temporary secretarial services. When we receive a call from the patient we turn to our roster of nurses and locate the nurse who can commit to the hours required for the job. We pay the nurse at the end of each week and bill the patient. The spread is our profit.

What kind of profit spread is there between what you charge and what you pay?

We pay the registered nurses $10.50 an hour and bill the patient $18. Some patients require only licensed practical nurses and we pay them $7.50 an hour and bill $14. For Medicaid patients we bill the state and are limited to a $14 reimbursement for RNs. Because of the low rate and delays in payment we try to stay away from Medicaid patients. Fewer than 5% of our patients are on Medicaid. Medicare is another matter. We can charge them our customary rates and have no trouble collecting within three weeks. With so many of our patients over 65, we probably have 50% of our billings directed to Medicare. I wish all our patients were on Medicare. We wouldn't have so many problems getting our money in.

What types of nursing or home health care services do your nurses provide?

Many of our patients are only convalescing from hospitalization. They may need nursing services for one or two weeks on an around the clock basis. The geriatric patient may need a nurse for an extended period. Our nurses do everything you'd expect under hospitalization.

That brings up the obvious question. If your patients are in need of constant nursing care, why don't they seek hospitalization or nursing home care?

For a variety of reasons. Many patients prefer to convalesce at home, they don't want to be hospitalized. In many other cases the patient is discharged, but finds he or she still needs nursing assistance from time to time. This is particularly true with the post-operative patient.

Mary, how did you perceive the need for your service?

Home health care is rapidly escalating. It may be the fastest growing segment of health services. The emphasis is on non-institutionalized medicine and third-party reimbursement agencies such as Medicare, Medicaid, and Blue Cross. They're pushing for home health care instead of prolonged hospitalizations. It's not only less expensive but helps the patient towards faster recuperation. So we know there would be a dramatic increase in the number of patients needing home health care services.

That brings me to my next question. If a patient needs a special-duty nurse, why do they have to go through your agency? Why can't they advertise directly for a nurse?

Many patients do. Many nurses advertise their own services, and local hospitals and the nursing associations have a roster of nurses looking for this type of work. But patients come to us for two reasons. One is that they don't know about these free referral services. Oftentimes the decision to hire a nurse is an emergency and they don't have the time to look around. A second reason is that we screen our nurses. There are some second-rate nurses around and patients don't want to take a chance on hiring someone who may not be reliable—or even competent. We stand behind the quality of our nursing staff.

How difficult is it to find nurses available for special-duty care?

It varies from locality to locality and also runs in cycles. The Miami area always has a shortage of nurses because such a large percentage of the population are geriatrics. There's a constant shortage of all health professionals. On a national basis there's a surplus of nurses. While we have problems finding good nurses, the upside is that the shortage keeps the number of nurses directly advertising their services down. In some parts of the country you can find a half-page of classified from nurses looking for private-duty work.

How competitive is your field?

We have three other firms in the Dade-Broward County areas who do pretty much what we do. Since we are the newest we also are the smallest. However, we hope to catch up with the competition by capturing a larger percentage of the market each year. Right now we do about 10% of the business and even if we don't grab more of the business, the increased demand should give us a healthy growth. It's still a competitive business and we expect new competition as time goes on.

What do you offer that other firms don't offer? What's your competitive advantage?

We really don't have any. All the home health care firms in the area provide essentially the same services for about the same rates. You can't really outdo the competition. All you can do is hope to obtain a reasonable portion of the business.

Do you have a particular approach to advertising?

We do what everyone else in our business does. We advertise daily in the metropolitan papers and send out brochures to hospitals and physicians. Most of our business is from physician referrals.

Pat, can you give us an idea of how much of your business grosses and the sales increases over the years?

During the first year we grossed $400,000 in billings. This year we're up to $700,000. Within a year or two we hope to hit the one-million mark.

Now that we know what your business is like today, let's go back to how you conceived the idea. What made you select this business?

Mary is herself a nurse so she was familiar with the technical end of the business and how to recruit, screen, and evaluate performance. My experience was in personnel work as an assistant personnel manager for a hi-tech firm. This business seemed like the ideal way to merge our talents in what we saw as a field with dynamic growth.

What type of planning did you do for the venture?

We spent about six months trying to find out everything we could from similar firms from around the country. Essentially it was six months of "picking brains." We then worked up a comprehensive business plan covering everything from start-up needs to operational policies and financial projections. We were on target with everything but our financial projections. That's where we fell down.

Let's get to that in just a moment. What did you estimate as needed for start-up costs?

Setting up an office was the simple part. We rented a $500-a-month office in Miami, and to outfit the office with equipment cost another $7000. We knew we needed a computerized operation so we leased an IBM for $800 a month. The software was expensive. We needed to program our own software to meet our needs and that cost us over $12,000. So our physical plant alone cost us almost $25,000.

The promotional program—flyers, advertising, and direct mail—for our launch was accurately projected at $20,000, with sustained advertising at $2000 a month thereafter.

How did you capitalize these costs?

We invested $10,000 of our own funds and borrowed $50,000 from the SBA. We figured this would give us $30,000–35,000 for working capital.

How difficult was it to obtain SBA financing?

We tried the banks first, and in fact, we had to be turned down by two banks before the SBA would consider us. The SBA was more "red tape" than we hoped for, but it was the only way to cement our financing. From the time we filed our loan application to the date we received our money was almost six months.

What are the terms of the SBA loan?

We have a seven-year payback which is longer than a bank would give us. We're paying 15½% interest or about 1% more than bank rates. Our loan is made through a local bank and guaranteed by the SBA, so it's a participation rather than a direct loan. For collateral we pledged the assets of our business and gave a second mortgage on our home.

Was the $35,000 sufficient working capital for your business?

No, we fell short on our projected capital needs by at least $70,000 and it's been the bane of our existence since. You can say we're strangling to death because we didn't have the financial backing.

How did you fall short on your working capital projections? I'm curious how you could underestimate your capital needs by so much.

This is an accounts receivable business. When we started, we calculated that we would have to finance about three weeks receivables or $35,000. We pay our nurses each Friday and simultaneously bill the patient (or Medicare) the same day. We expect our patients to pay within seven days and discontinue service if payments are not received within 14 days. There is no discontinuance under Medicare or Medicaid billings because we're relying on the government's credit. In theory, our receivables should turn over within three weeks but that's not how it happens in practice. Many private patients don't pay. We have over $40,000 in uncollectable receivables on our books. We set up no reserve for bad debts when we made our projections. We were naive. Our average collection period is not 21 days as we hoped, but closer to 35 days. To compound the problem, we're doing business at the rate of $750,000 a year. That means we have over $70,000 in current receivables on the books on top of the $40,000 we had to write off. We just weren't geared to finance $110,000 in receivables—not when you only have $35,000 to work with.

What impact does this have on operations?

Obviously, the money has to come from somewhere to cover the short fall in cash flow. We don't have an inventory to play with, so a buildup of receivables can only come from a buildup in payables. Right now we're behind two weeks in paying our nurses, three months behind in our rent, and seriously behind in virtually every other operating expense. Our checkbook has a constant overdraft of $10,000–15,000, and we've bounced more than one check. Falling behind with suppliers is one thing, it's something else when you can't make payroll or pay the rent. They don't let you fall behind 60–90 days.

Have you tried to refinance to obtain the needed working capital?

Half our time is spent looking for fresh money. We need a line of credit of about $180,000 to clear up the problem. Forty thousand dollars is needed to pay off the SBA, and $140,000 to properly finance the receivables and give us a few extra dollars for growth.

So far we've been unsuccessful. Banks don't consider our profit and loss statement strong enough to justify such a large loan. I also found that banks shy away from receivables as collateral. They prefer tangibles.

How about factoring your receivables? Many firms solve their receivable financing problems by assigning their receivables to a factor for immediate payment.

Factoring is not a workable solution for us. We can't assign the receivables to a factor unless we first pay down the SBA, as a factor wants the receivables free of liens. The second problem is that factoring doesn't work with consumer receivables. There's too much paperwork for the small amount due on each bill. Also, Medicare and Medicaid won't pay a third party such as a factor.

What we are after is a receivable loan. We'd retain ownership of the receivable and the bank would lend an amount equal to 70–80% of the outstanding but collectable receivables. So far we have no takers.

Part of your problem is your growth. Wouldn't you be in a better cash position if you had smaller sales and fewer receivables to finance?

It's a "Catch-22." We would have some alleviation to our cash flow problems, but we'd also have operating losses. So what do you do—cut back on sales to conserve cash or go after more profits? We walk that tightrope every day.

How profitable is your business now?

We lost $12,000 the first year and $56,000 last year. The large loss last year was because we wrote off the $40,000 in uncollectable receivables as a bad debt expense. This year we expect to make a $20,000 profit, assuming we can stay within our bad debt allowance of $15,000. Health care is still a marginal operation whose profitability depends on how you assess the collectability of the receivables.

Pat, if you can't re-finance would you consider bringing in a partner?

Partnership is our last alternative. Mary and I enjoy working together. Only a passive or silent partner would be interested in hooking up with a husband-and-wife team and a silent partner isn't likely to want to part with $100,000–150,000 for an interest in the business.

How do you know? Perhaps an investor will see growth potential that can lead to profitability once you overcome the cash crunch.

Maybe, but we want to stick it out as long as we can until we're sure re-financing is no longer a possibility.

What steps have you taken to cut back on expenses?

It's a bare bones operation now. We don't know where else we can cut back. In a sense we're retrenching because our creditors are forcing us to. For example, three newspapers will no longer accept our ads without COD payments. More times than not we don't have the money for ad space so we save on the cost at the expense of lost sales. Many of our better nurses won't work for us any longer. Why should they wait two weeks to get paid when other agencies pay on time? In the past year we probably lost 50 of our top nurses to competitive agencies. When you lose quality personnel in this field, it hurts.

Pat, speaking frankly, it appears that your business is going in the wrong direction. How much longer can you hang on if you can't raise capital?

That's very difficult to answer. A major slowdown in receivables could knock us out of business in a month. The business is at the breaking point now. On the other hand, if we stabilize at our present volume and can keep the cash flowing in on a regular basis and begin to build profits, then eventually the retained earnings may in a year or two substantially improve our cash flow position. There's no doubt about it though, we are at the fork in the road where the business must turn in one direction or another.

Since your one possibly fatal error has been in calculating the working capital needed to finance receivables, I'm interested in the help your accountant provided in the cash flow projections.

We had a CPA work with us during the planning stage. Mary and I worked up a rough cash flow projection and in retrospect our accountant only rubber-stamped it. It was partially our fault. We needed someone with strong experience in credit oriented industries. It's very tricky to plan your capital needs when receivables are part of the equation. Our new accountant has the experience, but he can't rectify the problem of starting with too limited capital.

What does your accountant recommend? At this stage you obviously need some professional guidance if you expect to survive.

He came up with one idea. His primary recommendation is to trim the business back to $300,000–400,000 a year and concentrate on patients who will prepay for their services. Improving cash flow is his only concern at this point and in theory I agree. The problem is in its practicality. You can't find the patients who'll prepay—not when your competitors defer their billing. So we look at it as only a textbook solution.

How much salary do you and Mary draw each week?

Right now I take only $450 a week from the business. I can't live on less. Mary is on the books for $400 a week but has deferred her salary for the last few months as a loan due from the corporation.

Pat, have you considered the idea of selling shares in the company to the nurses on your roster? The corporation could become a "nurses-owned cooperative," with the shares paid for from present earnings. Many troubled firms are becoming "employee owned," funded by salary reductions. It seems to be catching hold in labor intensive businesses such as yours.

No, I never did consider it. Of course, it sounds complicated and may mean that I'd lose ownership control of the business, but it is one alternative that beats bankruptcy.

Pat, you've had a rough ride with your business. Are you sorry you started?

I can't honestly answer that one. If the business fails, I'll probably lose my home and several years hard work. When you consider the salary cuts Mary and I took to begin this business, and add it to what we might lose, you're talking about a possible $200,000 loss. We're not rich people and you can't afford too many of those mistakes in a lifetime. If this is the winter of my discontent, you can say I'm discontented. Still, I am a perennial optimist—as every entrepreneur is—and for our breed, hope always springs eternal.

MOLLY-BEE MUFFINS, INC.:

Building a Better Business from a Better Muffin

In the Providence, Rhode Island, area they say you haven't really tasted a blueberry muffin until you tried a Molly-Bee muffin. I accepted the challenge from Michael Shapiro, Molly-Bee's 57-year-old founder, who was found with a tall white baker's hat perched on his head, unloading another batch of muffins from his overworked ovens. The townsfolk were right. Molly-Bee was the best muffin in town. I could see—and taste—how Molly-Bee came to be a $2-million-a-year enterprise from a humble $6000 investment. As with a good idea—you can't stop a good muffin whose time has come. Mike Shapiro, an affable type, mopped his brow and removed his chimney-like hat and told how it all happened as he joined me over a cup of coffee—and of course—several Molly-Bee muffins.

Mike, you seem to have a good size operation here. How large is it?

In terms of sales, we expect to crack $3 million this year. That's up 20% over last year. We have 27 employees and a fleet of nine delivery trucks. It gives you a pretty good idea of what we're about.

You bake a great muffin. Who do you sell to?

The way we look at it is that the consumer is our true customer. If they like our product, it will sell. Of course, we don't sell retail but only to restaurants, hotels, canteen services, and even other bakeries. Because we have to deliver "fresh" every day, our accounts are all within a two-hour radius of Providence.

Mike, tell us how you happened to start a muffin bakery. It's not the kind of business you hear about every day.

The army trained me as a baker back in 1944. Since then I worked as a baker in several bakery firms and a large hotel. I held my last job for over 16 years with a retail bakery firm, which went bankrupt in 1975. So I was out of a job, and when you're unemployed you begin to worry. I decided to take the plunge and bought my ex-boss's equipment from the Bankruptcy Court and set up shop.

They say that around Providence you're the muffin king. Why did you decide to become a wholesale muffin-maker instead of opening a full line or retail bakery?

I'd rather be good at one thing instead of mediocre at many. There was a demand for a good quality muffin, and nobody was turning out that top-notch muffin. My hunch was that restaurants would pay for a better-quality product, and I was right.

You bet your survival on the fact that you can turn out a better-quality muffin. What gives your muffin the edge over the competition's?

Size and quality. Our muffins are 30–40% larger than your average muffin. And they're lighter, fresher, and tastier. We use only natural products, put more into the muffin, and insist on the customer being served a fresh muffin.

Is it based on some secret formula or trade secret, or can any bakery match your muffin if they wanted to?

We have a few tricks which we won't discuss. Beyond that it's just a matter of demanding that the best quality ingredients go into our muffins. And we try to give the customer more for his money. For example, our blueberry muffins are loaded with fresh blueberries. We don't scrimp. You can say that our approach to muffins is the same as Frank Perdue's approach to chickens. Build a quality product and people buy. It's not difficult to understand.

How many people can appreciate a better muffin? I mean, will customers really select one restaurant or coffee shop over another because they sell Molly-Bee muffins instead of someone else's?

Muffin lovers will. Understand that for many people a muffin is their breakfast or lunch. It's a meal. And people who do know muffins can tell the difference. It's very much like good coffee. A restaurant can buy the least expensive or the top brand. For the restaurant it becomes a part of their operating philosophy—do they want to serve a quality product or go second-class.

I imagine most of your accounts are the top-quality restaurants?

If you mean the most expensive restaurants, you're wrong. Canteen services, coffee shops, and truck stops are the easiest places to sell. They're more quality-oriented than hotel restaurants, for example, who are basically selling atmosphere. There's something to be said about eating where the truckers stop.

What do you have for competition? You can't be the only muffin distributor in the area.

There are several bakery wholesalers who distribute various types of baked goods—donuts, cakes, breads, and rolls. With our larger accounts we have to convince them to buy our product rather than bake their own muffins. It's not an easy selling job to a hotel, for example, with its own bakery. In either situation our selling point is that we provide a better product than they can either buy elsewhere or make themselves. And for them it means repeat business.

How do your prices compare to your competition's?

We're about 25% higher. On a per muffin basis it's only a matter of another 8–10 cents. But the muffin may be the draw to attract a customer who'll spend $3–4 on a meal.

Now that we have an idea on the background of your company, let's go back to the beginning and find out how you put it all together and made it grow to its present size. Did you pre-test the idea before you committed yourself to the start-up?

I had a pretty good idea of the demand. The bakery I was working in had several accounts buying muffins and I figured that they would start as a nucleus of my business. Beyond that I talked to a few restaurant owners who expressed an interest in a quality muffin, if I could deliver at the right price and on a daily basis. If you know your business you have a pretty good idea of what you can sell.

I understand your starting capital was only $6000. How did you put together a shop for so little money?

What you see today is the result of seven years of expansion. We started out on a very small scale with only a few baking ovens, some miscellaneous equipment, and one delivery van. Our $6000 capital didn't last very long.

How did you finance the purchase of the equipment?

The equipment went at auction for $8000. Used bakery equipment has a very low liquidation value. The same equipment new would cost over $60,000. Because I was able to swing a great price, a local bank agreed to lend me $15,000 against the equipment. The extra $7000 was needed to move and install the equipment, at my location. Riggers charge a fortune to move heavy equipment.

Did you need any other equipment or were the items you picked up at auction sufficient to get started?

We needed a few small items, which we bought on credit from a bakery supply firm. It only amounted to $4000, and we paid it off several months later. The delivery van was another matter. I traded my Chevy sedan for the van, so the van became my family car.

It looks like you now occupy about 3000 sq. ft. of space. Is this the location where you started?

Yes. Originally we rented about 1500 sq. ft. in the building, but I chose this location because it offered the space to expand. I didn't want to outgrow my space and move again. To move the equipment you now see would cost over $50,000. When you talk heavy equipment you try to plan ahead so you can stay put.

What kind of a lease arrangement did you have when you moved in?

The building was originally used as a furniture warehouse. At one time it was used as a retail store, but it's no longer a decent retail location. That's why I was able to negotiate a good lease. When I started, I had a ten-year lease and paid $2 a sq. ft. or $3000 a year. Now my rent for the entire 3000 sq. ft. is about $9000.

Did you have to do any renovations to the building when you moved in?

The floor needed more supports, but the landlord took care of that. There was one expense I overlooked. My lease provided I'd have to pay any increased insurance costs on the building. The insurance on the building jumped from $600 a year to over $5000, because a bakery is a high-fire risk. The only way I could cut the costs was with a sprinkler system which set me back $8000. In my second year I had a plumber friend install the system and he agreed to a 12-month payout.

How much beginning inventory did your business need?

Inventory turns over very fast in this business, about once every two weeks. Our opening supplies totalled about $3000. Trade credit was no problem because I knew most of the suppliers. They were happy to work with me.

How did you go about staffing the business?

We started with myself as the baker and I hired one man for delivery. We start to work at midnight and bake until 6:00 a.m. The van starts its delivery runs at 6:00 a.m. and finishes its rounds about noon.

That's considerably different from what you have now in personnel.

Now we have eight full-time bakers, nine route drivers, two people in the office handling the books, and several people handling a variety of jobs. Our payroll is almost $500,000 a year now. In my first year it was $25,000 including my own $12,000 salary.

Your growth seems to have been steady in all directions, gradually adding staff and equipment to match the buildup of accounts.

My idea has been to keep volume ahead of my increases in expenses. We won't hire more help unless absolutely necessary.

The same is true with equipment. We can't afford idle time with either manpower or equipment.

How steady has your sales growth been? Do you see the company reaching the saturation point?

Our first years gross was about $200,000. By the end of our third year we were at the $1-million mark. Sales have been up about 20% each year since. We think the business has the potential to do $5 million a year before it begins to level off.

Mike, how do you go after new accounts?

I'm the only salesman for our company. When I started I'd walk into a restaurant and leave the owner a dozen muffins and my business card, telling him I'd be back in a few days. There was no sales spiel. The muffins did the selling. A few days later I'd return to see if the customer was ready to do business. It's still my approach, although now many of my new accounts come to me because they know the Molly-Bee reputation. When you have a quality product you have to let the product itself do the selling. Advertising hype doesn't mean much.

Starting with virtually no capital must have created some cash flow problems in your early years. How serious were your problems?

I don't think a new business ever has enough cash, no matter how much is invested. We ran behind 60–90 days with many of our vendors at the beginning, but they could see what we were doing and our purchases were always increasing. Vendors usually work with you when they see the cash flow problems are due to growth. They get nervous when they think it's a business in decline. In large measure, we've been able to avoid serious problems because we have a high gross profit, a fast inventory turnover, and have always managed to keep our expenses in line with sales.

Do you sell your customers on credit or is it COD?

When we started out we sold only on COD. It caused resistance with some customers, but we had no choice. With no working capital behind us we weren't in a position to finance receivables, and to handle receivables you need bookkeeping. It was an added expense we didn't need. In 1981 we switched to a seven-day billing. We were in a better position to finance receivables, but the major reason for the switch was to improve efficiency with our route drivers. If a route driver has to pick up a COD payment it cuts down on the number of deliveries a day he can make.

How did you finance the equipment you've added since opening?

We started with two baking ovens. We now have six. All my ovens were acquired used. There's always an auction on a bakery somewhere, and the spread between used and new is too great to go shop for new. Besides, an oven never seems to wear out. Unlike other types of equipment it doesn't become obsolete. I estimate we saved over $100,000 over the years, and that's money you need to finance growth.

Are there ways in which you can improve efficiency in this type business?

Every business can become more efficient. Back in 1975 we baked about 250 dozen muffins a day. Today we're up to 4000 dozen. Fifty thousand muffins a day is a lot of muffins. We've automated our mixing process and use automatic conveyor belt feeds wherever possible. Where our operation is labor intensive is in deliveries. There are very few ways you can cut costs here, except through better routing.

Is it fair to say you financed growth and expansion through retained earnings or did you use outside financing?

Increases in our capital costs have only been in the areas of added equipment and delivery vehicles. We lease the vehicles so we had no upfront costs. New ovens have been paid for out of cash reserves. We have no long-term debt and except for our original loans never have.

What about expansion, Mike? Where do you see Molly-Bee Muffins going in the next few years?

Our immediate goal is to continue to build sales to $4–5 million. Then we'll have the best possible profit picture. We have added capacity without bringing in more equipment and the output in relation to labor would increase. The only costs that go up in direct proportion to sales are the delivery costs.

Do you see Molly-Bee expanding into other bakery products?

Not in the foreseeable future. Once you begin with a mix of products you have a very different operation. Efficiency goes downhill because you can't use an assembly line method.

How about expanding by packaging your muffins for food store sales?

We've intentionally stayed out of that market. To package muffins for retail sales you need a muffin with a long shelf life and that means preservatives. Molly-Bee muffins have only natural ingredients and that means sold fresh and served fresh.

Mike, did you foresee this kind of growth when you first opened?

Not really. But I'm not sure any business person can predict what a business will be six or seven years into the future. You take a premise—an idea—and use it as a starting point. From there 100 factors can influence the future size and shape of the company.

How carefully did you plan your business? For example, did you use any outside help in preparing your financial projections?

My numbers are in my head. From the day I opened I was able to tell where I stood. On a weekly basis I would review sales, accounts payable, and cash on hand. The only budget I had was to keep payroll within 15% of sales. The only time you need a more refined financial statement is when you're in a merchandising business or have heavy accounts receivable to contend with.

What would you say your major mistake was since you opened?

Not spending enough time on sales. For the first six months I did the baking and could only spend an hour or two a day shopping for new accounts. That was a mistake. To conserve on payroll I was doing the work of a $300 a week baker. I was worth more to the company on the road building sales faster. I imagine a lot of people make that mistake. When you're in business you really have to spend your time where it will do the most good.

How do you allocate your time now?

I still work 60–70 hours a week. I come in about 4:00 a.m. to make sure we're ready for a 6:00 a.m. shipping. Those are the critical hours. From 9:00 a.m. to 12:00 p.m. I try to see several new accounts. The company is now set up on a departmentalized basis—with one supervisor for bakery operations, one for delivery, and one as an office manager. My job is to straighten out problems that can't be handled by the department heads, and of course, I'm still the one-man sales staff.

Any regrets with the business, Mike? As profitable as it may be, it sounds like a tough business to run.

The business is a killer from the viewpoint of hours. It's not only crazy hours but a seven-day week. And it's also a tension business. You work on a tight time schedule. Delivering 50,000 muffins to 500 accounts within a two-hour space. But still it gives me satisfaction to see the business grow. Last year I turned down $600,000 for the business. That's not a bad return on a $6000 investment. It's one form of satisfaction.

Mike, any parting words for other shoestring entrepreneurs about to start their own venture?

Only the same advice I'd give any new business person. Don't go into the venture unless you're 120% committed to making it work. The shoestring entrepreneur only has to work harder to make it work. But it's worth it.

EPILOGUE

What does the future hold for the entrepreneurs you've just met? Can we really predict who will find their formula for success and build their business beyond anything they can imagine today?

Could Royal Little predict back in 1923 that his $10,000 loan to start a small, humble, synthetic yarn processing plant would today be Textron worth over $3,000,000,000?

Did Frank Seiberling realize when he borrowed $13,500 to start Goodyear Rubber and Tire Co. that it would someday produce sales in excess of $7,000,000,000?

You wonder whether Atlanta druggist, Dr. John Pemberton, could conceive his $50 investment becoming the mammoth Coca-Cola Company ringing up $4,000,000,000 in sales when he concocted his first batch of syrup in 1886.

How could David H. McConnell foresee his $500 loan becoming the giant Avon Cosmetics, worth over $4,000,000?

What clairvoyance did George Eastman have when he scraped together $3000 to begin the Eastman Kodak success story?

Can $40 in borrowed capital create a company valued at $4,000,000,000? It happened to Isaac Merit Singer, founder of the now famous Singer Sewing Machine Co.

What would the future be for Hewlett-Packard, when William R. Hewlett and David Packard scraped together their last $538 in 1939? It was a question these two budding entrepreneurs couldn't answer.

These are a few of the stories of the past. Each, in their own way, is a success story of people with the courage to risk, the ability to create, and the determination to achieve. But the stories continue. During the past 20 years we have seen the largest bumper crop of new stories. Starting on a shoestring and making it work does not belong to an era, but to people who believe the opportunities are always there. They'll provide the stories for the future. Yours may be one more story to be told.

APPENDIX

The network of resources for the small business entrepreneur is extensive. Here are the resources that can help you with a successful start.

ASSOCIATIONS

American Association of
Small Research Companies
8794 West Chester Pike
Upper Darby, PA 19082
(Helpful in matching small R&D firms with larger contractors.)

Center for Family Businesses
Box 24268
Cleveland, OH 44124
(Membership organization for family-owned businesses.)

Human Economy Center
Box 551
Amherst, MA 01004
(Focuses on small technology firms.)

National Association of
Women Business Owners
2000 P St., N.W.
Washington, DC 20036
(Has many local chapters to assist women entrepreneurs. Newsletter, workshops.)

National Association of
Women in Commerce
1333 Howe Ave., Suite 210
Sacramento, CA 95825
(Membership association for women in career planning or business start-ups.
Workshops.)

National Federation of
Independent Business
150 W. 20th Ave.
San Mateo, CA 94403

(Small business association with 600,000 members.)

National Small Business Association
1604 K St., N.W.
Washington, DC 20006
(Membership association, lobbying group. Procurement search service, newsletters.)

National Venture Capital Association
2030 M St., N.W., Suite 403
Washington, DC 20036
(Trade association for venture capital professionals.)

Rural American Women, Inc.
1522 K St., N.W. Suite 700
Washington, DC 20005
(Membership association for rural women. Includes assistance to women entrepreneurs, co-ops.)

Small Business Foundation of America
69 Hickory Drive
Waltham, MA 02154
(Gives and receives research grants, conducts seminars, does regional and federal advocacy.)

Small Business Service Bureau
544 Main St., Box 1441
Worcester, MA 01601
(Membership association effective in retail trades and five-or-less employee businesses. Offers monthly magazine.)

BOOKS WORTH READING

Business Planning Guide
Upstart Publishing Co.
366 Islington St.
Portsmouth, NH 03801
(Good book for business planning.)

Encyclopedia of Business Information Sources
Gale Research Co.
Book Tower
Detroit, MI 48226
(Over 1200 reference categories.)

Have You Got What It Takes?
by Joseph Mancuso
Spectrum Books
Prentice-Hall, Inc.
Englewood Cliffs, NJ 07632
(Another good Mancuso book, with short blurbs on entrepreneuring.)

How to Become Financially Successful in Your Own Small Business
by Albert J. Lowry

Simon & Schuster
Rockefeller Center
NY, NY 10020
(A compendium of very helpful start-up tips.)

How to Start, Finance and Manage Your Own Small Business
by Joseph Mancuso
Prentice-Hall, Inc.
Englewood Cliffs, NJ 07632
(A broad overview of general management of the start-up.)

In Business
by Jerome Goldstein
Charles Scribner's Sons
NY, NY 10020
(Offers good examples of non-traditional ventures.)

Setting Up Shop
by Randy Baca Smith
Warner Books
665 Fifth Ave.
NY, NY 10020
(A nuts-and-bolts look at starting a small business.)

Small Time Operator
by Bernard Kamoraff
Bell Springs Publishing
Box 640
Laytonville, CA 95454
(Emphasizes bookkeeping for the start-up.)

The Entrepreneur's Guide
by Diver Brown
Macmillan Publishing Co.
NY, NY 10020
(Practical information, especially for the small manufacturing or marketing firm.)

SMALL BUSINESS PUBLICATIONS

Entrepreneur
631 Wilshire Blvd.
Santa Monica, CA 90401
(Focuses on unusual and profitable opportunities.)

In Business
18 So. 7th Street
Emmaus, PA 18049
(*In Business* is a magazine with a combination of nature and small business, fascinating start-up example.)

Inc.
38 Commercial Wharf
Boston, MA 02110
(The focus of Inc. Magazine is directed to the market managers of small business in the range of $1 million to $25 million.)

Journal of Applied Management
1200 Mt. Diablo Blvd.
Walnut Creek, CA 94596

(On the technical side, but increasingly slanted toward the entrepreneur.)

Small Business Report
550 Hartnell St.
Monterey, CA 93940
(*Small Business Report* is a helpful magazine with an orientation to the people side of business.)

The Business Owner
50 Jericho Tpke.
Jericho, NY 11753
(Designed for the small firm. Good case examples.)

The Professional Report
118 Brook St.
Scarsdale, NY 10503
(*The Professional Report* is a tax and management newsletter of well-established quality.)

Venture Magazine
35 W. 45th Street
NY, NY 10037
(Editorially slanted toward the larger start-up. Very popular magazine.)

ENTREPRENEURIAL PROGRAMS

Association for Chairs of Private Enterprise
School of Business
Georgia State University
Atlanta, GA 30303
(Write for list of schools with academic chairs in fields of entrepreneurship and free enterprise.)

Babson College
Entrepreneurial Studies Program
Babson Park
Wellesley, MA 02157
(Entrepreneurial studies; graduate and undergraduate degree programs.)

Center for Entrepreneurial Management
311 Main St.
Worcester, MA 01608
(Newsletter, seminars, workshops.)

Center for Industrial and Institutional Development
University of New Hampshire
Durham, NH 03824
(Identifies availability of information risk capital.)

Center for Venture Management
207 E. Buffalo St.
Milwaukee, WI 53202
(Write for detailed list of schools and course descriptions on new ventures and entrepreneurship.)

County Business Services
22 Main St.
Brattleboro, VT 05301
(Seminars for starting/buying an operating business.)

"Entrepreneurship Education in 1980"
by Karl H. Vesper
University of Washington
Graduate School of Business Administration
Seattle, WA 98195
(Catalog of all courses in entrepreneurship.)

Hankamer School of Business
Baylor University
Waco, TX 76703
(Offers degree program in entrepreneurial studies.)

International Council for Small Business Management
University of Wisconsin, Extension
929 N. 6th Street
Milwaukee, WI 53203
(Membership association for academicians in fields of small business management.)

New School for Democratic Management
589 Howard St.
San Francisco, CA 94108
(Offers courses in co-op management and more.)

The East-West Center
1777 East-West Road
Honolulu, HI 96848
(Seminars in identifying and developing entrepreneurial capabilities.)

The Entrepreneurship Institute
90 E. Wilson Bridge Road, Suite 247
Worthington, OH 43085
(Courses for entrepreneurs.)

The School for Entrepreneurs
Tarrytown House
East Sunnyside Lane
Tarrytown, NY 10591
(Specializing in New Age business attitudes; directed by Robert Schwartz.)

Uncollege Management Training Center
P. O. Box 736
Point Pleasant, NJ 08742
(Counseling on marketing, advertising, packaging, time management, etc.)

FEDERAL GOVERNMENT RESOURCES

Directory of State Small Business Programs
Small Business Administration
Washington, DC 20416
(State-by-state breakdown of loan, procurement, technical

assistance programs, and more.)

Federal Trade Commission
Washington, DC 20580
(Write for listing of regulations affecting your industry.)

Internal Revenue Service
Washington, DC 20224
(Free tax handbooks plus free seminars. Write for local listings.)

International Trade Administration
Business Counseling Section
Office of Export Development
Room 4009
Department of Commerce
Washington, DC 20230
(Export assistance.)

Minority Business Development Agency
Public Affairs Office
Department of Commerce
14th and Constitution, N.W.
Washington, DC 20230
(Many regional and local offices. Technical assistance and financing for minority-owned business. Publishes free bimonthly. Access with new laws, resources, and profiles.)

National Center for Appropriate Technology
P. O. Box 3838
Butte, MT 58701
(Research grants for many appropriate technology businesses: recycling, energy, health, farming. Offers good technical reports.)

National Science Foundation
Small Business Innovation Office
1800 G St., N.W.
Washington, DC 20550
(Research grants, patent assistance, workshops, reports.)

National Technical Information Service
Department of Commerce
5285 Port Royal Road
Springfield, VA 22161
(R&D arm of federal government. Write for report catalog.)

Patent and Trademark Office
Department of Commerce
Washington, DC 20231
(Free booklets on patents and inventions.)

Register of Copyrights
Library of Congress
Washington, DC 20540
(Free information on copyrights.)

Security and Exchange Commission
Office of Small Business Policy
500 N. Capitol St.
Washington, DC 20549
(Rules and regulations for

public or private offerings. Write for free pamphlet, "Q & A: Small Business and SEC.")

Small Business Administration
1441 L St., N.W.
Washington, DC 20416
(Main government agency for small business. Offices include Advocacy, Procurement, Lending, Technical/Management Assistance, Publications.)

SMALL BUSINESS LOANS

The SBA has authorized some large, nationwide financial service organizations to provide and prepare guaranteed loans, in addition to many banks. Credit Financial Corporation, a subsidiary of Control Data Corporation, was incorporated for the sole purpose of lending under the SBA Guaranteed Loan Program. Their loans are being made via 13 Control Data Business Centers and 30 Satellite Centers.

The following list provides information on the 13 Control Data Business Centers; they will supply you with information with regard to their Satellite centers too.

Commercial Credit Services Corporation Business Centers

ATLANTA, GA
Business Center
180 Interstate North
Suite 115
Atlanta, GA 30339

BALTIMORE, MD
Business Center
22 W. Padonia Road
Timonium, MD 21093

CHARLOTTE, NC
Business Center
Arnold Palmer Center
P. O. Box 34189
3726 Latrobe Drive
Charlotte, NC 28234

CHICAGO, IL
Business Center
2001 Midwest Road
Suite 105
Oak Brook, IL 60521

CLEVELAND, OH
Business Center

Western Reserve Bldg.
1468 W. 9th St., Suite 100
Cleveland, OH 44113

DALLAS, TX
Business Center
Control Data Bldg.
14801 Quorum Drive, Suite 101
Dallas, TX 75240

DENVER, CO
Business Center
8000 E. Prentice Avenue
Building D
Englewood, CO 80111

LOS ANGELES, CA
Business Center
18831 Von Karman Avenue
Suite 300
Irvine, CA 92715

LOUISVILLE, KY
Business Center
Triad East, Suite 150
10200 Linn Station Road
Louisville, KY 40223

MINNEAPOLIS, MN
Business Center
5241 Viking Drive
Bloomington, MN 55435

SAN FRANCISCO, CA
Business Center
One Bay Plaza, Suite 330
1350 Old Bayshore Highway
Burlingame, CA 94010

KANSAS CITY, KA
Business Center
Executive Hills Office Park
11011 Antioch
Shawnee Mission, KA 66210

TAMPA, FL
Business Center
Suite 285
4511 N. Himes Avenue
Tampa, FL 33614

BUSINESS DEVELOPMENT CORPORATIONS

The purpose of Business Development Corporations is to attract and retain business in their respective states, and thus increase employment. Although they sound like government agencies, they are not. BDCs operate within a state. Business development corporations are specifically designed to provide long-term capital to small businesses.

Industrial Development
Corporation of Florida
801 North Magnolia Avenue
Suite 218
Orlando, FL 32803

First Arkansas Development Finance Corporation
910 Pyramid Life Building
Little Rock, AR 72201

Alaska State Development
Corporation
Pouch D
Juneau, AK 99811

Statewide California

Business & Indus. Dev. Corp.
717 Lido Park Drive
Newport Beach, CA 92663

Connecticut Development Credit Corporation
99 Colony Street
P. O. Box 714
Meriden, CT 06450

Business Development Corporation of Georgia, Inc.
822 Healey Building
Atlanta, GA 30303

Iowa Business Development Credit Corp.
247 Jewett Building
Des Moines, IA 50309

Kansas Development Credit Corp.
First National Bank Tower
Suite 620
One Townsite Plaza
Topeka, KA 66603

Business Development Corp. of Kentucky
1940 Commonwealth Bldg.
Louisville, KY 40202

Development Credit Corp. of Maine
P. O. Box 262
Manchester, ME 04351

Development Credit Corporation of Maryland
1301 First National Bank Bldg.
Baltimore, MD 21202

Massachusetts Business Development Corp.
One Boston Place
Suite 3607
Boston, MA 02108

First Missouri Development Finance Corp.
302 Adams Street
P. O. Box 252
Jefferson City, MO 65101

Development Credit Corp. of Montana
P. O. Box 916
Helena, MT 59601

Business Development Corporation of Nebraska
Suite 1044, Stuart Bldg.
Lincoln, NE 68508

New Hampshire Business Development Corp.
10 Fort Eddy Road
Concord, NH 03301

New York Business Development Corp.
41 State Street
Albany, NY 12207

Business Development Corp. of N. Carolina
505 Oberlin Rd.
P. O. Box 10665
Raleigh, NC 27605

North Dakota State Dev. Credit Corp.
Box 1212
Bismark, ND 58501

Oklahoma Business Development Corp.
1018 United Founders Life Tower
Oklahoma City, OK 73112

RIDC Industrial and
Development Fund
Union Trust Building
Pittsburgh, PA 15219

Southeastern Pennsylvania
Development Fund
3 Penn Center Plaza
Philadelphia, PA 19102

Business Development Co.
of Rhode Island
40 Westminster Street
Providence, RI 02903

Business Development Corp.
of S. Carolina
Palmetto State Life Bldg.
P. O. Box 11606
Columbia, SC 29211

Virginia Industrial
Development Corp.
201 Mutual Building
P. O. Box 474
Richmond, VA 23204

Business Development Corp.
of Eastern Washington
417 Hyde Building
Spokane, WA 99201

Index

INDEX